INDIA'S CHINA DILEMMA

The Lost Equilibrium and Widening Asymmetries

B.R. Deepak

PENTAGON PRESS LLP

India's China Dilemma: The Lost Equilibrium and Widening Asymmetries
B.R. Deepak

ISBN 978-93-90095-45-2

First Published in 2021

Copyright © RESERVED

All rights reserved. No part of this publication may be reproduced, stored in a retrieval system, or transmitted in any form or by any means, electronic, mechanical, photocopying, recording or otherwise, without the prior written permission of the Publisher.

Disclaimer: The views and opinions expressed in the book are the individual assertion of the Author. The Publisher does not take any responsibility for the same in any manner whatsoever. The same shall solely be the responsibility of the Author.

Published by
PENTAGON PRESS LLP
206, Peacock Lane, Shahpur Jat,
New Delhi-110049
Phones: 011-64706243, 26491568
Telefax: 011-26490600
email: rajan@pentagonpress.in
website: www.pentagonpress.in

Printed at Aegean Offset Printers, Greater Noida, U.P.

Contents

Introduction   ix

I. INDIA'S CHINA DILEMMA

1. Finding a New Equilibrium with China   3
2. Galwan: Border is not China's Biggest Agenda   7
3. Death of LAC and CBMs Between India and China   12
4. China won't Accept "status quo ante"   16
5. China Debates India-China Disengagement   20
6. China's Narrative of the Border Standoff   26
7. The Doklam Standoff: Dangerously Diverging Interpretations   31
8. The Dalai Lama's Reincarnation and the Tibet Issue   36
9. Chinese Media and India's anti-terror Strikes Inside Pakistan   41
10. Shifting Balance of Power and Nepal's "Equidistance Policy" Towards India and China   45
11. Kyaukpyu Port Construction and China-Myanmar Economic Corridor   49
12. China's Footprints in India's Neighbourhood   53
13. Significance of Mamallapurm Modi-Xi Informal Summit   57

14	India-China and the RCEP	62
15	India's Myopic China Policy Needs to Change	66
16	India in China's Strategic Calculus	70
17	Disruptions of Global Supply Chains and India's Options	75

II. PEOPLE-TO-PEOPLE RELATIONS

1	India-China High Level Mechanism on People-to-People Exchanges	83
2	Why Civilisational Dialogue?	87
3	India and China Need a Civilisational Rebalancing	91
4	How Lord Ram Reached China?	97
5	Know Yourself, Know Your Enemy	101
6	Influence of Sanskrit on Chinese Language	105
7	Xu Fancheng: A Chinese Yogi in India	110
8	Hanuman and Sun Wukong: Integration of the Chinese and Indian Literary Images	114

III. INDIA AND THE US

1	India-US Defence Partnership: Why is it not an Embrace?	121
2	India-US LEMOA: A Strategic Master Stroke or a Blunder?	124
3	James Mattis' India Visit: Deepening India-US Defense Cooperation	127
4	India-US 2+2 Dialogue and China	131
5	China Sarcastic and Suspicious about Donald Trump's India Visit	134
6	Quad 2.0 will not 'dissipate like sea foam'	138

IV. CHINA AND THE US

1	China's "Sharp Power" and the Hegemonic Contest	145
2	The Marginalisation of China in the Korean Crisis	148
3	China, US, War Clouds over North Korea and India's Predicament	151
4	Behind the US-China Trade War	154
5	US-China Trade War Kicks Off	157
6	US-China Economic War gets Colder	160
7	China and the Indo-Pacific	163
8	Donald Trump's Asia Policy: Will it be a 'fight a bit and talk a bit' Strategy?	167
9	Trump-Xi Summit in Florida: Can the US Avoid Thucydides Trap?	171

V. MULTILATERALISM

1	India's Entry into the Shanghai Cooperation Organisation: A Boost to Regional Stability?	179
2	BRICS: The Driver of Global Growth and Governance?	183
3	Community of Shared Future: Win-Win Partnership to Benefit Both India and China	188

VI. THE BRI

1	Yunnan in the Belt and Road Calculus: Building Capacities for Sub-regional Economic Cooperation	195
2	China's Belt and Road Forum: Should India get Back on Board?	199
3	Belt and Road Initiative will not Fail	203
4	A New Roadmap for the Belt and Road Initiative	208

VII. COVID-19

1	Coronavirus: A 'Black Swan' for China and the World	215
2	COVID-19 and the Politics of Compensation	218
3	Post-Coronavirus New World Disorder	222
4	China's "Two Sessions" and post-COVID-19 Blueprint	226
5	Tracing the Origin of COVID-19	230

VIII. CHINA'S GOVERNANCE

1	Understanding China	237
2	The Philosophical Foundations of Xi Jinping's 'New Era'	241
3	China's Constitutional Amendments for 'Longlasting Security of the Party - State'	244
4	Xi Jinping's Governance of China	248
5	China's Rise and 40 Years of Reforms	251
6	The 19th Party Congress: Clearing Factional Fog and Xi Jinping's 'Doctrine'	255
7	Made in China 2025: Cause for a Cold War between China and the US?	259
8	Destruction and Construction in China: A 'Millennium Plan' for Building Xiongan—A New Area and a New Capital City	263
9	China's Foreign Policy in the Last 70 Years	266
10	China's War on Poverty	271
11	The Two Sessions further Consolidate Xi Jinping's Power	275
	Index	278

Introduction

If we use civilisational perspective to understand India-China relations, we will be able to explore its historicity, continuity and interconnectedness whether amongst the major polities of India and China of ancient time or between the smaller polities inside or outside their empires. The interconnectedness and its driving force – the circulatory movement of ideas, people, technologies and commodities has been well recorded in the textual as well as oral traditions of both the countries. There is no denying the fact that the uninterrupted dialogue between the two, not only enriched their civilisations, but various other polities in the vicinity also benefited from this exchange. For example, Buddhism emerged as a new entity in China creating innumerable new images such as Vimalkirti, Guanyin, and Mulian and associated sutras unfamiliar to the Indian Buddhism (Yu and Liu 2015, 41-53). As a result of the sutra translation in China, various thought systems of India and Central Asian polities such as astronomy, literature, music, theatre, languages etc. made their inroads to China enriching the knowledge systems of the region. Technologies such as sugar making, paper manufacturing, steel smelting, silk, porcelain, tea etc. travelled from China to other countries and the world without being patented by anyone. Nonetheless, there were aberrations too, which have been shunned by both the sides either intentionally or due to the lack of understanding of history.

There are references to regime changes in Jibin kingdom (Kashmir) and the killing of Azes II by the Chinese forces (Geng 1990, 10; Sen 2004, 3-4). Similar episode was repeated in Kannauj when Harshvardhan's usurper maltreated Tang envoy Wang Xuance, who in turn with the help of Tibetan and Nepalese forces defeated the usurper and took him as a prisoner along with his family to Tang capital Xi'an (Geng 1990, 197-198; Ray 2011, 57; Sen 2004, 23-24). During Zheng He's voyages in the Indian Ocean (1405-33), there were also similar incidents. China's regime change in Annam (Vietnam), extending Chinese tributary system to Siam (Thailand) and Java prior to Zheng He's voyages, but the defeat of Palembang (a Srivijaya principality) ruler Chen Zuyi and his decapitation in Nanjing during the first voyage (Fei Hsin 1436, 53), as well as the dethroning of Sinhala (Sri Lanka) king Alagagkonara (Fei Hsin 1436, 64-65), and taking him all the way to China in 1411 during the third voyage, albeit he was released and sent back the next year, are some examples revealing the ugly side of the geopolitics during ancient and medieval times. We may also argue that such incidents in the history of two thousand years of exchanges are miniscule.

The colonial connection between India and China are mostly looked through the prism of great power rivalries and their interest maximising behaviours reflected in their territorial as well as trade expansionism. The eyewitness accounts of Huang Maocai, Ma Jianzhong, Wu Guangpei and Kang Youwei remain important to construct the Chinese narrative about India and Indian people under the British rule through this perspective. If Huang Maocai invoked the nostalgia of the 'Five Indies', Ma Jianzhong and Wu Guangpei held Indian people responsible for their own fate, for they called the Indians as ignorant and their government impotent as they were unable to defend themselves against the British colonisers. Indians were treated as "people of a lost century" and "no more than slaves" (Lin 1994, 39; Sen 2017, 264; Deepak 2018, 300-303). A little later, the fugitive official of the Reform Movement, Kang Youwei, lamented how tragic is it to be a subjugated nation. So much so, Lu Xun, one of the tallest writers of the 20th century China, despised Rabindranath Tagore as a 'poisonous *dhatura*' and Indian people as 'inferior slaves' in a cage (Deepak, 2014, 152). In his opinion, colonised India had become a 'shadow country', namely, a defeated country, and therefore, it was impossible for India to produce great writers and works any longer (Liu 2013). Obviously, for a better understanding, one also needs to appreciate the socio-political environment and literary feud that was predominant in China at that time.

Therefore, there is a need to decolonise this narrative which is full of negativity, for there were stories of camaraderie and support and sympathy for each other. There are instances of Indian soldiers stationed in China, switching over to the Taiping rebels during the Taiping Uprising (1850-64) and fighting shoulder to shoulder against the imperialists and the Qing government (Deepak, 2005, 139-149). The memoirs such as *Cheen Mein Terah Maas* (Thirteen Months in China) by Gadadhar Singh (1902), an Indian soldier in China who sympathised with the Boxer Rebellion are not even known to the people of India and China. This rapprochement continued when more organised struggle for national independence was launched by the Indian and Chinese people. Activities of the Indian and Chinese nationalists joining hands in Japan and China; Ghadr Party vehemently opposing deployment of the Indian troops in China by the British and even joining the Chinese revolution in the 1920s went unnoticed as these were the people hounded by the British intelligence (Deepak 2012, 147-170; Deepak 1999, 439-456). Mahatma Gandhi, Jawaharlal Nehru, Rabindranath Tagore supporting and even raising funds for China's war against the Japanese aggression in the 1930's and 1940s, and India dispatching a team of five doctors to China talks volumes about the mutual support and sympathy amidst their anti-imperialist struggle.

In modern and contemporary times, the narrative is either dominated by invoking the glorious civilisational connect or the negativity and animosities of the British period and those of the 1950s and 1960s. It is perhaps during the colonial period, that contemporary images of India and China find their foundations. Negative images constructed during the colonial times were further underscored by the northern expansion of the British as well as the westward expansion of China, especially their respective military expeditions in Tibet. The inheritance of the very colonial and imperial legacies by both India and China exacerbated the situation as both looked at each other with suspicion. The contradictions came to surface during the Asian Relations Conference organised by the Indian Council of

World Affair in New Delhi in early 1947, where Tibet was one of the delegates. Noted Irish historian Nicolas Mansergh (1947, 295-306) has noted that China was opposed to India's cultural leadership in the region and its representatives lost no opportunity of saying that all nations in Asia were equal that there was no question of leadership; similar play of words was seen during the Bandung Conference in 1956. India's neutrality and its leadership aspirations were denounced, and China levelled India as a "double-dealer nationalist country that harboured the desire to expand outward" (Yang 1992, 253). The Tibetan rebellion of 1959 and the flight of the Dalai Lama to India were pronounced as the handiworks of India, for according to China, India "practically wants to turn Tibet into their colony or protectorate" (PRC 1959, 80-97). The hostilities along the border, the Dalai Lama's flight to India in the aftermath of the Tibetan uprising in 1959, and India's refusal to renew the 1954 agreement on Tibet, brought the relationship to a nadir culminating into a brief armed conflict over the Himalayas and then a deep freeze in diplomatic relation for almost three decades. As a result, the 'cultural cousinhood' of ancient time, and 'colonial cousinhood' of the anti-imperialist era was lost in no time. The US-China rapprochement at the height of the Cultural Revolution, the end of the Cold War, and the globalisation facilitated a new equilibrium and understanding between India and China as both accorded priority to economic development that desired peace and stability in the region. The newly found equilibrium improved the security as well as trade and investment environment between the two unprecedentedly. The equilibrium was built on the premise that both were at the same level of development, and hence need to give full play to their complementarities and potentialities. When Rajiv Gandhi visited China in 1988, the first by an Indian Prime Minister after the 1962 conflict, India's GDP was US$ 296.59 against China's US$ 312.35. India's per capita income in the same year was US$ 354, way ahead of China's US$ 284.[1] It was this parity that a series of Confidence Building Measures (CBMs) were signed between 1988 and 2013.[2] The CBMs were instrumental in maintaining peace and tranquillity along the border, as both pledged to strictly respect and observe the Line of Actual Control (LAC) and keep their border military presence to a minimum level compatible with the friendly and good neighbourly relations.

As the CBMs proved successful in managing the border and guarantying peace, both diversified relations into other areas such as trade and investment, people to people exchanges, cooperation in science and technology on the one hand and collaborated on the global issues of common concern like climate change and global governance on the other. In tandem, both created new institutions of global governance such as the Asia Infrastructure Investment Bank (AIIB) and the BRICS New Development Bank (NDB), considered to be challenging the Bretton Woods Institutions of the West. Both underscored the significance of multi-polarity, initiated or became members of an array of multilateral mechanisms such as the BRICS, the Shanghai Cooperation Organization (SCO), the East Asia Summit (EAS) and the G-20. This in turn, besides improving bilateral relations, also stabilised relations with smaller countries in the vicinity, as both talked of taking care of each other's core interests and sensitivities.

Trade flourished between the two and China became the largest trade partner of India. No wonder, in a short span of two decades, bilateral trade approached $100 billion. China's accumulative investment between 2017 and 2019 reached a whopping $9.5 billion, mostly investing in the "Digital India" start-ups. Presently, 17 out of 24 unicorns are supported by capital from Chinese brands such as Alibaba, Tencent and Global Data. As the labour, intensive industries started to become unviable at home, China started to relocate supply chains such as mobile telephony, electronics, home appliances, etc., to India, localising production and penetrated deep into sectors such as e-commerce, energy, telecom, automobiles etc. Though balance of trade remained heavily in favour of China owing to the economic structure of both the countries, however, China did make unfulfilled promises to rectify this by making more investments in India and providing greater market access to India's pharmaceutical and information technology companies. Meanwhile, Indian movies and Yoga captivated the imaginations of a million Chinese people, some of the blockbusters like *Dangal* earned more revenue at box office in China than in India. Both identified themselves as civilisational states and advocated that civilisational dialogue between them through stronger people to people bonding should be initiated, resulting in inking High Level Mechanism on Culture and People to People Exchanges in 2018.

The equilibrium had started to develop fissures as face-offs between the border troops of India and China became frequent, implying that the CBMs were challenged. There were transgressions in Depsang in 2013, Chumar in 2014, culminating into the Doklam in 2017 and finally bloody clashes at Galwan in June 2020. The accessibility of the LAC by the People's Liberation Army (PLA) through rapid infrastructure development and subsequently India playing a catch up; India abolishing Article 370 in Jammu and Kashmir, which according to some scholars in China "greatly increased the difficulty in resolving the border," "strategic troubles" such as India joining the "Indo-Pacific Strategy" of the US for containing China, besides "Hindu nationalism" and India's "great power mentality" have been cited as some of the reasons for these face-offs.[3] Some scholars and practitioners like India's former foreign secretary, Vijay Gokhle, believes that the "most fundamental misperception between the two countries is the inability to comprehend each other's international ambitions, yielding the fear that their foreign policies are targeted against the other."[4] While these appear to be logical arguments, however, the border standoffs are not one off incidents, had it been the case, number of incursions and the above mentioned face-offs would not have occurred at all.

It is the power shift that has disrupted the equilibrium between India and China. The shift could be attributed to China's massive economic growth in the last four decades. Last decade is particularly worth noting as China's 2010 GDP of US$ 6 trillion catapulted to US$ 14 trillion, whereas India's US$ 1.7 trillion only rose to US$ 2.8 trillion.[5] This resulted widening of India's asymmetries with China, while China bridging its economic and technological gaps with the US. It is the embryonic bipolarity which has made China to believe that the regional and well as global balance of power has tilted in her favour. This on the ground looks so, as China has emerged as the leading trade partner of most of the countries in the region. In 2020, ASEAN became the largest trade partner of China, bilateral trade touched a whopping US$ 731.9 billion.[6] China's trade with South Asia that reached US$ 126.7 billion in 2017 is steadily rising.[7] However, trade with India fell from US$ 95.7 billion in 2018 to US$ 92.89 billion in 2019, and it fell further to US$ 77.7 billion in 2020 owing to the COVID-19 pandemic and post-Galwan tensions. Bilateral trade has since rebounded with a 62.7 per cent growth in the first half of 2021 to reach to US$ 57.48 billion.[8] No wonder, Chinese researchers such as Liu Zongyi (2021) posits that "to a certain extent "Made in India" and *Atmnirbhar Bharat* (self-reliant India) etc. policies implemented by the Indian government have encountered setbacks." China's economic footprints in Asia and beyond has emboldened it to push the narrative of the "East is rising and the West is declining."[9]

Moreover, since the narrative of "emerging India", which was based on India's robust economic growth, demographic dividend, and capacity to handle domestic and global challenges pragmatically, enters unpredictability, India and the world faces a more assertive China. China sees no compulsion to accommodate India's regional and global aspirations. This has been demonstrated by China ignoring India's sensitivities by building China Pakistan Economic Corridor (CPEC) that runs through the Indian claimed territories, China's rebuff to India on issues such as cross-border terrorism, blocking India's efforts to bring terrorists like Masood Azhar under the scanner of 1267 sanction committee, blocking India's entry into the Nuclear Suppliers Group (NSG), and unilaterally wanting to claim Jampheri in the Doklam and change the status quo on the border. Even though India adhered to "one-China policy" from the very beginning but China made no concessions, rather issued stapled visas to Indian citizens from Kashmir, and now wish to create a new issue of Ladakh. Therefore, under present circumstances, status quo ante in the Western Sector looks a remote possibility. Instead, China has created new hot spots in the Gogra Heights, Hot Springs and Depsang. Given the economic superiority of China, the amassment of forces, establishment of new permanent structures along the LAC, China wants India to accept the new modus vivendi on the border and normalise relations in other areas, which India has found unacceptable.

The kind of equilibrium and understanding India and China had reached post-Cold War is in shambles and there is a need for a reset. Finding new equilibrium and understanding will not be easy given India's asymmetrical relationship with China. It will depend on how quickly the narrative of India's rise regains traction. There are scholars (Choudhry et.al. 2020, 169-180) who posit that post Covid-19, India has an "opportunity to participate in global supply chains, as multinationals are losing trust in China." Indeed, there is an attempt to ameliorate business environment for attracting foreign investment, and it has been witnessed that India's FDI inflows are bullish. India's foreign exchange reserves have crossed US$ 600 billion for the first time. Whether it is an endorsement of India as a preferred destination is debateable, for compared with many developing countries, India's "cost of doing business" is still very high, notwithstanding the fact that India has climbed up to the 62nd position in 2020 from 140th in 2014 as far as the "ease of doing business" is concerned. The costs of land, labour, capital, raw materials and electricity are highly uncompetitive. Logistics costs alone, account for 13-15 per cent of the product cost, compared with a global average of 6 per cent (Deepak 2020, 5-8).

Decoupling with China will certainly not help in restoring the equilibrium. Notwithstanding India changing its FDI policy in 2020 and banning Chinese apps, bilateral trade in the first half of 2021 rose by 62.7 per cent. According to the Trade Promotion Council of India (TCPI), India imports 53 APIs and critical key starting materials (KSMs) from China accounting for 70 per cent of its API requirements.[10] Even though the government is thinking of building new pharma parks, but the low cost of the API and medical equipment from China will continue to attract the Indian pharma sector. Given these realities, India emerging as the next supply chain destination in short run looks rather a hype and exaggeration, for it took China 40 years to develop a supply chain ecosystem with the support of its detractors such as the US and Japan. It may take many more decades for India to realise the same, but shutting doors to Chinese investment may further prolong it.

The new equilibrium and understanding will also depend on India's relationship with major and middle powers, especially the kind of partnership India is able to build with them in the field of trade and investment, technology and defence. India may have missed the BRI train, but aligning its connectivity initiative such as US$ 2.2 billion *'Bharat Mala'* and *'Sagar Mala'* project with neighbouring countries, the SAGAR as well newly established Build Back Better World (B3W) vision of the G7 countries will be crucial. Strategic and economic partnership with BIMSTEC and ASEAN countries is an absolute necessity, and India remaining outside

RCEP will certainly deprive of her being part of the global supply chains. India's role in the Quad and Indo-Pacific Strategy of the US will also determine the nature of India-China coexistence, cooperation and competition in various areas. Finally, as long as India's growth trajectory remains weak, social cohesion and communal harmony remain in disarray, the kind of understanding India seeks from China will be impossible.

It is in the view of these currents and undercurrents of India-China bilateral as well as multilateral relationship that I thought of organising some of my articles written for the *Sunday Guardian* in this compilation and dedicate to readers. These have been arranged in eight sections, namely: India's China dilemma; peoples to people relations; India and the Unites States; China and the United States; multilateralism; the Belt and Road Initiative; Covid-19; and the governance of China. The articles are demonstrative of Indian, Chinese, the US and many other perspectives, and could be useful to academicians, policy formulators, researchers and students alike.

NOTES

1. Statistics Times. "Comparing China and India by economy," May 16, 2021. https://statisticstimes.com/economy/china-vs-india-economy.php (accessed July 7, 2021)
2. For detailed discussion on these CBMs, see Deepak, B. R. *India and China: Beyond the Binary of Friendship and Enmity*. Singapore: Springer Nature, 2020:63-68.
3. Wang, Shida. 《印度已经被"双重自信"冲昏了头脑》 "India blinded by 'double confidence'" *Guanchazhe*, June 4, 2020 https://m.guancha.cn/WangShiDa/2020_06_04_552877.shtml (accessed July 14, 2021); Yuan Jirong. 《示好换不来和平与友谊，对印要立足立威》 "Goodwill cannot be exchanged for peace and friendship: China must stand up and establish its prowess against India" *South Asia Bulletin*, July 7, 2020, and Eurasian System Science Research Association. https://www.essra.org.cn/view-1000-818.aspx (accessed July 14, 2021). For Indian perspective see, Malik, V. P. "If LAC not marked soon, build up like on LoC likely." *The Indian Express*, 5 June 2020. https://indianexpress.com/article/india/express-interview-vp-malik-lac-india-china-6443187/ (accessed July 16, 2021); Deepak, B. R. "China knows it cannot meddle in Kashmir post 370 Decision." *Sunday Guardian*, August 24, 2019. https://www.sundayguardianlive.com/opinion/china-knows-cannot-meddle-kashmir-post-370-decision (accessed August 24, 2019)
4. Gokhle, Vijay. "The road from Galwan: The future of India-China relations," *Carnegie Endowment for International Peace*. 2021. https://carnegieendowment.org/files/Gokhale_Galwan.pdf (accessed July 18, 2021)
5. Statistics Times. "Comparing China and India by economy," May 16, 2021.
6. Global Times, "ASEAN becomes China's largest trading partner in 2020, with 7% growth," January 14, 2021. https://www.globaltimes.cn/page/202101/1212785.shtml (accessed July 18, 2021)

7. Ministry of Commerce, PRC. "2017年中国与南亚贸易额达1267.7亿美元." The trade volume between China and South Asia reached US$126.77 billion in 2017. *Country-specific trade and investment environment information*, June 25, 2018. http://trb.mofcom.gov.cn/article/zuixindt/201806/20180602758892.shtml (accessed on July 27, 2021)
8. India Today. "India-China trade grows 62.7% in 1st half of year, crosses $57 billion," July 14, 2021. https://www.indiatoday.in/business/story/india-china-trade-grows-62-7-in-1st-half-of-year-crosses-57-billion-1828018-2021-07-14 (accessed on July 27, 2021)
9. He, Bin. "在县级领导干部学习贯彻党的十九届五中全会专题研讨班上的发言" Speech at the special seminar for county-level leaders to study and implement the Fifth Plenary Session of the 19th Central Committee of the Communist Party of China. *Qilian News*, February 25, 2021. https://web.archive.org/web/20210226222555/http%3A%2F%2Fwww.qiliannews.com%2Fsystem%2F2021%2F02%2F25%2F013341147.shtml (accessed on July 27, 2021)
10. BioWorld. 2020. "India looks to cult reliance on China for APIs," BioWorld 6 April 2020. https://www.bioworld.com/articles/434213-india-looks-to-cut-reliance-on-china-for-apis

REFERENCES

Choudhry, Monika, Sondhi, P.R., and Das, Shankar "Effect of COVID-19 on Economy in India: Some Reflections for Policy and Programme." *Journal of Health Management* 22(2) (2020).

Deepak, B. R. "Revolutionary activities of Ghadr Party in China." *China Report* 35 (4) (New Delhi, Sage, 1999)

Deepak, B. R. "1857 Rebellion and the Indian involvement in the Taiping Uprising of China." In Thampi, Madavi. 2005. *India and China in the Colonial World*. (New Delhi: Social Science Press, 2005).

Deepak, B. R. "The colonial Connections: Indians and Chinese nationalists in Japan and China." *China Report* 48 (1-2) (New Delhi, Sage, 2012).

Deepak, B. R. "Lu Xun's critique of Tagore: Sardonic irreverence and misunderstanding." In: Zhang Xiaoxi. 2014. In《比较文学与比较文化研究丛刊》 *Comparative Literature and Comparative Culture Studies Series*. (Beijing: Zhongyang Bianyi Press, 2014).

Deepak, B. R. (Tr.) *Ji Xianlin: A Critical Biography*. (Delhi: Pentagon Press, 2018): 300-303. Original Chinese book by Yu Longyu and Zhu Xuan.《季羡林评传》(Jinan: Shandong Education Press, 2016)

Deepak, B. R. Book Review of Sen, Tansen. 2017. *India, China and the World: A Connected History*. Maryland: Rowman and Littlefield. *China Review International*, vol. 23 (3) (Hawai: University of Hawai Press, 2018)

Deepak, B R. *India and China: Beyond the binary of friendship and enmity*. (Singapore: Springer Nature, 2020).

Fei Hsin 费信 《星槎胜览》(The Overall Survey of the Star Raft) Originally published in 1436, translated by JVG Mills, Revised, annotated and edited by Roderich Ptak, Harrassowitz Verlag (1996).

Geng, Yinzeng.《汉文南亚史科学》 *Historical Data of South Asia from Chinese Sources*. (Beijing: Peking University Press, 1990).

Gokhle, Vijay. "The road from Galwan: The future of India-China relations," *Carnegie Endowment for* International Peace. 2021. https://carnegieendowment.org/files/Gokhale_Galwan.pdf (accessed July 18, 2021).

Lin, Chengjie. 《中印人民友好关系史: 1851-1949》 *A History of Friendly Relations between Indian and Chinese People: 1851-1949*. (Beijing: Peking University Press, 1994).

Liu, Jian. 2013. "Indian studies in China: An assessment" https://indiachinainstitute.org/wp-content/uploads/2014/04/Liu-Jian_Submission_2013_Edited.pdf (accessed on July 28, 2021)

Liu, Zongyi. "印对华贸易依赖度高," India highly dependent on China for trade, *China Business News*, February 24, 2021. https://finance.sina.com.cn/stock/usstock/c/2021-02-24/doc-ikftpnny9487288.shtml (accessed on July 18, 2021)

Malik, V. P. "If LAC not marked soon, build up like on LoC likely." *The Indian Express*, 5 June 2020. https://indianexpress.com/article/india/express-interview-vp-malik-lac-india-china-6443187/ (accessed on July 30, 2021)

Mansergh, Nicholas. "The Asian Conference." *International Affairs (Royal Institute of International Affairs 1944-)* Vol. 23, No. 3 (Jul., 1947): 295-306

PRC [People's Republic of China]. *Concerning the Question of Tibet*. (Peking: Foreign Language Press, 1959).

Ray, H. P. *Chinese Sources of South Asian History in Translation*. (Kolkata: The Asiatic Society, 2011).

Sen, Tansen. *Buddhism, diplomacy and trade: The realignment of Sino-Indian relations 600-1400*. (Delhi: Manohar, 2004).

Sen, Tansen. *India, China and the World: A Connected History*. (Maryland: Rowman and Littlefield, 2017).

Singh, Gadadhar. *Cheen Mein 13 Maas* (Thirteen Months in China). (Lucknow: Dilkusha, 1902).

Wang, Shida. 《印度已经被 "双重自信" 冲昏了头脑》 "India blinded by 'double confidence'" *Guanchazhe* 4 June 2020 https://m.guancha.cn/WangShiDa/2020_06_04_552877.shtml (accessed on July 30, 2021)

Yang, Gongsu.《中国反对外国侵略干涉西藏地方斗争史》 *History of China's Struggle and Resistance to the Foreign Invasion and interference in Tibet*. (Beijing: China's Tibetology Publications, 1992).

Yu, Longyu and Liu, Chaohua.《中外文学交流史: 中国-印度卷》 *The History of Sino-Foreign Literary Exchange: China-India Volume*. (Jinan: Shandong Education Press, 2015).

I
INDIA'S CHINA DILEMMA

1

Finding a New Equilibrium with China

The so-called equilibrium and understanding between India and China was built on the premise that both are at the same level of development, and hence need to give full play to their complementarities and potentialities. It was on such a basis that both countries signed a series of confidence building measures to stabilise the border and security environment in the vicinity. Both came together on various issues of common concern and were instrumental in initiating multilateral mechanisms such as BRICS, the AIIB, the NDB, SCO etc. It was a golden period of their bonhomie as both advocated that there was enough space for them to develop and rise simultaneously. This equilibrium has visibly been lost three decades after its inception.

The reason for the collapse is China's massive economic growth in the last four decades. The last decade is particularly worth noting as China's 2010 GDP of 6 trillion US dollars catapulted to 14 trillion US dollars, whereas India's 1.7 trillion only rose to 2.8 trillion US dollars. This also resulted in China bridging its technological and economic asymmetries with the US, while India's asymmetrical relationship with China widened drastically. The loss in equilibrium and understanding is due to a visible shift in the balance of power favouring China.

Though analysts on both sides have attributed it to India forging closer security ties with the United States, the creation of a "mini NATO" in the Indo-Pacific, the abrogation of Article 370 and bifurcation of Jammu and Kashmir into two union territories, which China said has posed a "challenge to the sovereignty of Pakistan and China" and "dramatically increased the difficulty in resolving the border issue", India's rebuff to China's Belt and Road Initiative, and India beefing up border infrastructure, in particular roads like Durban-Shyok-DBO and Dharchula-Lipulekh etc. issues. Undoubtedly, these could be considered as some of the triggers for the Galwan, Pangong Tso, Hot Spring and Naku La standoffs. However, the border standoffs are not one off the incidents, had it been the case, incidents like DBO-Depsang (2013), Chumar/Demchok (2014) and Doklam (2017) would not have happened at all; the number of incursions along the entire Line of Actual Control (LAC) would not have jumped to such a proportion. Therefore, more than anything else, it is the power shift that has disrupted the equilibrium, and is the fundamental reason for China's behaviour along the LAC, the region and beyond.

This has also been aided by the United States' retrenchment from global governance as well as the narrative of "emerging India" entering a state of unpredictability. The narrative was based on India's robust economic growth, demographic dividend, and capacity to handle domestic and global challenges pragmatically. Therefore, China's assertiveness that has been witnessed in the reclamation of islands, reefs and rocks in the South China Sea, China crossing the median line in the Taiwan Straits, changing the status quo on the LAC along the India-China border, and its "wolf-warrior" diplomacy will continue in one form or another. In the face of such a scenario, is a new equilibrium possible?

Finding a new equilibrium and understanding with China will depend on a number of factors. At the outset, it will depend on how quickly the narrative of India's rise regains traction. How strong India's growth trajectory will be in the post-COVID-19 era. In this context, India must incessantly create and ameliorate its business environment so as to become a top investment destination, for the cost of doing business in India is still very high. India needs to unfold a workable connectivity strategy within and with our neighbouring countries. China unfolding a strategy of economic corridors across its borders is not difficult to understand if we peep into the kind of corridors and a network of roads, rails and waterways it has created within its territories. Our own new initiatives such as *Bharat Mala* a network of 5000 kilometres of roads connecting all the Himalayan states of India with a capital of US$ 2.2 billion need to be carried out in letter and spirit and at war footing. In the same vein, the *Sagar Mala* project, whereby all coastal cities in India would be interconnected through road, rail, ports and airports through a special development package needs to be moved very quickly. Simultaneously, the nodes of these projects need to be extended to India's immediate and extended neighbourhood and aligned with the SAGAR and IORA vision. It is necessary that neighbours see an economic opportunity in India and integrate their development strategies with those of India's.

Second, connectivity will pave the way for strategic and economic partnerships with various regional entities such as BIMSTEC, SAARC and ASEAN. The RCEP is an opportunity to integrate Indian economy with the region. In fact, the Act East Policy, Quad and Indo-Pacific Strategy will gain momentum, if India's economic integration with the region and beyond is realised.

Third, India's relationship with major and middle powers needs to be strategically crafted. The same would be tested by the kind of partnership India is able to build with them in the fields of trade and investment, technology and defence. Going by the recently declassified "U.S. Strategic Framework for the Indo-Pacific" it is clear that the U.S. has made its strategic choices clear, i.e. cooperate with India and other likeminded countries to "counterbalance China." To this end, the U.S. is willing to "accelerate India's rise and capacity to serve as a net provider of security and major defence partner." Though India has forged closer security cooperation with the U.S. has she made the choice to contain China, even if China believes so? India's relationship with Russia, which the classified report labels as "a marginal player in the Indo-Pacific" will remain a concern as was pointed out by the outgoing U.S. ambassador, Kenneth Juster.

Fourth, decoupling from China, as has been expected around the world is a far cry. Even if it happens, Southeast Asia is a better destination as has been proved by the investment flows to Vietnam, Thailand, Myanmar etc. countries. Undoubtedly, some decoupling will happen in the field of new technologies, where the West fears China's dominance. As regards the relocation of labour intensive supply chains from China, India must not shy away from attracting Chinese investment, especially manufacturing, infrastructure, and food processing to name a few. The 78 billion U.S. dollars of bilateral trade between India and China from January-November 2020 amidst the COVID-19 and Galwan clashes prove the decoupling and boycott China theory utterly wrong. In fact, owing to price advantage, some of the Chinese companies have bagged lucrative infrastructure projects, even as the military standoff continues between the two. India needs to engage with China constructively by identifying certain sectors where trade and investment can be realised and stand against it when it comes to protecting India's core interests.

Finally, all the above factors together with India's capacities to handle domestic and external challenges will enable her to establish a new equilibrium and understanding with China, and possibly the resolution of unsettled border too. Interestingly, another report titled "Global Britain, Global Broker" released by the Chatham House, U.K. on January 11, 2021 puts India in a very bad light and clubs it with illiberal democracies, which it says are difficult to deal with. Therefore, as long as India's growth trajectory remains weak, social cohesion and communal harmony remain in disarray, the kind of understanding India seeks from China will be impossible.

2

GALWAN:
BORDER IS NOT CHINA'S BIGGEST AGENDA

"...From the very beginning of the war, the firepower of the Indian army was extremely fierce. After two hours of fierce fighting, though the Chinese army occupied the Galwan Valley, it had paid a heavy price. 874 Chinese soldiers fell in the icy snow of this river valley. It was not until the beginning of the 1980s that the bodies of more than 800 soldiers were brought back from the frozen snow." Thus, wrote Sun Xiao, a People's Liberation Army (PLA) officer in the *Snow of the Himalayas: Sino-Indian War Records* (Chinese edition 1991). Sun says that in 1982 when he visited Xinjiang, he was witness to the remains of these soldiers being transported from Ngari (Ali) in Tibet to Urumqi in Xinjiang. The Indian official version of the 1962 conflict, the *History of the Conflict with China, 1962*, (unpublished report) edited by S. N. Prasad (1992) says that "the Chinese attack on the [Galwan] post started with heavy artillery and mortar bombardment on the 20th of October at 0530 hours.... After an hour of shelling the Chinese carried out a battalion strength attack on the forward positions. The men who had moved into said forward trenches fought a bitter last-ditch battle....it was only towards the evening that the Chinese finally succeeded in overrunning the post. In all, the Chinese launched three attacks. The casualties suffered by the defenders, 36 killed out of a total 68 all ranks, show how bitter the fighting was"! The Chinese official version of the conflict entitled *History of China's Counter Attack in Self-defense Along the Sino-Indian Borders* (Chinese edition 1994) gives the total Chinese casualties in the entire western sector as 97 all ranks!

It is the same Galwan valley that is in news again as we hear about the intrusions of the PLA beyond their claim line of 1960. This is a new development and bad news for both India and China. Alistair Lamb, who had done considerable research on the India-China border remarked in 1964 that "the extent of Chinese claims seems to increase slightly from time to time" in the Western Sector. Rightly so, as there are three Chinese claim lines in the Western Sector. One is the claim line of 1956, which intersects Aksai Chin almost in the middle; the second is the line separating the Indian and Chinese forces on 7 November 1959, and the third, the line reached by the Chinese after the 1962 conflict. China did go back 20 kilometers behind the line of actual control in the Eastern Sector, i.e. Arunachal Pradesh, but not in the Western Sector where they reinforced their 1960 claim line. The Chinese message was clear: accept our claims in the Western Sector, we will accept the McMahon Line. It was the stand China had hinted at in various semantics, although she had gone back from the 1956 claim line and demanded more territories beyond the 1956 line in 1960. Neville Maxwell, while accusing India for its "forward policy" has remained tight-lipped about China establishing forward posts beyond their 1956 claim line. Thus, he has accepted different claim lines put forth by China in the Western Sector as their legitimate right. Therefore, to say that the entirety of Aksai Chin was under Chinese jurisdiction is not correct, though the status quo has been drastically changed by China. If the reality of China's different claim lines, together with the Shyam Saran Report of 2013 and professor P.A. Stobdan's study is to be believed, Ladakh has been shrinking in size!

This has been demonstrated by ever increasing transgressions, mostly in the Western Sector by the PLA – the Galwan valley; the Srijap range where India's claim line extends to Finger 8 but doesn't control the areas beyond Finger 4; and Naku La in Sikkim. India must be watchful for similar flashpoints in the Middle Sector in areas such as Nilang-Jadang,

Bara Hoti, Sangchamalla and Lapthal, Shipki La and Spiti as these are also claimed by China. Interestingly, having reinforced its 1960 claim line in the Western Sector, China is playing the victim and blaming India for "provoking the incident" in the Galwan valley "intentionally" and "trying to change the status quo unilaterally"; the version since 18th May has appeared in various print and social medias in China. Social media has been carrying reports of the 1962 flash points in this area and singing praises of the PLA's valor. Wang Dehua, a veteran of India-China relations in an article in sohu.com on 19th May 2020 has even warned Prime Minister Narendra Modi that "Boundless is the sea of misery, yet a man who will repent can reach the shore nearby." Why is China behaving like this?

First of all, the border is not the biggest agenda for China at this point in time. China believes that it has not reached the stage where a resolution is a must, therefore, peace and stability in the neighbourhood remain the top priority, along with transforming China into a 'moderately developed power' by 2049 when it will realise the second centenary, i.e. a century of the establishment of the People's Republic of China, and perhaps the unification of China too. Therefore, the 'maintenance of peace and tranquility', and 'managing' rather than solving the problem will be its top priority.

Second, it is also not a big agenda for China, as it has easy access to the Line of Actual Control (LAC) owing to the state of the art infrastructure it has created. China knows that the CBMs that both sides have created will not be enough to resolve the problem, hence no stone should be left unturned as far as infrastructure development in Tibet and Xinjiang is concerned. For example, the "Thirteenth Five-Year Plan" (2016-2020) allocates 200 billion RMB (US$ 20.5 billion) for infrastructure development in Tibet. Today 99 per cent of the villages there are connected to highways, as the network in the region has increased from 65,000 kilometers to 90,000 kilometers. These roads are further connected with major railway lines and airports inside Tibet and Xinjiang.

Third, since India is also ramping up its border infrastructure 'rapidly', it has caused uneasiness on the other side of the LAC. Although the 255-kilometers-long Darbuk-Shayok-Daulat Beg Oldie (DS-DBO) took us

19 years to complete (not to talk about the scandals associated with these projects), nonetheless, it will make accessible many areas of the LAC for patrolling and will keep an eye on the Chinese movements in the Aksai Chin, which is a few kilometers away. There are 60 more such projects that are part of the 3,300-kilometer road network along the border, the work of which was supposed to be completed in 2019 but according to BRO officials is only 75 per cent done. Surveys for border rail projects such as Bilaspur-Manali-Leh, Misamari-Tenga-Tawang, North Lakhimpur-Bame-Silapathar, and Pasighat-Teju-Parsuram Kund-Rupai are on and are supposed to be completed by 2025. It is perhaps this new 'development' which has been a cause of concern to China. Therefore, it has been making forays into new areas simply for "holding the line" as they perceive. India perhaps will too "hold the line" if more areas are accessible once the infrastructure is laid. This however, will give rise to Galwan and Doklam like confrontations, which could lead to a larger conflict. It is also out of this thinking that China is contemplating the demilitarisation of the LAC. India too perhaps could think of such a proposal if she feels comfortable with the notion of equal and mutual security, for the cost of maintaining 'peace and tranquility' is becoming higher for both India and China.

Fourth, many scholars and analysts in both the countries have related the Galwan and Naku La standoff with the COVID-19 situation in India, and China taking advantage of that, which I believe is not quite logical. More than that it is the power shift and India cozying up to the US as far as India's security interests are concerned; it has something to do with India's close coordination with the quad and Indo-Pacific strategy. India's support for a COVID-19 probe can also be seen in this light. Some of the Chinese scholars believe that India has been fishing in troubled waters as Sino-US relations have nosedived. Professor Wang Dehua even warns India that "recently, due to the rapid deterioration of Sino-US relations, New Delhi has forgotten its history and has started to bloat a bit" which I believe is uncalled for.

Finally, rather than flaring up jingoism, both India and China must go back to the "consensus" reached in Wuhan and later in Mahaballipuram, reactivate all available confidence building mechanisms and restore the status quo ante. They must quickly dis-engage, for both cannot possibly push their economies back further, which are already reeling in negative growth trajectories in the backdrop of COVID-19. This is the 70th anniversary of the establishment of diplomatic relations between India and China; both have planned 70 events to celebrate the year, but unfortunately we have started the anniversary on a very negative note.

3

DEATH OF LAC AND CBMs BETWEEN INDIA AND CHINA

The death of Indian soldiers in Galwan, the first after 1962, has dealt a heavy blow to the confidence building measures (CBMs) India and China signed between 1988 and 2013, as well as the "Wuhan Spirit" and "Chennai Connect" that talk about the "consensus" between Prime Minister Narendra Modi and Chinese President Xi Jinping that both sides "will not allow their differences to turn into disputes." China, rather, has thrown down the gauntlet to India telling India that all the disputed territory between India and China belongs to it, and that it will continue to change the status quo and pass it as fait accompli to India with brute force. This is the maximalist position of China. Let us examine how China has reached this far.

In fact, this is the shadow of our own maximalist position on the border in the 1950s that we absolutely mismanaged, demonstrating strategic myopia in settling the border. India could have settled the border including the Kashmir issue in the year 1954 when India accepted Tibet as a part of China and signed the "Agreement Between the Republic of India and the People's Republic of China on Trade and Intercourse Between Tibet Region of China and India." India could have opened up the border issue and settled it on a quid pro quo basis. But rather than demonstrating strategic vision, Nehru and his advisors harped about Panchsheel as "little short of a no war pact" that will "ensure peace to a very large extent in a certain area of Asia." All these lofty ideals and rhetoric were belied by the PLA incursions in Bara Hoti soon after signing the agreement.

India Could have settled it in 1960 when Chinese Premier Zhou Enlai visited India in the backdrop of the Tibetan rebellion and the subsequent flight of the Dalai Lama to India, and the bloody incidents at Kongka La in the Western Sector and Longju in the Eastern Sector. The summit between Nehru and Zhou was inconclusive, as India's maximalist position failed to read Zhou's message that the "settlement of the boundary question between the two countries should take into account the national feelings of the two peoples toward the Himalayas and the Karakoram Mountains" subtly reflecting his earlier statement that "an overall settlement of the boundary question should be sought by both sides, taking into account the historical background and existing actualities." To be fair, Nehru's "tough posture" was a reflection of the negative role played by the cacophonous press and opposition, which pronounced Zhou as a "murderer" and that if at all Nehru wished to talk to Zhou "China must accept two prerequisites set by New Delhi, i.e. accept the McMahon Line and evacuate Aksai Chin.

There was an opening in 1979 as well when Deng Xiaoping in his meeting with the then Foreign Minister of India, A.B. Vajpayee proposed the idea of a "package deal" for the resolution of Sino-Indian boundary issues. Vajpayee's reply was that "this was an old Chinese proposal and that a beginning could be made by trying to tackle those areas where there was less dispute" according to former ambassadors Ranganathan and Khanna in their book published in 2000. Henceforth, it was because of this "sectoral" approach that China now asked for more concessions in the Eastern Sector if India wanted China to cede more territories in the Western Sector. The 2003 Special Representative (SR) Mechanism according to China's SR, Dai Bingguo, who negotiated the border issue with four Indian SRs between 2003 and 2013 points to another opportunity lost to resolve the border issue in his memoir *Strategic Dialogue: Reminiscences of Dai Bingguo*.

However, it wasn't really an opportunity, for India had conveyed to

China that through this mechanism we would explore the guiding principles for resolving the issue, but would not involve specific negotiations for border demarcation and work on the maps. It is indeed intriguing as to why the exchange of maps was omitted since it was already there in Article X of the 1996 CBM. Nevertheless, the SR mechanism did result in the 2005 protocol on the Political Parameters and Guiding Principles for the Settlement of the India-China Boundary Question. However, Article VII that envisages "in reaching a boundary settlement, the two sides shall safeguard due interests of their settled populations in the border areas" has been abandoned by the Chinese as it essentially jeopardizes the principle of give and take according to them.

It could be discerned that China over the years, and after carrying out an extensive modernisation of the PLA and beefing up its border infrastructure in Tibet and Xinjiang along the LAC, has adopted a maximalist position blended with sectoral approaches in the form of "early harvest" proposals. China's approach is to take advantage of the undefined Line of Actual Control (LAC) on the ground, occupy it, militarise it, change the status quo and pass it as a fait accompli relying on brute force as it has done in the South China Sea. Any student of history and border studies will know about the various differing claim lines of China in the Western Sector, and how these have been shifted westward over the period of time owing to the undefined nature of the border as well as the LAC. It is also owing to this reason that China will not be interested in resolving the border and also the identification of the LAC. Moreover, seeing the changing nature of the conflict restricted by the CBMs not to open fire, China for long has embedded "gedou" (gladiator) contingents armed with "langyabang" (wolf teeth iron maces) along the LAC.

In the face of these ground realities, what could be India's options? Take stock of India's China policy in tandem with opposition parties, experts hailing from military, diplomatic, economic, technological, sinological etc. fields and draw a long-term, sustainable strategy to deal with China. Draw a blueprint for closing the differential gaps with China in various fields, which will require building huge capacities across the spectrum. India will be forced to take sides between the "Washington Consensus" and the

"Beijing Consensus" which is nothing but a choice between authoritarian and liberal models of growth. India obviously will tilt towards Washington irrespective of Chinese scholars threatening India to maintain a distance from the US. If China's behavior on the ground smells of coercion and brutality, there perhaps won't be buyers for the "China Dream" and "Community of shared future" etc., jargons in the world. India will forge closer defense and economic ties with the US and its allies as envisaged in the relevant agreements.

If China remains insensitive towards India's sensitivities, India may not care too much for China's sensitivities in Tibet, Taiwan and Xinjiang etc. Coversely, India must be watchful of China flaring up insurgencies in India as it did post-1962. Economically, the relationship is bound to take the brunt, but it may augur well for India for the revival and revitalisation of its own industrial supply chains. Nevertheless, here again, India should identify sectors where investment could be attracted and utilised for enhancing its capacities, but the question remains whether it is plausible if relations spiral downward. At a tactical level, if the LAC does not exist for China, it will not exist for India as well. Implying that henceforth, both countries are likely to occupy vantage points and challenge the other side and turn the border hot through their existing "fistfights", limited conflicts or even a full-blown war along all the sectors. If the pattern of China's posturing along the LAC since 2013 is analyzed, it becomes clear where both are heading towards. Additionally, the ramping up of border infrastructure would also demand that Indian army is fully informatised, equipped, and have access to quick logistical support which certainly is not reflected on the ground in Galwan. Finally, if diplomacy prevails and both settle for an East-West swap, it would be the best option, as finding a solution based on history, customs, maps, military, CBMs, and an LAC as a border has proven futile.

4

CHINA WON'T ACCEPT "STATUS QUO ANTE"

On 2nd July 2020, China's *Global Times* interviewed me on the current state of India-China relations. Most of my arguments were incorporated and published except for a few answers to a question – "Some Indian experts believe the recent border clash leads to a "worrisome and extremely serious" turning point in India-China relations. What is your take?" My answer was:

> "In India, we believe that China has altered the status quo in the Western Sector. If the satellite images are to be believed, China has crossed its own Line of Actual Control (LAC) in Galwan and moved a few kilometres westward in the finger areas of Pangong Tso. The coordinates provided by China to India as regards the boundary in the Western Sector during the 1960 border negotiations, and later reinforced on the ground after the 1962 war, including on its maps of the official history of the 1962 conflict titled *History of China's counter attack in self-defence along the Sino-Indian borders* (Chinese edition) published by the Chinese Academy of Military Sciences in 1994 have been violated, implying that China seeks a boundary beyond these coordinates."

I also argued that "some of the Chinese scholars have pointed out that 'China has actually learned this from the Indian experience' perhaps referring to the Doklam standoff, even though India didn't change the status quo in Doklam or in any other sector. India's security establishment and scholarship has come to believe that China is adopting the 'three step strategy' of acquiring territory from the South China Sea to the India-China border, i.e. to change the status quo by the reclamation and militarisation of territory. Therefore, we believe that it translates into the collapse of the confidence building measures (CBMs) and the very Line of Actual Control between India and China. It is in the face of such a shift from China, that many in India believe that China must be confronted rather than accepting the fait accompli of the territory. From this perspective, yes, it is a 'worrisome and extremely dangerous situation', which will impact adversely on various facets of India-China relations." I did manage to make some of these points in another interview during a show called *Dialogue* with China Global Television Network (CGTN) on 3 July 2020.

The above facts, which are indeed worrisome, have been vindicated by many articles written in Chinese mainstream and social media. One published on 3rd July in junshi.china.com, a website dedicated to military affairs, in the backdrop of the 3rd round of talks between the corps commanders of India and China posits that "the most important reason as to why the two sides cannot reach consensus on disengagement is that the Indian side has insisted on the restoration of the "status quo ante" in areas such as the Galwan Valley and Pangong Tso. However, China will obviously not pull back from the Galwan Valley area, and as for the important "Finger 4" area, China said it will never compromise!" According to the article, "India is also reluctant to accept China's demands. The Indian side stated that they will not retreat from Pangong Tso area, nor would they retreat 2-3 kilometers away from Pangong Dao [perhaps finger 3]. In addition, the patrol points of the Galwan Valley and the Hot Springs were also discussed, but the two sides failed to reach a consensus."

The main reason for not retreating from the Galwan standoff site has been given as its "commanding height" which if lost will be "difficult to recapture". The article states that "From the satellite images, it could be seen that the Chinese embankment in the Galwan Valley is still intact. This position is very important, for this is the place where one man can hold out ten thousand men. From here, our army can see the Indian camp opposite us very clearly. More importantly, when the water level rises in the river, many places in the vicinity will be submerged, except this commanding height. Once concessions are made, it will be difficult to recapture it. Therefore, we can understand why China is determined not to retreat." The article further states that "In order to defend this vital place, China has deployed more than 100 military vehicles and established 16 encampments nearby. This place is a key part of the Galwan region, and China will not retreat easily until India doesn't show enough overtures for peace!"

Another argument, which has been debated in China is that border skirmishes are just one of the facets of the India-China relationship and should not hamper relations in other areas. Hu Shisheng, director of the Institute of South and Southeast Asian and Oceanian Studies under the China Institutes of Contemporary International Relations has aired such views in a discussion on CGTN on 27th June. Similar arguments were aired on the 3rd July Dialogue show where I repeated my earlier arguments given to the *Global Times* that "The killing of soldiers and trade with China cannot go on as usual. As far as banning 59 Chinese apps, I believe this is an indication in this direction originating from two concerns. One, the security implications in terms of big data security, China's sharp power that makes inroads into other's societies while the same is denied to others. Two, the revenue earned by these apps in the Indian market is also huge. For example, Tiktok alone has over 300 million downloads in India with over 1 billion-dollar revenue." Cancellations of Chinese contracts in other sectors by India should be seen in this light too.

It is also in this context that the Chinese will often ask you as to "what forms the core of India-China relations?" "Of course, it should be mutual development and exhibiting sensitivity towards each-other's sensitivities and core interests. I believe the understanding that China will not threaten India's security, and respect its interest in the neighbourhood has been undermined, and that this could be discerned from China's pivot to Asia where China's focus is not on consolidating its ties with India but with the smaller countries in the vicinity. This is reflected in China's investment and diplomatic engagement in the region. "The Sino Pak entente cordiale, and China's stance on cross-border terrorism, have made Indians believe that China's strategy is to pin India down to South Asia" I argued while answering another question from the *Global Times*. Many commentators in China are equally enthusiastic about reminding India of the asymmetric economic, military, and technological relationship between India and China. It may be so, but that does not mean that countries will not stand up against China!

5

China Debates India-China Disengagement

On 10 February, Wu Qian, spokesperson of the Ministry of National Defence of China, announced that according to the consensus reached at the ninth round of the commander level talks between China and India, "the Chinese and Indian frontline troops at the southern and northern bank of the Pangong Tso Lake start synchronised and organised disengagement from 10 February." This was confirmed by Wang Wenbin, spokesperson Ministry of Foreign Affairs during a conference on the same day. On the following day, Rajnath Singh, Minister of Defence (MoD) also told the Rajya Sabha in a statement that India and China have agreed to disengage from the Pangong Tso area in eastern Ladakh.

Rajnath Singh told the House that "In response to the Chinese mobilisation of large number of troops and armaments along the Line of Actual Control (LAC) as well as in the depth areas," India responded to the "unilateral action of China" and "showed valour and courage on both South and North bank of Pangong Tso". The minister revealed that India's approach during talks with China was that "(i) both sides should strictly respect and observe the LAC; (ii) neither side should attempt to alter the status quo unilaterally; and (iii) all agreements and understandings between the two sides must be fully abided by in their entirety." The agreement envisages that the "Chinese side will keep its troop presence in the North Bank area to east of Finger 8. Reciprocally, the Indian troops will be based at their permanent base at Dhan Singh Thapa Post near Finger 3. A similar action would be taken in the South Bank area by both sides." MoD's statement also read that "both sides will cease their forward deployments in a phased, coordinated and verified manner" and that "any structures that had been built by both sides since April 2020 in both North and South Bank area will be removed and the landforms will be restored".

How did this happen and at what cost? What do the Chinese state and social media say about it? What kind of future awaits an unsettled border? In India, most people, including the Army, believe that it was China that unilaterally violated the Confidence Building Measures (CBMs) as well as the LAC, and that it was after the Indian Army took control of the commanding heights in Kailash range and Finger 4 that the Chinese side was forced to come to the negotiating table. This perspective is best reflected in Lt Gen Y.K. Joshi's interviews to the Indian print and electronic media. Lt Gen Joshi calls it a win-win for both the sides. However, he gives the impression that the status quo ante that existed before April 2020 has been restored, which is only partially true. It is true for the reason that the People's Liberation Army (PLA) has been forced to go to the east of Finger 8, the Indian claimed LAC. But it is also true that status quo has been altered by forcing a "buffer zone" between Fingers 4 and 8, and neither side will be able to execute any military activity in this area including patrolling. This is similar to what China imposed at patrolling point 14 in the Galwan valley.

On the Chinese side, the narratives are varied, some declaring victory, some expressing disappointment the way the PLA left the occupied areas, and still others declaring it a loss of face for China. Starting from 19 February, the Chinese media launched a large-scale propaganda in the form of a series of videos and articles in the state media accusing India of "nibbling Chinese territory" and held India responsible for provoking the conflict. It was also hyped as a victory aimed at inciting patriotism. China's news agency, *Xinhua* posted a video titled "Video from ground zero of the conflict in the Galwan River Valley revealing desperate struggle between our soldiers and foreign troops"; the *People's Daily* and the *PLA Daily* also published an article entitled "Heroes stood their ground at Karakoram: Heroes and soldiers defending the country and border approaching the New Era"; while an opinion article by the PLA Paper titled "Sing the heroic song, strive to win with a strong army" declared victory against the "foreign army" by the New Era soldiers made of "iron and steel" having the "Party, People, Responsibility and Commandments in Heart". The articles also revealed the names of the Chinese soldiers who lost their lives in the bloody clashes. Besides there are many other articles by anonymous writers on portals such as xilu.com, huanqiu.com and dongfangjinbao between 20 and 24 February.

It is perhaps the revelation of the names after eight months of secrecy, and the manner in which the PLA had to vacate the occupied areas, that drew the ire of the Chinese netizens and commentators in China and beyond. A netizen with the screen name "Crayon Xiaoqiu" (labi Xiaoqiu) commented, if those who went to "rescue" our soldiers were also martyred, it implies that the number of fatalities is more than four. No wonder India was the first to declare its casualties, said the netizen. Chinese social media was abuzz with similar posts which forced the Party to crack down on such people, pronounced as "bedbugs" (chouchong) by one of the earlier-mentioned articles published by the official media. The article said that these "bedbugs" have been "criticising and discrediting the heroes". Fortunately, such "social bugs" have received their "due punishment". Not surprisingly, "Crayon Xiaoqiu", along with one certain Chen from Beijing, and another netizen named "well-known Zed" (Zhiming Zed) from Mianyang, Sichuan were detained by the public security bureau on 20 and 21 February. Li Muyang, a US based Chinese commentator says in the News Insight broadcast on 20 February that the Chinese suffered heavy losses and lost face in the process of the standoff, albeit his channel is critical of mainland China.

Li opines that if the TASS report is to be believed, China lost 11 times more than the reported fatalities. In the same vein, Shen Dan, a US based critic says in an article written on 20 February, on a website called www.aboluowang.com that the CCP (Chinese Communist Party) rather than winning, failed both strategically and tactically on the Sino-Indian border. According to Shen, "It is more likely that the CCP originally intended to provoke conflict and divert attention, for the CCP has been all along wanting to assert power and further consolidate its military strength through local war along the Sino-Indian border. In the end, they failed to achieve their goals and had to claim victory and conceal their actual defeat". Shen further says that unable to cope with two fronts, "the CCP is forced to retreat from the west to deal with the military pressure emanating from the South China Sea, the East China Sea, and the Taiwan Strait". The article further argues that strategically, the conflict cemented India-US relations further and gave birth to the "Mini NATO" in the Asia-Pacific. Another article in xilu.com titled "Sudden withdrawal of troops on the Sino-Indian border is a calculated move by India", on 24 February does acknowledge that "China's core interests still exist in the southeast coast and the South China Sea", but is quick to mention that "it is also impossible for the PLA to retreat unconditionally to areas prior to April 2020", an indication that China's withdrawal from other areas of friction is going to be a tough task.

China may have retreated from Finger 4 to the east of Finger 8, owing to India's control of the Kailash range, however, it is just a minor disengagement from a small pocket; other areas such as Depsang, Hot Spring and Gogra heights remain plausible flash points. India needs to be prepared for the long haul and possibly for a live northern border. As pointed out by the xilu.com commentator, "we may still see escalation in the next few months along the Sino-Indian border".

Secondly, India has sent a strong signal to China that irrespective of stark economic and military asymmetries, India will not allow China to replicate the "three step strategy" (laying claims, reclamation by force, changing the status quo and presenting it as fait accompli) of South China Sea along the India-China border. In fact, as a "psychological warfare" tactic, China has been boasting of better weaponry, infrastructure and logistics support before, during and after the standoff. It is strange to note that some Chinese analysts have argued that India's very economic asymmetries with China were behind India's "offensive" on China along the LAC. An article entitled, "This is the basic reason and motive for India to provoke China" in Fenghuang Net and Jinri Toutiao on 20 February, argues that India's GDP, electricity, steel, cement, production, petroleum consumption is merely 20 per cent, 23.2 per cent, 11 per cent, 12.5 per cent, 37.8 per cent, of China's, respectively. It says that India dreams to become the "Centre of the world manufacturing" but has been "bullied and pushed over" by the biggest "hegemon" China, therefore, by way of "border provocations", "flaring up anti-China sentiments" and "boycotting Chinese goods" India wishes to achieve this goal. Behind India's military provocation, there are economic reasons, argues the anonymous author. It cautions that "In the long run, India is likely to emerge as the biggest geopolitical adversary of China, and it would be foolish to underestimate a country as large as India. For such an ambitious and arrogant neighbour, it is necessary to formulate a long-term response and even a fundamental solution" concludes the article.

Thirdly, from the sequence of events, China's posturing, and negotiation strategy, it is obvious that by way of realising "buffer zones" in friction areas, China is reinforcing the idea of establishing a demilitarized zone (DMZ) along the border. In fact, China has been advancing such a thinking for quite some time in unofficial talks, but India's response has been somewhat lukewarm, as the DMZ, according to India, will not be based on the concept of "equal and mutual security" enshrined in the CBMs. Nonetheless, it could be established if the LAC is identified, but since China has shown no interest in the identification of the LAC, such a possibility is ruled out.

Fourthly, the internal dynamics in China is also in play in the disengagement. Factional politics in China is heating up as is visible from the crackdown on Jack Ma's Ant Group, for the investors have been found related to the Shanghai clique. This is important because China is about to hold the Two Sessions in March, the first centenary of the CPC in July, and finally the 20th Party Congress next year. Any blunder on the border will be detrimental to Xi Jinping's power and image and could intensify the latent faction feud inside China.

Finally, since both India and China have not given up their respective territorial claims in all sectors of the India-China boundary, the best way forward is the East-West swap as suggested by Premier Zhou Enlai in 1960 and elaborated by Cheng Ruisheng, a former ambassador of China to India. According to Ambassador Cheng, China would agree to hand over 90,000 square kilometres of disputed land (in Eastern Sector) to India and make major compromise...and India would hand over 33,000 square kilometres of land in Western Sector to China. As rightly pointed out by Professor Zhang Jiadong of Fudan University, "Neither of them has the ability and willingness to force the other side to accept its claims by military means."

6

CHINA'S NARRATIVE OF THE BORDER STANDOFF

With the military standoff between India and China entering its fifth month, the possibility of complete disengagement and de-escalation in the Western Sector of the India-China boundary appears remote given the adamancy of China in changing the status quo on the ground by force in places like the Depsang plains, the finger areas along the northern bank of Pangong Tso and the Gogra heights, and presenting the same as a fait accompli to the Indian side. This could be attributed as the main reason for a bloody brawl that took place on the 15th June and resulted in 20 fatalities on the Indian side and an undeclared number on the Chinese side. Undoubtedly, the incident has further flared up public opinion and nationalistic sentiments on both sides. Indian troops taking a leaf out of the Chinese playbook on 29-30th August along the high grounds on the Southern bank of Pangong Tso, and the People's Liberation Army's attempt to replicate the 15th June incident in one of the points in this area on 7th September, demonstrates that we are sitting on a powder keg, which may explode anytime.

The new development in the south bank of Pangong Tso has rattled China, and its media and scholarship has minced no words in stating their rhetoric of humiliating India yet again. In order to peek into China's narrative of the standoff, let's examine the following:

One, the debate in China is that since the Indian government has failed to contain the COVID-19 pandemic and the economy has encountered huge difficulties, therefore, the government, in order to divert the attention of its people has picked up a fight with China at the border. They are quick to point that India has beaten Brazil to become the second worst hit country in the world, and that India's second quarter GDP has experienced an unprecedented decline of 23.9 per cent, the worst among the world's major economies. Feng Chuanlu of the Research Institute for Indian Ocean Economies, Yunnan University of Finance and Economics is one of the many Chinese scholars airing such views. In an interview to the *Red Star* News reporter, Feng said, "India's actions and attitude towards China have been to a certain extent related to the out-of-control Covid pandemic, economic downturn, and rising populism." A series of moves from Modi are indeed designed to calm the mood of the domestic public and the opposition parties..." Li Bingxian, a regular contributor to Fanhua, draws an analogy that "there is leakage all over in the big Indian ship."

Two, Chinese scholars have maintained that India has been "nibbling Chinese territory" all along. China has been portrayed as a victim, the one exercising restraint, and never crossing the LAC. Conversely, India has been blamed for her so-called "assertiveness" and "frequent cross-border provocations." Such views are reflected by Long Xingchun of China West Normal University, Lin Minwang of Fudan University, Liu Zongyi of the Shanghai Institute of International Studies and many others. Huang Hancheng, editor in chief of Trigger Trend pronounces the same as India's "wolfish nature" (langzi yexin) and "obsession" (zhinian) with Chinese territory. However, he rebuts his own words when he says "Whoever controls Tibet can control the subcontinent." In fact, India "nibbling Chinese territory" is an old narrative propounded by China's political class as well as older generation scholarship like Wang Hongwei, Yang Gongsu, Wang Dehua etc. and inherited by the present scholarship. The present scholarship argues that India wants to repeat a Doklam in the Western Sector and unilaterally change the status quo but was thwarted by the PLA. However, they fail to explain as to why China's claim line in the Western Sector has been moving westward. As regards the Indian patrolling in finger areas along the north bank of Pangong Tso and Depsang plains, they argue China had "allowed" India to go to the areas she claimed, but China has learnt its lessons since the Doklam standoff.

Three, most of the Chinese scholars are quick to remind India that China's comprehensive national strength is five times bigger than India, its defense budget more than three times that of India, China's weaponry far more advanced than the weapon systems purchased by India from a "thousand countries", and that in event of a conflict, China will definitely win the war and India will have to suffer a humiliation worse than that of 1962. Huang Hancheng is quick to indicate the prevailing asymmetry as regards military assets between India and China. According to him, China has 2.29 times more fighter jets than India; 12.22 times more attack helicopters; 3.8 times more armored combat vehicles; 9.96 times more rocket launchers; 4.6 times more submarines and 3.6 times more destroyers. Moreover, he states that China has better logistical support and infrastructure along the LAC. In the same vein, Feng Chuanlu says that "India cannot afford to fight a war, and would not be able to bear the outcome of defeat. Similar views are mirrored by Gao Feng, a military affair analyst. Moreover, if the standoff enters winter, Indian forces do not have the requisite winter paraphernalia and logistical support, assert the Chinese scholars.

Four, though most of the writings do have a threatening tone, they also advocate that rather than confronting India directly, the game must start from the small countries around India. China must initiate a strategic thinking of "aligning with smaller countries to stabilise the big" (hexiao wenda). For example, strengthening strategic cooperation with countries such as Nepal and Pakistan will help counterbalance India's tough posture against China. This certainly has been part of China's pivot to South Asia for quite some time, however, it remains to be seen if China would be successful in converting some of them into pivot states in the line of Pakistan.

Five, China believes India punches above its weight. Right from the 1950s, "India claimed to be the center of Asia. Nehru once dreamed of establishing an Asian federation with India as its nerve center" asserts Huang. According to Feng, ever since Modi ascended to power in India, he declared India's ambitions to become a "global leader." However, he maintains that India is mistaken that the balance in the "Dragon-Elephant Contest" has tilted in favour of India. The Chinese scholar posits that "against the background of America's hawkish strategy towards China, India believes that it is currently in a period of international strategic opportunities, and has unique geographic superiority to take full control of South Asia and overlook the entire Indian Ocean." In such a scenario, he believes that it would be unrealistic to obtain external support for furthering Indian interests. Many Chinese scholars including Lin Minwang have argued that India has already become a pawn of the US, which could be ascertained from its approach towards border and other regional issues including the Indo-Pacific strategy of the US.

Six, China officially doesn't consider Ladakh as a "part of China", however, China's position on Kashmir and some of the Chinese scholars openly advocating that it is part of Tibet and hence Chinese territory is worrisome. Some of the scholars like Hu Zhiyong of Shanghai Academy of Social Sciences, Wang Dehua of Shanghai Municipal Centre for International Studies and others hold such views. In the wake of the abrogation of Article 370, Chinese analysts made noises that "India assimilates Chinese territory Ladakh into India" and "violates Chinese sovereignty." Scholars such as Lu Yang of Tsinghua University, Zhao Gancheng, a researcher with the Shanghai Institute of International Studies, Lan Jianxue of the China Institute of International Studies, Hu Shisheng of the China Institute of Contemporary International Relations has also published articles reflecting such views.

Seven, as far as India's economic measures against China are concerned, China is in disbelief as to how that could happen. Chinese scholars believe that India is highly dependent on China, if India has taken moves such as banning Chinese apps, cancelling contracts etc. it will harm India rather than China. It is true that in the short and medium term Indian supply chains in electronics, telecommunication, automobile and pharmaceutical sector are bound to be disrupted, but in the long run, it may make India self-reliant in these sectors and boost domestic manufacturing.

Finally, it is obvious that China's perception about the standoff is diametrically opposite of India's. No one needs to tell the world as to which country has been doing and simulating military exercises since early 2020, and altering the prevailing status quo in the Western Sector. The only thing India has been negotiating with China is the restoration of the status quo ante. If it doesn't happen, the repetition of capturing higher ground in all the sectors of the India-China boundary by both cannot be ruled out. The very exercise will push both to the razor's edge as has been witnessed at the northern and southern banks of Pangong Tso. The tone and tenor of External Affairs Minister S. Jaishankar and his counterpart Wang Yi's meeting in Moscow has raised hopes for a diplomatic settlement. However, both sides need to walk the talk, both must activate all channels at their disposal including another Modi-Xi summit to inject positive energy to the relationship and save it from further derailment.

7

THE DOKLAM STANDOFF:
DANGEROUSLY DIVERGING INTERPRETATIONS

In order to understand the present standoff at Doklam, it is necessary to revisit the great game between colonial India and imperial China regarding their spheres of influence in the Himalayan states. The much-referred 'Convention between Great Britain and China relating to Sikkim' on the 17th of March, 1890, was a spinoff of the 1886 Tibetan invasion of Lingtu, a place eighteen miles within the Sikkim frontier.[1] However, the Tibetans and Chinese maintained that the post was within Tibetan territory, and even if it was not, it had all the right to do so since Sikkim was its vassal state.[2] The British demanded the withdrawal of Tibet from Lingtu but Tibet refused to budge; on the contrary, Tibet demanded the British withdraw from Sikkim and Bhutan. Wen Shuo, the Chinese Amban or imperial resident in Lhasa, supported the Tibetans but was admonished by the Qing court and dismissed in 1888 for fomenting trouble. A new Amban, Sheng Tai, was appointed in his place.[3] The British resorted to force and ejected the Tibetan army from Lingtu; Sheng Tai memorialised the throne on June 18, 1888, apprising that the Lingtu affair was settled for good. The British had recalled their forces, and the status quo that existed two years back had been restored.[4]

Contrary to Sheng Tai's assurances to the Qing court, the affair was not settled as yet, for the Tibetans were preparing for another battle. It was under such circumstances that the Manchus sent Sheng to Calcutta to conduct further negotiations and sign a treaty with the British to settle the Sikkim-Tibet boundary, which he signed on March 17, 1890. According to Alistair Lamb, even after ten years of long discussions from 1894 to 1903, the British and Chinese failed to persuade the Tibetans to accept the 1890 boundary, which had been arranged on their behalf.[5] The Chinese consulate in Manchester also adheres to this view when a post on its website says that 'They (the Tibetans) even managed to destroy the border stones erected by Britain in an open protest against the border division and the unfair treaties.' Chinese scholarship on the other hand is of the view that ever since the signing of this convention; China lost its *sovereignty* over Sikkim.[6]

Notwithstanding the Tibetan disagreement, the convention did decide the Sikkim-Tibet boundary. Article 1 of the convention reads:

> "The boundary of Sikkim and Tibet shall be the crest of the mountain range separating the waters flowing into the Sikkim Teesta and its affluent from the waters flowing into the Tibetan Mochu and northwards into other rivers of Tibet. The line commences at Mount Gipmochi and follows the above mentioned water parting to the point where it meets Nipal territory."[7]

China has made use of this convention for claiming the tri-junction of India-China-Bhutan at Gipmochi or *Gymochen or* Jimu Mazhen in Chinese. However, according to geographical features, the 'watershed' and 'the crest of the mountain range', don't stretch beyond Batang La, 6 kilometres north of Doka La. It is this interpretation which Bhutan and India are holding to and which has infuriated China the most. China has built a motorable road to Shinche La or Shenjiula in Chinese since the early 2000s. However, when China presently wanted to extend it to the Jampheri Ridge near Doka La, roughly over 2 kilometres north of Gipmochi, Indian forces entered the third country to stop the construction.

The area of the standoff is a disputed territory between Bhutan and China and both have concluded 24 rounds of talks to resolve the dispute.

China has expressed its interest to swap the area with disputed areas in Northern and Eastern Bhutan, but owing to its special relationship with India, Bhutan is unable to strike a deal with China. Moreover, according to Bhutan, there is a written agreement of 1998 between Bhutan and China, which says that both will safeguard peace in the area and maintain the status quo. India's former National Security Advisor, Shiv Shankar Menon has also maintained that this is China's attempt to change the status quo at the tri-junction.

This is the tri-junction which China's *People's Daily* has issued in its official blog, warning India that the 'border line is the bottom line.' On July 11, 2017 the same paper posted an image from its September 1962 front page editorial titled, "If this can be tolerated, what cannot?" *People's Daily*'s sister newspaper *Global Times* has provided a lot of ammunition to provoke India by spitting venom in its dozens of articles and commentaries, unprecedented in the modern history of India-China relations. Even though serious Chinese scholarship on the Indian side has brushed these aside, nonetheless, there is a view in India which holds that perhaps for the first time, Chinese diplomacy has been hijacked by the papers and social media.

What are the reasons for such behaviour? At the outset, the global political and economic architecture is undergoing a fundamental transformation, and there is no doubt that China is instrumental in driving this change, as it contributes to over 30 per cent of global economic growth. As far as regional contours are concerned, China outsmarts India in political, economic as well as military domains. Economically, it is the largest trade partner of almost each and every country in the Asia-Pacific. China's military build-up continues to grow as it is able to pump four times the money India uses, into defence expenditure. Globally, contrary to its traditional non-interventionist tendencies, China increasingly behaves like a great power, and demands respect from the established hegemon, the US.

However, it is India which many believe is holding its ground against China, be it through the question of boycotting China's Belt and Road Forum in Beijing on account of its sovereignty concerns in the China Pakistan Economic Corridor; India's forays into the Pacific Ocean to the displeasure of China; raising its voice against China's increased interests in the Indian Ocean Region; or building intimate relations with China's adversaries like the US, Japan and Vietnam. Therefore, as India starts to play the balance of power game more seriously, it has disrupted the Chinese calculations of establishing a new regional and perhaps global order in face of the US retrenchment, albeit India has joined many initiatives of China such as the AIIB, BRICS New Development Bank, and more recently the Shanghai Cooperation Organisation.

That said, the ongoing standoff is seemingly heading towards a dangerous confrontation. Given the Indian military presence in Bhutan, China may assert more pressure on Bhutan, and also build more structures in the disputed territory. Similar behaviour and interpretations during the 1962 conflict resulted in an all-out war between the two countries. China opening up new fronts in line of the 2013 and 2014 standoffs in the Western sector will aggravate the already volatile situation. The only possible way to end the present standoff is the restoration of the mid-June status quo – i.e. the Indian troops withdrawing to the Indian side of the border and Chinese assuring that the status quo would not be changed. After all, the foundation of any cooperation between India and China has been that both will leave jittery issues for future consideration.

This consensus indeed created a conducive environment for economic development and enabled the two sides to sign a series of confidence building measures to control and manage their differences on border issues. Though these mechanisms fall short of resolving the complex border issue, they nonetheless have paved the way for a comprehensive development of bilateral relations. There are huge complementarities between the two, if this potential is tapped, both could be partners in each other's development. This brinkmanship will lead the two countries nowhere!

NOTES

1. Bell, Charles (1924). *Tibet Past and Present*. Oxford University Publication, London. p. 60; Lamb, Alastair (1966). *The McMahon Line*, Volume I and II. Routledge and Kegan Paul Ltd., London. p. 127.
2. Yang, Gongsu 杨公素(1992). 中国反对外国侵略干涉西藏地方斗争史 (*History of China's Struggle and Resistance to the Foreign Invasion and interference in Tibet*). China's Tibetology Publications, Beijing. pp. 73-74; *Qingji Waijiao Shiliao* 清季外交史料 (*The Sources of*

Diplomatic History of Late Qing Dynasty) Wenhai Publishers, Taipei (1964). Vol. 3, Juan 75, p. 214.
3. Li Wenhai comp. 李文海 (2000). 清史便年 (*Annals of Qing Dynasty*). Peoples University Press, Beijing. Juan 2, p. 481.
4. Li Wenhai comp. 李文海 (2000). Juan 2, p. 488.
5. *Qingji Waijiao Shiliao* 清季外交史料 (1964: 38).
6. Wang Hongwei 王宏纬 (1998). 喜马拉雅山情节：中印关系研究 (*The Himalayas Sentiment: A Study of Sino Indian Relations*). China Tibetology Publication, Beijing. p. 56.
7. Convention between Great Britain and China relating to Sikkim, available at http://treaties.fco.gov.uk/docs/pdf/1894/TS0011.pdf

8

THE DALAI LAMA'S REINCARNATION AND THE TIBET ISSUE

On 18th March 2018, the *Reuters* published an exclusive interview with the Dalai Lama in which the Dalai asserted that "In the future, in case you see two Dalai Lamas come, one from here, in a free country, one chosen by Chinese, then nobody will trust, nobody will respect (the one chosen by China). So that's an additional problem for the Chinese! It's possible, it can happen." On 19th March, Geng Shuang, the spokesperson of China's Ministry of Foreign Affairs responded to it by saying that:

> "Reincarnation of living Buddhas, as a unique institution of inheritance in Tibetan Buddhism, comes with a set range of rituals and conventions. The Chinese government implements the policy of freedom of religious belief. The reincarnation system is respected and protected by such legal instruments as Regulations on Religious Affairs and Measures on the Management of the Reincarnation of Living Buddhas. The institution of reincarnation of the Dalai Lama has been in existence for several hundred years. The 14th Dalai Lama himself was found and recognised following religious rituals and historical conventions and his enthronement was approved by

the then central government. Therefore reincarnation of living Buddhas including the Dalai Lama must comply with Chinese laws and regulations and follow religious rituals and historical conventions."

This statement emphasises two things. One, that the incarnation of the Dalai Lama must follow *rituals and historical conventions*. And two, it would be decided by such *legal instruments* as "Regulations on Religious Affairs and Measures on the Management of the Reincarnation of Living Buddhas." Now, as regards the rituals and conventions, these were laid down by the Qing Emperor Qianlong, once his 170,000 strong army defeated the Gurkhas in the aftermath of the latter's invasion of Tibet in 1791. Amongst these, the most prominent and often quoted by the Chinese is the "29-Article Ordinance for More Effective Governance of Tibet" which stipulated that the *Ambans* or the Qing imperial resident commissioner in Tibet will enjoy the same status as the Dalai and the Panchen; the reincarnation of the Dalai Lama, the Panchen and various Hotogtu Rinpochs must follow the procedure of drawing lots from the golden urn under the supervision of the Ambans and the same must be reported to the imperial court for approval; a new uniform currency bearing the title of the emperor was issued; traders were required to carry a passport; all communication with neighbouring states was to be conducted through *Ambans*. Some Chinese scholars, for example, Li Tieh-Tseng in his book *The Historical Status of Tibet* traces real Chinese sovereignty over Tibet from 1791, contrary to most scholars tracing it from the Yuan Dynasty. As regards the 'legal instruments', the "Regulations on Religious Affairs and Measures on the Management of the Reincarnation of Living Buddhas" was issued by the State Administration for Religious Affairs of the People's Republic of China on 18th July 2007 and went into effect from 1st September 2007. These provide the legal basis for China rejecting any incarnation announced outside Tibet. In all, there are 14 articles in these 'Regulations'. However, article 2 remains most crucial as it stipulates that:

> "Reincarnating living Buddhas should respect and protect the principles of the unification of the state, protect the unity of the minorities, protect religious concord and social harmony, and

protect the normal order of Tibetan Buddhism. Reincarnating living Buddhas should respect the religious rituals and historically established systems of Tibetan Buddhism, but may not re-establish feudal privileges which have already been abolished. Reincarnating living Buddhas shall not be interfered with or be under the dominion of any foreign organisation or individual."

The two requirements flagged by Geng Shuang make it clear that China will designate its own Dalai Lama and any name proposed by the Dalai Lama or any organisation outside Tibet would be deemed illegal. The statements regarding the incarnation by the Dalai Lama and their castigation by China is not new. The Dalai Lama has been saying many things as regards his reincarnation. For example, he has been saying that the issue of reincarnationa would be decided by his believers; that there would be no Dalai Lama after his death; or rather a beautiful maiden may be his reincarnation, or his reincarnation would be outside China, and even outside the planet. China has castigated such remarks by the the Dalai Lama as non-serious and laughable. It has argued that since the Dalai is aging, and because the prospect of "Tibetan independence" seems bleak, he has indulged in such talks. Zhu Weiqun, *Director* of the Ethnic and *Religious Commission* of the Chinese People's Political Consultative Conference has termed the Dalai Lama's remarks on re incarnation as 'extremely non-serious.'

This time, we have not witnessed the kind of criticism China poured on the Dalai in the past so far, though the Chinese approach remains the same. For example, since the 2008 Lhasa riots, Zhang Qingli, the then general secretary of the Communist Party in Tibet has pronounced the Dalai Lama to be a "wolf in monk's robes." Zhang had said that he actually quoted the words of Zhou Enlai to describe the Dalai Lama in that way. Zhang also made comparisons between the Dalai Lama and Rebiya Kadeer, a Uygur separatist leader from Xinjiang. Reacting to the Dalai Lama's announcement of retirement, Qiangba Puncog, the then Chairman of the Standing Committee of the Tibet Autonomous Region's People's Congress said on the sidelines of the NPC session on 11 March 2011 that the Dalai's retirement is "absolutely meaningless." He said, "Since no country recognises his self-declared 'Tibetan Government in Exile', whatever he does in his illegal political organisation is nonsense and Tibet will not be affected at all." Puncog admitted that the "Dalai Lama, as a Living Buddha and religious leader, does have some influence on his believers," but also said that "his death is expected to have a minor impact on Tibet, the overall social situation will remain stable, and we are prepared to handle some minor turbulence here and there after his death."

Therefore, the fundamental perceptions of the Tibetan émigrés and China are very divergent. As far as the Dalai Lama headed 'TGIE' is concerned, it has adopted the 'middle way' approach for the resolution of the Tibet issue. In brief, the Dalai Lama demands "genuine autonomy" within the constitutional framework of the Peoples' Republic of China. However, part one of the Strasbourg proposals that deal with the history of Tibet and deem Tibet as an independent country before 1949 is troublesome and has not gone well with the Chinese government. The second part is forward looking and deals with the future of Tibet. China would remain responsible for Tibet's foreign policy, but Tibet would be governed by its own constitution. The government of Tibet would comprise a popular elected chief executive, a bicameral legislature and an independent legal system. The other major hurdle is the demand to restore the whole of Tibet known as greater Tibet. The greater Tibet or the so called 'Cholka–Sum' is the ethnic Tibet which consisted of three provinces, namely, U Tsang, Kham and Amdo. Genuine autonomy is sought for all 6 million Tibetans in China, not just the 2.6 million Tibetans living in the Tibet Autonomous Region (TAR).

As far as China is concerned, whether it was the issue of the Dalai Lama's retirement or the recent reincarnation, it cares little, and describes the Dalai Lama's proposals or the demand for 'genuine autonomy' as a ploy to seek independence, semi independence or even independence in disguised form, for according to China the 'Charter of the Tibetan in Exile' promulgated in 1991, maintains that efforts shall be made to transform a future Tibet into a Federal Democratic Self-Governing Republic and a zone of peace throughout her three regions, and the Dalai Lama as a head of such a future entity. Therefore, to Beijing, the real motive of "genuine autonomy" could be best described as a "sanbuqu" (Trilogy) to secure

Tibetan independence: i.e. one, to secure the return of the Dalai Lama to Tibet through negotiations; two, to gain political power through "genuine autonomy"; and three, to realise "Tibetan independence" through a "referendum."

It could be discerned that these are extremely divergent positions and there is no meeting ground for the two sides. China is eagerly waiting for the demise of the Dalai Lama as is evident from the statements of its officials in Tibet. Nevertheless, it would be wishful thinking on China's part if it believes that the Tibetan movement will die with the demise of the Dalai Lama. The émigrés feel that the TGIE has matured as an institution and would continue to be an umbrella organisation for Tibetan émigrés throughout the world, and continue to follow the course of non-violence and engage China in dialogue. Organisations such as the Tibetan Youth Congress (TYC), Tibetan Women's Association (TWA), National Democratic Party of Tibet (NDPT), Gu-Chu-Sum Movement (GCSM) Students for a Free Tibet (SFT), the International Tibet Support Network (ITSN) and the Tibetan Writers Organisation (TWO) etc. which have been pronounced by China as 'radical' and at times 'terror outfits' are likely to continue their struggle through the tactics of the mass movement on the one hand, and arouse international support and sympathy for their cause on the other. Everyone acknowledges that the void left by the Dalai Lama would be difficult to fill in. It would not only be a huge loss for Tibet and the émigrés but a loss for China too, for China will never find a personality like him, who could wield the support he did, and secure a peaceful resolution of the Tibet issue.

9

CHINESE MEDIA AND INDIA'S ANTI-TERROR STRIKES INSIDE PAKISTAN

In the wake of India's air strikes on the Jaish-e-Mohammed (JeM) training camp in Balakot, Pakistan, the Chinese media is abuzz with all kinds of reports and analysis, but one and all maintain that the source of the present tension between India and Pakistan is India holding Pakistan responsible for the Pulwama terror attack. They posit that India "without any real evidence", "identified the Pakistani government as a "behind-the-scenes manipulator" of the attack irrespective of the fact that "Pakistan has denied having any track with the outfit." Cheng Xizhong, a Senior Research Fellow at the Chahar Institute, holds that India "unilaterally crossing the Line of Control" is solely responsible for the current tensions. According to him, "unilateral air strikes against the so-called 'terror camp' is a serious violation of the [ceasefire] agreement reached between India and Pakistan."

According to a CNR (China National Radio) Defense Time military observer, Fang Bing, the Indian airstrikes were not carried inside Pakistan but in 'Pakistan controlled Kashmir'. The Chinese version of the Indian 'preemptive' and 'non-military strikes' on the JeM training camp in Balakot matches the reports emanating from Pakistan. It says that since the strikes were carried out in the wee hours at around 3.30 am, Pakistan could not scramble enough fighter jets to intercept the incoming Mirage fighters of India. Moreover, the ZDK03 early warning aircraft was also not airborne. However, once the Chinese made JF17 (xiaolong or Thunder) was employed to intercept the Indian Mirage fighters, the Indian jets prematurely emptied their ammo onto a hilltop, causing the 'death' of ten trees and "did not achieve the desired effect." A partial photograph of the bombing site displaying the caption "My name is pine tree and I am not a terrorist", perhaps lifted from a certain Pakistani social media post, was embedded in the article. Another article questions the worth of around US$ 10 billion surgical strike by India whose military assets have been "manufactured in a thousand countries".

As regards the "retaliatory strikes" by the Pakistan Air Force, the Chinese local media has all the praises for its third generation JF 17 successfully shooting down the "comparatively low grade MiG 21" and capturing an Indian pilot alive, whose photographs along with his service pistol, maps and survival on land booklet are being flashed in the media with headlines like "Captured!", and "After being shot down the pilot dropped his pistol and surrendered" etc. Some of the reports also say that the Chinese made jet also shot down a SU-30 MKI, and that if the report turns out to be true, the 'superior features' of the Chinese aircraft and the "professional capabilities of the Pakistani pilots" have been established. Another piece that featured in Tencent News, reports the loss of two IAF fighter jets – one falling in "Azad Kashmir" and the other in and around the LOC area. In addition, it said that two Indian pilots have died and one was captured. It further adds that "Pakistan has not only gained the advantage in this military conflict, but has also taken the initiative to appeal to the Indian side for dialogue and achieved the moral high ground."

As regards India's air defense shooting down a Pakistani military unmanned aircraft, one report says that according to India, the unmanned aircraft had been bought by Pakistan from a 'neighbouring country', and was shot down by newly procured SPYDER missiles from Israel. It also reports the Indian claim of shooting down a Pakistani F-16 but buys the Pakistani argument that its F-16s were not used in combat. Some articles are even speculating that India and Pakistan are at the verge of fighting a fourth war, and that India's only aircraft career Vikrmaditya is eyeing Karachi. Nevertheless, they say that so far, "Pakistan has clearly gained the upper hand in the conflict initiated by India." Even the loss of 7 Indian Air Force personnel in an accidental MI-17 helicopter crash was adjudged as a "big gain for Pakistan" in another headline.

An article posted on Tencent News titled "Is the US brazenly protecting India and unreasonably depriving our Iron Brother, Pakistan of its right to counterattack?" argues that Secretary of State Pompeo's statement that "the two sides should avoid further escalation" cannot hide the US conspiracy to protect India. According to the anonymous analyst, "the US has not persuaded the two allies to stop the conflict in a fair and just manner. On the contrary, it has unreasonably demanded that the Iron Brother Pakistan "refrain from further military action"; to put it bluntly, the US is asking the Pakistanis "to not fight back", thus creating a space for the Modi government to "win this war." It says that in the context of the Indo-Pacific, India figures more prominently than Pakistan in US strategy, for India can afford to buy high-value US military equipment at a higher price, and also has the ability to contain Russia. Conversely, Pakistan, besides playing a role in the Afghan issue, has little value for the US. Obviously, Pakistan will not submit to India in accordance with the wishes of the United States, concludes the analyst.

It could be discerned that though the mainstream English newspaper *China Daily* and *Xinhua* have reported responsibly, various media outlets, especially those on social media which cater to domestic consumption, have reported events differently. No wonder, for right from the early 1960s when China formed an entente cordiale with Pakistan, it has portrayed Pakistan as a victim in its domestic media, even if the latter has been the aggressor in all the wars it has fought with India. Therefore, China sympathising with Pakistan and its proxies like LeT and JeM should not be surprising. We have seen how the Chinese press has reported on the Kargil War of 1999, the 2001 terror attack on the Indian Parliament, the Pathankot and Uri terror attacks in 2016, and even absolved Pakistan from the 26/11 Mumbai terror attack and blamed it on some 'Hindu fundamentalists' as Ajmal Kasab and the other attackers were supporting the Hindu sacred thread on their wrists. China knows who Masood Azhar is, and how he was exchanged for the safety of hijacked Air India flight IC 814 and much more. However, India must know that even if China supports the fresh proposal of the US, the UK and France to designate the JeM head as a global terrorist in the UN Security Council, chances of which seem remote, nothing much will change on the ground except his international travels and seizure of funds. Therefore, India needs to have a sound security apparatus, and above all, a lean and mean hi-tech integrated force to deal with any contingency.

10

SHIFTING BALANCE OF POWER AND NEPAL'S "EQUIDISTANCE POLICY" TOWARDS INDIA AND CHINA

Post-1791-92 when Chinese forces trounced the Nepalese army from Tibet, Nepal was reduced to a "tributary state", sending tributes to China once every five years, the last being in 1910. Nepal played the so called "China card" against British India during the Anglo-Nepalese War of 1814-1816, but China refrained from helping it, and pronounced the "Ghurkhas as bullies and insatiably avaricious, responsible for fomenting trouble in the south-western frontier." When Nepal tried to play the "British India card", threatening China with shifting its allegiance to the British, China got irked and rebuked Nepal: "if you throw your allegiance to the British, then you would not be entitled to send tributes to the Celestial Empire...As regards dealing with the tribes outside our frontiers, the Celestial Empire will not extend military assistance to any of the warring sides [referring to the Nepalese invasion of Sikkim]. The Celestial Empire is least bothered if your country concludes peace or goes to war with the British, approaches or eventually throw your allegiance to the British." (Deepak, B.R. *India and China 1904-2004: A Century of Pace and Conflict,* p. 13).

Today, when China has emerged as the second largest economy of the world and the challenger to the established global hegemon, to expect China to be indifferent to the smaller countries in the vicinity and beyond, as shown above would be wishful thinking. As for Nepal or any other country, choosing not to benefit from China's deep pockets, would be equally foolish and ignorant of ground realities. As for India, rather than helping Nepal overcome the devastation wreaked by an earthquake in 2015, it threw Nepal further into the abyss of misery by 'supporting' the Madhesi blockade. Furthermore, then Nepali Prime Minister Oli had blamed India for removing him "by remote control" when he concluded trade and energy deals with China in the wake of the blockade. China and Nepal were likely to announce the Lhasa-Kathmandu rail link under the "Belt and Road Initiative" of China during Chinese President Xi Jinping's prospective Nepal visit that had to be cancelled in the wake of Oli's resignation. In the December 2017 parliamentary elections, the alliance of Communist parties in Nepal registered an impressive majority amidst anti-India sentiments, and Oli was sworn in as Prime Minister once again in mid-February 2018.

It is in this background that K.P. Oli is visiting India, although there are already noises in Nepal saying that the visit has been announced unilaterally by New Delhi, not giving enough time to Oli to prepare for it. Will he be able to convince New Delhi that his policy of "equidistance" is not an embrace with China? Will he buy New Delhi's argument that China's entrenchment in Nepal remains a concern for India? Will he be able to extract as many benefits from India as he has been able to extract from China, especially when the Modi government is already in election mode? And, will India introspect as to why a culturally close neighbour has moved away from its so called "sphere of influence"? There are no easy answers to these questions. However, we may find some answer if New Delhi introspects the question of Nepal moving away from its influence.

It is economics, stupid! In November 2017, during a two-day Nepal Investment Summit, 89 companies from China committed an investment of US$ 8.3 billion in various sectors, compared to an investment of US$ 317 million committed by 21 Indian companies present at the Summit. Even Bangladeshi and Sri Lankan commitments far exceeded the Indian investment. China is executing projects such as the building of Pokhara airport, budgeted at US$ 216 million, the Melamchi Water Supply Project, valued at US$ 294.4 million, and the US$ 3 billion Lumbini Project that will have an airport, hotels, convention centre, temples and a Buddhist university, all connected with a system of highways. The US$ 2.5 billion Budhi Gandaki hydroelectric project that Nepal scrapped last year is certainly going to be given back to China. The 750 MW project to be built on the West Seti River is also being built by China.

Prime Minister Narendra Modi blamed previous Indian governments for letting Nepal down during his Nepal visit in 2014. In tandem with his counterpart, he unveiled a plaque for the police academy that India had promised to Nepal in the 1990s. Like much of the 'foundation stone' ceremonies in India, the academy remained an empty promise. The Chinese seized the opportunity and built a swanky academy with a cost of US$ 350 million in a record time of two years, and gifted it free of cost to Nepal in June 2017. India's other projects in Nepal such as the Rs. 33108 crore Pancheshwar multi-purpose project on the Mahakali river envisaged in the 1990s and revived during Modi's Nepal visit have not made much progress. During the Nepal Infrastructure Summit 2017, India announced that it would build Delhi-Kathmandu and Kolkata-Kathmandu railways to increase Nepal's connectivity with India. It is likely to remain nothing but an announcement for times to come; China meanwhile plans to complete the Lhasa Kathmandu line between 2020 and 2022. It is this noncommittal approach of India, added to its arm twisting of Nepal that has led to China's deep entrenchment in Nepal's infrastructure, energy and transport sectors today. By signing the "Belt and Road Initiative" with China, Nepal would be connected even better with China through rail, road, dry ports, optical fibres and so on and so forth.

Simultaneously, China has been assisting Nepal in strengthening its armed forces. In 1989 when Nepal imported arms from China, India imposed economic sanctions and closed 13 of the 15 transit points on the India-Nepal border. This was at a time when India enjoyed exclusive influence. Today however, Nepal is not only buying military equipment, it has also concluded its first ever military exercise named "Sagarmatha Friendship 2017" with China in April 2017. Moreover, while India has taken its cultural ties for granted with Nepal, China has invested US$ 80 million to boost its soft power in Nepal. Dozens of China Study Centres, a Confucius Institute in Kathmandu University and a few Confucius

Classrooms are imparting Chinese language and culture training to thousands of Nepalese. It has been reported that the Confucius Institute alone has trained over 20,000 Nepalese in a decade. These include members of the armed forces, police, bureaucrats, businessmen, and so on and so forth. The Ministry of Education of Nepal has announced that it will offer courses in Chinese. Today, over 3000 Nepalese students are studying in Chinese universities on Chinese government scholarship programs.

Why has Nepal embraced China, along with other neighbours of India? It didn't happen overnight. It has been happening since the economic rise of China began 40 years ago. In these years, starting from India's parity with China, the latter's economic muscle has become 5 times bigger than India at US$ 13 trillion and the gap is yawning. Indian blockades, be it in the 1960s, 1989 or 2015 have crippled the Nepalese economy, and added salt to injuries and flared anti-India sentiments in Nepal. Conversely, will China salvage Nepal from its difficulties? Maybe to some extent but, replacing India's 15 transit points along the open India-Nepal border with a 900 kilometre Nepal-Lhasa road is just impossible. India alone can have the magnanimity of opening its border to Nepal, not any other nation. This magnanimity needs to be replicated in other spheres, and India needs to act more and be less cacophonous at home and abroad.

India needs to lie low, strengthen its domestic economic drivers, build capacities and make itself attractive to its neighbours and the World. Until that happens, India must strategise how to engage with and integrate these nations into its economic development, show magnanimity in various disputes and increase its footprints in these countries. In this context, India may have to selectively approach China's Belt and Road Initiative, and reap benefits from bilateral and multilateral engagement with China. The trans-Himalayan region, with Nepal at its heart, would be crucial for transport, trade and tourism. We must think beyond the security prism as far as 3Ts are concerned, if at all we would like to make this shared neighbourhood a better place to live! From this perspective, Oli's India visit is extremely important, even if his coalition government at home may already have run into some difficulties. Here again, India must assure him that she aspires to see a stable and prosperous Nepal.

11

Kyaukpyu Port Construction and China-Myanmar Economic Corridor

On 19th November 2017, China's Ministry of Foreign Affairs revealed that during his meeting with the State Counsellor and Foreign Minister Aung San Suu Kyi in Nay Pyi Taw, Foreign Minister Wang Yi proposed the establishment of a China-Myanmar Economic Corridor (CMEC) which will connect China's southwestern province of Yunnan to Mandalay in central Myanmar, and stretching East till Yangon and West to the Kyaukpyu Special Economic Zone (SEZ), forming an equation of three-terminal support (*sanduan zhicheng*) and three-legged cooperation (*sanzu dingli*). Wang Yi pointed out that the CMEC will open up new vistas for building the 'Belt and Road Initiative' between China and Myanmar. At that time, the news hardly made any headlines, for it was overshadowed by China's three-phase proposal to address the Rakhine State issue. On 9th September 2018, China's National Development and Reform Commission (NDRC) issued a statement that China and Myanmar have signed an MoU to build the CMEC. This would be the second bilateral economic corridor after the China-Pakistan Economic Corridor (CPEC) and perhaps another flagship of Xi Jinping's pet project, the BRI. It was only on 8th November when China and Myanmar signed a renewed agreement as regards the

Kyaukpyu port, that it made headlines in the Indian press pronouncing it as a third 'pearl' in the 'string', after Gwadar in Pakistan and Hambantota in Sri Lanka.

The CMEC is envisaged as having a Kyaukpyu deep sea water port (US$ 1.3 billion) with two berths in its initial phase including Kyaukpyu SEZ (US$ 2 billion); a China-Myanmar oil and gas pipeline (US$ 5 billion); a Mandalay Yida Economic and Trade Cooperation Zone (US$ 4 billion); a Tagaung Taung (*Dagongshan*) Nickel Industry Development Project (US$ 820 million); an over Letpadaung copper mine project (US$ 1 billion); a Kunming-Kyaukpyu railway line; a Mandalay-Tigyaing-Muse expressway and a Kyaukpyu-Nay Pyi Taw highway project etc. Though the CITIC Myanmar CEO Yuan Xibin argues that China didn't want to have the present 70 per cent stake in the Kyaukpyu port, it is however widely believed that China wanted to have between 70-85 per cent stake owing to the aborted, US$ 1.5 billion Myitsone dam project, where China suffered huge economic losses. Also owing to debt trap issues, Myanmar cut the originally conceived ten berth port worth US$ 7.5 billion to the present scale of investment. Many of these projects predate the BRI and were negotiated by China taking the so called 'Arial route'.

It could be discerned that China's economic engagement has deepened irrespective of the government change in Myanmar. In 2017, bilateral trade between China and Myanmar totaled US$ 13.54 billion and registered a year-on-year increase of 10.2 per cent, of which 79.8 per cent was in the value of border trade. In terms of investment, according to the data provided by the Myanmar Investment and Corporate Administration, by 28th February 2018, China (including Hong Kong and Macao) ranked first in foreign direct investment (FDI) in Myanmar, investing in 344 projects totaling US$ 24.85 billion. The port is of great strategic and economic significance to China as it will give it access to the Bay of Bengal, diversify its energy routes, and cut short almost 5000 kms of sea routes, thus getting rid of the so-called Malacca dilemma. China would be able to stock its energy and other imports from the Middle East, Europe, Africa, India etc. in Kyaukpyu and transport these to China through the already functional pipeline, roads and proposed rail connections. As reported in July this year by various Chinese news reports, the pipeline has unloaded a record 10.98 million tons of crude oil. As of September this year, the cumulative transportation volume has been recorded at 21.426 billion cubic meters, of which 18.715 billion cubic meters were shipped to China.

The Myanmar government has allayed the security fears of India and Western countries, stating that there would not be any Chinese military presence at the port. However, since the lease is supposed to be for 50 years and extendable to another 25 years, apprehensions remain. Furthermore, since Rakhine State has seen the unprecedented Rohingya refugee crisis marred by sectarian violence and terror attacks, large-scale Chinese investments in Rakhine will surely call for more security measures. It can be expected that in order to protect its long-term interests, China will certainly demand that the Myanmar government provide security as it has done in the case of the CPEC, failing which it may leverage its influence in the Kachin and Kokang areas to drive home a point, albeit China has responded positively to Myanmar restarting the peace process in these areas. China's special envoy Sun Guoxiang even held talks with the leaders of the Myanmar-Northern coalition forces in Kunming. It is believed that the participation of rebel groups in the peace process owes itself to Chinese mediation.

As far as India is concerned, it has been out of the BRI owing to its core issue involving sovereignty, though it has rightly remained open to business transactions with China. The BCIM economic corridor where India is a stakeholder along with Myanmar and Bangladesh is yet to take off owing to various degrees of indifference shown by the respective parties. The CMEC will further dilute the multilateral corridor as China is increasingly taking the bilateral route. Therefore, it becomes pertinent that while engaging multilaterally, new bilateral corridors are negotiated with China with desired stakes, which then could be docked to our connectivity initiatives in the immediate and extended neighbourhood. The trans-Himalayan region from India's Kashmir to the Northeast would be crucial for transport, trade and tourism, and also for poverty alleviation and integrating these regions with the mainstream. While India must not compromise its security, she must at the same time think beyond the security prism as far as these issues are concerned.

Interestingly, though India has been wary of China's forays in the Indian Ocean, it has advocated for the inclusion of China in the Indo-Pacific pivot before and after the Wuhan unofficial summit, which is not necessarily bad thinking. At the same time, India has been hedging China's advances by concluding logistical agreements with the US, France, Japan etc. by linking its onshore facilities with the offshore facilities of its defense partners. Nevertheless, the kind of buffers and naval and overland infrastructure China has been able to create in the last four decades is unprecedented and India may have to play catch up for a long time. The logic is simple – as long as your domestic economic drivers are not strong, you may not be able to bridge the asymmetrical gap with China and others. Therefore, why not to take a cue from Deng Xiaoping's strategy of 'hide your capabilities and bide your time' for at least a decade or two.

12

CHINA'S FOOTPRINTS IN INDIA'S NEIGHBOURHOOD

In 1947, noted Irish historian Nicolas Mansergh wrote an article on the Asian Conference of 1946 in the *International Affairs* and remarked that China was opposed to India's cultural leadership in the region, and that its representatives lost no opportunity in saying that all nations in Asia were equal and that there was no question of leadership. China, which had just emerged victorious from the War of Resistance Against Japanese Aggression in which she lost 35 million of her people, found it indigestible to see a poor and backward Asian country like India asserting leadership not only in the region, but at the global stage too by way of creating the NAM. India's neutrality and its leadership aspirations were denounced by China from the day one.

Hostilities along the border, the Dalai Lama's flight to India in the aftermath of the Tibetan uprising in 1959, and India's refusal to renew the 1954 agreement on Tibet, brought the relationship to a nadir, culminating in a brief armed conflict over the Himalayas and then a deep freeze in diplomatic relations for almost three decades. It was beyond any doubt that in the wake of China's hostilities with India, it acted as a countervailing force in the region vis-à-vis India, encouraged anti-India forces in the subcontinent and supported military dictatorships in Pakistan, Bangladesh and Myanmar. Though China has never admitted to the "String of Pearls" theory to contain India, the port development it has undertaken in India's immediate neighbourhood has caused India to perceive these as a threat to its national security.

For example, China has built a naval base in Gwadar, Pakistan as part of the China-Pakistan Economic Corridor project, the flagship of the Belt and Road Project. Though it may be a commercial port, the facility could be used as a military base in case of hostilities. China arming Pakistan with J-17, S20 diesel-electric submarines based on the Yuan-class (Type 039A-series) design, and nuclear weapons demonstrates the utility of Pakistan as a pivot of China. China's investment in and lease of Hambantota port in Sri Lanka shows China's depth in the region. In Bangladesh too, the Chinese have built Chittagong Port that could be converted into a military one depending on the equations between India, Bangladesh and China. China is deepening its engagement in Myanmar, especially after the conclusion of the China Myanmar Economic Corridor (CMEC). The CMEC envisages having the Kyaukpyu deep sea water port (US$ 1.3 billion) with two berths in its initial phase including the Kyaukpyu SEZ (US$ 2 billion); a China-Myanmar oil and gas pipeline (US$ 5 billion); a Mandalay Yida Economic and Trade Cooperation Zone (US$ 4 billion); a Tagaung Taung Nickel Industry Development Project (US$ 820 million); a Letpadaung copper mine project (US$ 1 billion); a Kunming-Kyaukpyu railway line; a Mandalay-Tigyaing-Muse expressway and a Kyaukpyu-Nay Pyi Taw highway project etc.

In the same vein, infrastructure projects worth over US$ 10 billion are being executed in Bangladesh; in Nepal, China is executing projects such as the building of Pokhara airport budgeted at US$ 216 million, the Melamchi Water Supply Project at US$ 294.4 million, the US$ 3 billion Lumbini Project that will have an airport, hotels, convention centre, temples and a Buddhist university well connected with a highway, and recently, during President Xi Jinping's visit, both sides reached an agreement to connect Nepal to Tibet by rail. China's investment in the region has been astronomical, amounting to US$ 13.87 billion to Bangladesh, US$ 3.11 billion to Sri Lanka, US$ 1.34 billion to Nepal, US$ 970 million to the

Maldives, and US$ 12.9 billion to Pakistan. In addition, it has also increased its footprints in the Maldives and Seychelles. In 2016, China started to construct its first ever naval base abroad in Djibouti.

Today, when China has emerged as the second largest economy in the world and the challenger to the established hegemon, to expect China to be indifferent to the smaller countries in the vicinity and beyond, as shown above would be wishful thinking. As for smaller countries, to not benefit from China's deep pockets would equally be foolish and ignorant of ground realities. In the face of such challenges, what could India's options be?

At the outset, India needs to unfold a workable connectivity strategy with its neighbourhood. New initiatives such as *'Bharat Mala'*, a network of 5000 kilometres of roads connecting all the Himalayan states of India with a budget of US$ 2.2 billion need to be carried out in letter and spirit, and at war footing. In the same vein, the *'Sagar Mala'* project whereby all coastal cities in India would be interconnected through road, rail, ports and airports through a special development package need to be sped up. Simultaneously, the nodes of these projects need to be extended to India's immediate and extended neighbourhood, and aligned with the SAGAR and IORA vision.

Secondly, India must strengthen its strategic and economic partnership with BIMSTEC and ASEAN countries. The RCEP is an opportunity to integrate India's economy with the region. Meanwhile, the strategic location of India's northeast needs to be utilised for building bridges with the region. Without the development of Northeast India, Act East Policy will not reap many dividends. Rebuilding and reopening the Stillwell Road could be an option.

Thirdly, India needs to be magnanimous in its approach as far as resolving bilateral problems is concerned. Arm twisting by way of economic blockades in the case of Nepal, and stopping gas supplies to Bhutan will only harm India's own national interests. Furthermore, India's noncommittal approach needs to be changed for good, and whatever she commits needs to be delivered. For example, some of India's projects in Nepal such as the Rs. 33108 crore Pancheshwar multi-purpose project on the Mahakali river, which was envisaged in the 1990s and revived during Modi's Nepal visit in

2014, has not made much progress. A police academy promised to Nepal by India in the 1990s, revived by Prime Minister Modi in 2014 didn't make progress either. The Chinese seized the opportunity and built a swanky academy with a cost of US$ 350 million in a record two years' time and gifted it free of cost to Nepal in June 2017.

Finally, as can be discerned from the above, it's all economics! In November 2017, during a two-day Nepal Investment Summit, 89 companies from China committed an investment of US$ 8.3 billion in various sectors, compared to an investment of US$ 317 million committed by 21 Indian companies present at the Summit. Even Bangladeshi and Sri Lankan commitment far exceeded the Indian investment. Therefore, India needs to strengthen its economic drivers, build capacities in every field that will make it a competitive and attractive market not only for neighbours but globally too. In this context, it is necessary for India to forge closer economic ties with China, benefit from its over capacities and deep pockets and lay the ground for a better economic flight. The option of 2+1 in the vicinity could be explored for viable joint projects. India must think beyond the security prism as far as trade, transport and tourism is concerned, and certainly should not take its cultural ties in the region for granted.

13

Significance of Mamallapurm Modi-Xi Informal Summit

In April 2018 when Prime Minister Narendra Modi and President Xi Jinping met for an informal summit in Wuhan, I remember President Xi telling Prime Minister Modi through an interpreter that the bronze statue of an "antlered crane" that attracted PM Modi's attention in the Wuhan Museum dates back to 433 BC, and that it was discovered from the tomb of Marquis Yi of Zeng of the Spring and Autumn Period. A little later, PM Modi was seen striking the famous 64 *bianzhong* or chime bells discovered from the same tomb. It is in these bells that exact dates have been inscribed, showing that the artifacts are 2400 years old.

The Spring and Autumn Period was the time when Chinese Silk handicrafts had already entered India. India's *Arthasastra* mentions that *kauseyam cinapattasca cinabhumijah* (cocoons and Chinese fabrics are the products of China), and that Greek and Roman businessmen sailed to India a long time ago and bought Chinese Silk in Indian markets. The line "What characteristics does the moon have, that it perishes and rises again? What is that good thing it has? Isn't it that rabbit in its belly" in Qu Yuan's narrative poem *Questions to Heaven* of the 4th Century BC is believed to have come from the Indian legend of the 'rabbit on the moon'. These are the findings of the great Chinese scholar Ji Xianlin, on whom the Government of India conferred the Padma Bhushan in 2008 for his contribution towards Indology. Professor Ji is of the view that the line "God releasing his disc and decapitating Yin from Yang" from the above poem is the depiction of the *Samudra Manthan* story in which Indra decapitates Rahu and Ketu. Now, how many in India and China know that during the time period referenced, civilisational dialogue between India and China was already in place, and that traces of it could be discovered in the textual tradition of both countries?

In the same vein, the selection of Mamallapuram or Mahabalipuram, which falls within the district of Kanchipuram, the capital city of the Pallava Dynasty (275-897), also reinforces the civilisational linkages between India and China. For example, the first ever reference to Kanchipuram found in Chinese texts dates back to the 2nd century BC. A detailed description of the sea route between China and Kanchipuram, spelled as Huanhzhi (Kanchi) is found in Chinese historian Bangu's *Han Annals*. The reference states that "Huangzhi is big and its population huge, and abounds in exotic products…The interpreter, who is a royal official, accompanied other assignees to the sea to buy pearls, beryl (vaduriya), precious stones and other exotic products and bartered it with gold and varieties of silks… During the Yuanshi Era of Emperor Ping when Wang Mang executed government affairs, as he wished to show off the brilliance of his majestic virtue, sent rich gifts to the king of Huangzhi, in return Huangzhi sent an embassy along with the present of a live rhinoceros… To the south of Huangzhi lies the country of Sichengbu, (Present day Sri Lanka) it is from here that the Han interpreter returned."

It could be established that South India had good trade and diplomatic relations with China at least from 9 BC. This relationship was further strengthened throughout the Pallava Dynasty (275-897) and Kanchipuram became one of the major trading centers between the Pallavas and the Tang Dynasty (618-907) of China. Chinese and Roman coins have been found at Mamallapuram, exhibiting that it was a global hub of trade during ancient times. The great scholar-monk Xuan Zang who visited Kanchupuram in 640, records that the "city was 6 Chinese miles in circumference and that its people were renowned for their bravery, piety, love of justice, and veneration for learning." Bodhidhrma, the Pallava prince from Kanchipuram, who reached China in 547 is also an important link between India and China, as he is the one who is credited with disseminating Zen into China along with the Shaolin martial art. Therefore, the civilisational rebalancing between India and China during the summit will be the foremost theme. Both India and China will have a consensus to restore their civilisational glory.

Second, the rebalancing of political relations in the wake of the Wuhan Summit would be reiterated. Both sides will emphasise establishing strategic communication between the leaders, building consensus on certain issues and giving an overall direction to bilateral relations. For example, India and China agreeing to issue strategic guidance to their militaries to build trust and mutual understanding. Both sides reached a consensus that differences between the two should not become disputes, which has worked well for India and China so far. There won't be much headway on the border issue, though they will put an emphasis on maintaining peace and tranquility along the border. India will not shy away from objecting to the China-Pakistan Economic corridor, and reminding China to be sensitive towards each other's core interests, albeit PM Modi may thank the Chinese President for supporting India in declaring Masood Azhar to be an international terrorist.

Third, it is obvious that the rebalancing of trade and investment will dominate discussions. India-China bilateral trade has touched a historic US$ 95.54 billion, and is expected to reach the US$ 100 billion mark this year. This could be a difficult task as data available for the first five months of 2019 showed a decline of 3.59 per cent owing to the economic slump in both the countries. What should be a welcome sign is that the much talked about trade deficit of India came down by US$ 10 billion to US$ 53 billion in 2019. China passing a law allowing India's generic drugs in the Chinese markets is a welcome sign. In addition, India's marine products, especially fish and molluscs; tea, coffee and spices, cotton and fruits showed a massive jump in sales. China's exports to India such as electrical equipment, organic chemicals, plastics and fertilisers also registered sharp increases.

Conversely, Chinese investment in India has risen up exponentially. It has touched the US$ 10 billion mark, of which US$ 5 billion was pumped in by Chinese venture capitalists in Indian starts ups, mostly in the "Digital India" and "Make in India" programs, surpassing the investment from Japan and the US in 2018.

As China undergoes an economic restructuring, India and China are giving full play to their complementarities. It is no wonder that today, nearly 2000 Chinese companies have invested in India, providing employment to over 200,000 people. The entire supply chains as regards labor intensive industries such as mobile telephony, electronics, home appliances etc. have been shifted to India. For example, mobile phone manufacturing clusters in Noida, electronics manufacturing in Chennai, white electrical appliances facilities in Pune, optical fiber industry in Hyderabad, and solar panel manufacturing in Bangalore are some of the examples of China shifting their bases to India. This scope is likely to expand and diversify in other areas as China and the US continue to lock horns in the ongoing trade war. India's agricultural sector, including the food processing industry will certainly reap some of the benefits.

Fourth, there would a consensus on their global rebalancing in terms of multi-polarity, globalisation and global governance. Both India and China stand for a multipolar world and seek to share greater responsibilities in the global power structure. They are together on the question of global terrorism. Their joining hands in various multilateral institutions such as BRICS, SCO, G20, AIIB, East Asia Summit and convergences on issues like climate change speaks volumes of this. At the same time, it must not be construed that their coming together on these platforms is meant to reshape or challenge the rules of the existing order or replace existing institutions. Why should they challenge the existing international order when the same has benefitted both nations immensely? They know that it was in the process of globalisation that India and China have been able to alleviate over 300 and 700 million people from poverty respectively. The alleviation of over 1 billion people from poverty in such a short time is a miracle in the history of humankind.

Finally, both need to work hard on the resolution of problematic issues, for the above rebalancing could be rendered meaningless by any unpleasant standoff like Doklam. If the China-Pakistan axis is troublesome to India, so is the idea of Quad, the Indo-Pacific strategy and India cozying up to the US to China. Therefore, both may have to rebalance their approaches. China especially, should be willing to share power with India in the region rather than seeking parity for its pivots. Nevertheless, it would be wrong to put the India-China relations in the binary of either friends or enemies, for the relationship is too complex and encompasses elements of cooperation, coordination, competition and even conflict and confrontation. Therefore, to handle such a relationship, informal summits are a better bet.

14

INDIA-CHINA AND THE RCEP

On 4 November 2019, after negotiating for 7 years, India temporarily decided not to sign the Regional Comprehensive Economic Partnership (RCEP) until it satisfactorily addresses "India's outstanding issues and concerns" even though all other 15 countries (10 ASEAN and 6 Asia-Pacific including China, India, Japan, South Korea, Australia and New Zealand) agreed on the "text based negotiations" and declared that they were ready to sign the deal in 2020. Now, what are India's concerns? Why did it back out even after participating in all the 28 negotiations, 9 ministerial meetings and 3 summits, and how is China reacting to India's decision?

In the words of Prime Minister Narendra Modi, since the agreement doesn't augur well with respect to the interests of all Indians, therefore, "neither the talisman of Gandhiji nor my own conscience permit me to join the RCEP." What are these interests? The foremost concern of India is its burgeoning trade deficit of US$ 53.5 billion with China, US$ 21.8 billion with ASEAN, US$ 12 billion with Korea, US$ 9.6 billion with Australia, and US$ 8 billion with Japan. If India signs the RCEP, India would be forced to reduce duties on around 90 per cent of its imports over the next 15 years. Therefore, apprehensive of Chinese products flooding the Indian market in absence of an auto-trigger mechanism, India had sought to check the imports but had been rejected. However, the 7th ministerial meeting in Vietnam revealed that India was willing to reduce tariffs on 28 per cent of Chinese products immediately, and the remaining in a phased manner over 15 years.

India is also concerned about China circumventing the rule of origin, which seemingly has not been addressed either. Dairy products from Australia and New Zealand could adversely impact the domestic dairy industry. Other industries such as steel and textiles have also sought protection. Second, India has sought a greater movement of labour and services to RCEP countries, which seems to have fallen through in the face of stringent immigration laws in these countries. Third, India has sought 2014 as the base year for tariff reduction rather than 2013, when its import duties were lower. Fourth, India's request for exemption from Ratchet obligations (raising tariffs after signing the deal) also hit a wall. Fifth, the protectionist pitch raised by opposition parties and the ruling party's parent body [Rashtriya Swayamsevak Sangh (RSS)] has also made the government cautious about saying yes to the deal without enough safeguards. Finally, the economic slowdown in India manifested in a plummeting growth rate and rising unemployment could also be held responsible for India holding up the deal.

How has China reacted to India's negotiations and holding out of the deal? While most of the writings agree with the above proposition, many however, have also offered varied insights. For example, many articles have levelled India as a defiant "nail house" (dingzihu) resisting development around it. If India joins the RCEP, the largest ever free trade zone will cover 45 per cent of the world's population, nearly 40 per cent of the world's GDP, about 30 per cent of total world trade, and about 36 per cent of global foreign direct investment. According to a column in Kline.123.com.cn on 5 November, "India 'a nail house' for 7 years has opted out of RCEP". It says that India's decision was influenced by the pitch made by the US Secretary of Commerce during the Indo-Pacific Business Forum held on 4 November 2019. Arguing for India's participation, the article says that US$ 23 billion GDP of the block will essentially pave the way for India's economy to take off and reap the demographic dividend. If it doesn't, the same will become a population trap and aggravate India's economic situation further. In the same vein the *Global Times* also writes that joining the RCEP would have been beneficial to India, just as China's entry into the WTO (2001) "forced China's industrial progress and greatly promoted China's industrialisation process."

Second, India lacking a competitive industrial structure and relatively low national capacity has also been listed as one of the reasons by academicians and reporters like Mao Keji of the Yunan Academy of Social Sciences and Yuan Rongji of the *People's Daily*. They believe that such an industrial structure has made it difficult for India to transform reforms with openness like China. This has been proven by India's FTAs with other member countries like Australia, Korea, and Japan. For example, they argue, the trade deficit between India and South Korea has shot up from US$ 5 billion in 2009 to US$ 12 billion in the fiscal year 2018-19. Therefore, structural reforms are required in order to attract foreign investment, promote economic growth and create employment, which in turn would provide a breathing space for domestic enterprises. The RCEP, they argue would have had a positive effect on improving the above goals, however, "the most trouble-free choice" for the government to neutralise pressure from various interest groups undoubtedly is to step out of the RCEP.

Third, Chinese scholars argue that India backing out of the RCEP is owing to the excessive politicisation of India's economic problems. They have cited the examples of the Swadeshi Jagran Manch boycotting foreign products and nationalist parties and their outfits advocating swadesi, which they feel makes India extremely protectionist and a reluctant player to join the global supply chain. In such a domestic situation, "politicians can only choose short-term gains, allowing economic gains and long-term benefits to go by." No wonder, Modi claimed that "India staying out of the RCEP is in line with popular public opinion."

Fourth, geopolitically, if India is neither a member of the TPP nor RCEP, what will happen to India's "Indo-Pacific strategy"? Undoubtedly, the Chinese scholars have not spelled it out. Nonetheless, they admit that without an economic heft any talk of strategy is empty talk. Interdependence and economic integration make you an important stakeholder, not fence-sitting. In this context, some Chinese reports arguing that India opted out at the behest of the US is interesting.

Finally, China believes that the Indo-Pacific region is increasingly becoming the fulcrum of global geo-economics and geopolitics. China is already deeply integrated with the region, and the RCEP will undoubtedly consolidate its leading position in the region. China believes that India not joining the RCEP is temporary, and that China is willing to continue to negotiate and iron out issues facing the negotiations with India in the spirit of mutual understanding and mutual accommodation. China will welcome India's participation in the agreement at the earliest. It has stated that India not signing the RCEP will not have a negative impact on China-India economic relations.

15

INDIA'S MYOPIC CHINA POLICY NEEDS TO CHANGE

In the aftermath of the murderous Galwan attack, the change in the Chinese coordinates of the LAC in Galwan, the "disengagement" and creation of "buffer zones" at points of friction, and the continuous build up along the India-China border, it is time to re-evaluate India's China policy now, and undertake a comprehensive shakeup and calibration keeping in mind present and future challenges.

Having inherited imperialist and imperial legacies, India and China were bound to embark on this collision path, irrespective of a Nationalist or Communist regime in Beijing. Undercurrents of the coming storm were felt in 1947 when Luo Jialun, ambassador of the dwindling Chiang Kai-shek government objected to the map that showed Tibet outside China during the Asian Relations Conference in Delhi. Even though India severed relations with the Republic of China on 30 December 1949 and recognised the Communist government barely three months after its inception, the clouds over India's foreign policy challenges were about to darken, for both were poles apart in terms of ideology, social systems, approaches towards Tibet, the border and leadership roles in the region and beyond. India's "steadfast" neutrality in the East-West conflict, its policies of anti-colonialism and pan-Asianism as well as the ideals of world peace, in fact, put the need for understanding Mao's China in oblivion. This might have enhanced India's "international standing" at a particular point in time, but the same vanished when it failed to secure its borders, assist Tibet, and defend itself against China in 1962.

Even after its Himalayan blunder, India continued to support China's permanent membership to the United Nations Security Council in place of the Republic of China, which was functioning from Taiwan. India adhered to the principle of "One China policy" irrespective of the fact that China made an entente cordiale with Pakistan, took possession of the Shaksgam Valley in Indian claimed Pakistan Occupied Kashmir, and did not recognise Jammu and Kashmir as part of India, rather casting an evil eye on Ladakh. The historic handshake between Rajiv Gandhi and Deng Xiaoping hinted at a consensus that China would not a pose threat to India's security and that it would be sensitive to India's core interests. In order to normalise and diversify relations in other areas, both agreed to maintain peace and tranquility along the border by way of initiating various confidence building measures. However, China's desire to expand its imperial legacies on the borders and seas has tattered the consensus it has reached with India and other countries. Is China really behaving differently? I would say not really!

One, India has to acknowledge the reality of China's rise, asymmetries in relationship, dynamics of the global and regional balance of power, and major power relations. Undertake a comprehensive review of our China policy, restructure and recalibrate it leveraging all instruments of state policy. India must recognise what is workable and achievable and what is not, and accordingly reshape its engagement with China on the basis of pragmatic constructivism. Foreign policy and military affairs cannot be hijacked by sporadic outbursts of national sentiments, rather they need to be goal oriented, long-term and sustainable. There should be no room for cosmetic changes, knee jerk reactions, lip service, and lopsided approaches.

Two, India must recognise the fact that China has never treated India as an equal in its modern and contemporary history. Presently, when the regional balance is clearly tilted in China's favour, can India expect China to relent on issues such as NSG, UNSC and more importantly the border? China knows that these will make little difference to its relations with

India, as was demonstrated by her eleventh hour ban on global terrorist Masood Azhar, and that rather than earning India's goodwill, will place India on a high table, which has been punching above its weight all the while. There are rants being made for the identification of the LAC again, an absolutely futile exercise, for China is not interested at all in defining the same. The imposition of "buffer zones" along the points of friction, is nothing but China's long-term strategy to demilitarise the LAC on its own terms. Moreover, by way of challenging the established hegemon (US), China is emitting signals to other countries in the region and beyond. By doing so, she has announced the arrival of the G2 and forced nations to choose between the two, which perhaps is a strategic miscalculation. Contrary to Deng's notion, the China of today is willing to lead the South, drive a wedge between the US and its allies in the North, and browbeat those who are perceived as threats to the Chinese order, albeit China says she doesn't want to alter the liberal global order that has worked in favour of her so far.

Three, since China's pivot to Asia is here to stay, which will further undermine India's place and role in the region, India, though having deciphered it for long, has failed to take counter measures. The foremost policy calibration would have been to shift our focus from Pakistan to China for a number of reasons. Pakistan's asymmetries with India are far greater than India's with China; India's GDP alone, is over ten times that of Pakistan. India's LAC with China is almost 5 times longer than our LoC with Pakistan. Do we need to focus all our energies on Pakistan for a few myopic electoral gains by our politicians? Do we want to drag ourselves to the level of Pakistan, especially if India aspires to be a great power? Are we not playing by China's playbook by getting bogged down in conflict with Pakistan? At best, it should be treated as a little nuisance and dealt with without making noises about it. Similar questions can be asked as regards our relations with our smaller neighbours, but not without some self-examination.

Four, total decoupling from China is impossible. Therefore, we must formulate a pragmatic trade and investment policy, which hereunto has been haphazard, directionless and extremely muddled. Of late, we have been talking about erecting a great wall against Chinese tech companies, cancelling Chinese contracts and banning their participation. However, Chinese inroads in India's telecom sector started right after India's nuclear tests in 1998 when China vehemently lobbied for their rollback. In 2009-10, India attempted to restrict Chinese telecom companies from selling telecom gears to India's service providers due to the security threat, but when their executives met the officials from the Prime Minister's Office, home ministry, communications ministry and the National Security Council, things suddenly became normal. A few years down the line, most of the Chinese FDI was directed towards the Digital India campaign. The 'back office' of the world tag all of a sudden disappeared from public discourse! Rather than developing our own Apps and related platforms, India was flooded with Chinese apps, smartly on their own smartphones and ecommerce portals! The opportunity to attract investment in infrastructure was lost as it was not encouraged owing to 'security concerns'. Therefore, India must identify sectors where pragmatic cooperation with China could be realised and red flag those where quid pro quo is denied.

Five, India's security cooperation with the US, India's participation in the Indo-Pacific strategy, and the Quad has been viewed by China as its containment. I have been emphasising that security has to be accompanied by solid economic engagement, which at a bilateral level may be possible in certain areas, but could be a challenge at a multilateral level. The security budget allocated by the US to the Indo-Pacific is abysmal, a mere 0.3 per cent of its total military expenditure for the next one year! As for India, I don't think we have lodged the Indo-Pacific strategy in our foreign policy and military consideration, for India's economic, military and diplomatic engagement in the Indo-Pacific remains very low. India cannot be a lynchpin in this strategy as long as she doesn't enhance her internal economic and military capacities on the one hand and build solid economic and security alliances externally on the other, as both are mutually inclusive.

Finally, India's economic growth and her capacities to handle domestic and external challenges will enable it to seek an understanding from China along India's borders, as well as for its regional and global aspirations. As long as India's growth trajectory remains weak, social cohesion and communal harmony remains in disarray, the kind of understanding India seeks from a global player will be impossible.

16

INDIA IN CHINA'S STRATEGIC CALCULUS

After the establishment of the Communist regime in 1949, China's overall foreign policy at the first instance was the reversion of the so called "century of humiliation." This was incorporated as a national goal; therefore, transforming the image of China from a weak, bullied and humiliated one to a strong and self-confident China was projected as China's domestic as well as foreign policy goal. The goal consisted of building a military second to none; regaining "territorial integrity" that included Tibet and Taiwan; and earning foreign respect. Given the ostracization of China by the West, China "leaned to one side" and brushed aside the notion of a third road, in fact a dig at the non-alignment policy of India.

China, rather than accepting India as a non-aligned nation, viewed it as an ally of imperialism, a reactionary and "expansionist" nation, as she inherited British legacies in Tibet. Yang Gongsu, who was one of the members of the 1960 border negotiations, posited that the "Indian bourgeois elite and the leaders of ruling class were bred by the British imperialists and were bound together with countless ties, they not only had inherited the status and privileges of British imperialism in South Asia, but also harboured the desire to expand outward." Therefore, China's policy from the very beginning was an "alliance" with the communist block and a "struggle" against the capitalist block; India obviously fell in the second category, a "temporary friend" as Zhou Enlai had classified friends into "permanent and temporary", that could be joined hands with due to India's criticism of the imperialists on certain issues. Wang Hongwei, a veteran scholar of India-China relations posits that the main motive of China, besides promoting friendship between India and China, was to "secure India's neutrality in the Sino-US conflict, render the US encirclement of China bankrupt and create a peaceful environment for China's construction," which I believe has all along been the case.

China was successful in "eliminating imperialist influences" by making India accept Tibet as an integral part of China and relinquish her rights in Tibet, gaining India's support at the international forum; shelving the Tibetan plea at the UN due to India's reluctance to support the motion; and restoring China's seat at the UN. India not only didn't get anything in return, but also did not win Chinese confidence. China criticised India for illegally handing over 21,900 Korean and Chinese prisoners of war to the US under the influence of the US military and Chiang Kai-shek's secret agents; accused India of instigating the 1959 Tibetan revolt; and ridiculed India for thinking that amidst the "warm currents of fraternal love", China would give Nehru a "face" by softening her attitude on the border issue and compromise! In such a background, the 1962 border conflict was just a matter of time.

During the post-1962 deep freeze, China continued to pronounce India as a stooge of the US imperialism, Soviet revisionism and social imperialism. China's pivot to Asia had started with her befriending of Pakistan to contain India, and inciting insurgencies in India, including Naxalism. China justified its actions as she accused India of supporting Tibet's and Taiwan's independence. China supported Pakistan during the latter's military adventures against India in 1965 and 1971, and threatened India with similar actions. Anti-India posturing continued throughout the "Cultural Revolution" as thousands of red guards demonstrated outside the Indian embassy in Beijing and shouted anti-India slogans such as "Down with the Indian reactionaries", "Resolutely eliminate all spies of imperialism, revisionism and reaction."

The turbulent phase of wars, class struggle, struggle sessions came to an abrupt end with China initiating the policy of "reform and open door" in 1979. During Rajiv Gandhi's China visit, Deng Xiaoping told the visitor that "Let us forget the unpleasant phase in our past relations and do everything with an eye on the future." It was opined that the border issue should not become an obstacle in the improvement of bilateral relations. The Joint Working Group was created to discuss the border issue, which was taken over by the mechanism of Special Representatives in 2003. In the intervening period, Confidence Building Measures were signed with an aim to manage the border rather than resolving the issue. The year 2003 was perhaps the only time India forced China to accept Sikkim as a part of India in lieu of India accepting Tibet as a part of China in the official declaration of 1954. It may be remembered that the agreement India had signed with China on Tibet in 1954, was valid for eight years, implying that once it was not renewed by India in 1962, India no longer accepted Tibet as a part of China. Some Chinese scholars deem it as a mistake of China; they argue that Sikkim would have been a powerful card in China's playbook against India.

In 1998, ignoring the well documented history of its own proliferation in India's neighbourhood, China stated that India exploding a nuclear device reflected, "an outrageous contempt for the common will of the international community." China further blamed India for seeking hegemony in South Asia and called on the international community to adopt a common position in strongly demanding India to immediately stop its nuclear development program. China obviously had double standards, as she was clandestinely supplying her pivot, Pakistan with nuclear and missile technology, and sought parity for the same with India. China's support to Pakistan during the Kargil conflict (1999), the Mumbai terror attack (2008), cross-border terrorism, and the abolition of Article 370 (2020) is obvious to any reader.

Nevertheless, as the overcapacities in China's industrial sectors started to pile up, China pushed for aggressive trade and investment policies in the region and beyond, therefore, an all-round yet cautious expansion of economic cooperation with India, constituted an important dimension of this new approach. A Joint Study Group (JSG) was set up to examine the potential complementarities between the two countries. The JSG recommended an India-China Regional Trading Arrangement (RTA), comprising of trade in goods and services, investments, and measures for the promotion of economic cooperation in identified sectors. China was keen to push for an agreement, however, considering some apprehensions from the Indian side, the two sides agreed to appoint a Joint Task Force (JTF) to study in detail the feasibility and the benefits of the RTA and give recommendations regarding its content. By the year 2019-20, China's exports to India accounted for 14.9 per cent of India's total imports, making India highly dependent on APIs for its pharmaceutical industry, electronics, automobile spares, fertilizers, energy equipment etc. Conversely India's exports to China accounted only for 5 per cent of its total exports to the world. China's FDI that was nil in 2005, increased to 8 billion US dollars in 2019. As India's trade deficit with China burgeoned to 48.66 billion US dollars in 2019-20, India became apprehensive and went slow with the JSG and JTF recommendations, including its participation in the RCEP.

Irrespective of China becoming the largest trade partner of India, her stated anti-India posturing on International platforms remains unchanged. Though China continues to harp China's support for "India's aspirations to play an active role in the UN and international affairs", everyone knows that it is just rhetoric. The same could be gleaned from China's stiff opposition to India's entry into the NSG and India wanting to proscribe global terrorist Masood Azhar. China's insensitivity to India's core issues was revealed when she signed the US$ 62 billion CPEC with Pakistan that ran through disputed territory in Pakistan Occupied Kashmir. It is also constructing dams in the disputed Gilgit-Baltistan area and has stationed over 10,000 soldiers in the disputed territory between India and Pakistan. This is one of the main reasons for India to oppose the Belt and Road Initiative of China, of which the CPEC is a flagship. As differences grew wider, the consensus that the border issue would not become an impediment for developing robust trade and economic ties got a beating. Frequent standoffs along the border – 2013 in DBO-Depsang, 2014 in Chumar, 2017 in Doklam, and Galwan in 2020 revealed that the sanctity of the Line of Actual Control (LAC) and the Confidence Building Measures

(CBMs) had long been lost in the course of China ramping of its border infrastructure and making the LAC easily accessible for patrolling as well as for quick deployment. Creating "buffer zones" along the points of friction is nothing but to change the status quo on the ground. As India tries to play catch up as far as infrastructure building is concerned, the points of friction along the LAC are bound to increase and result in frequent standoffs and even fatalities as we witnessed in Galwan.

It could be discerned that China's India policy is goal oriented, very clear as to what she wants from India whether on trade or security. China has penetrated deep into almost every industrial sector in India, but has denied India market access in sectors like information technology and pharmaceuticals. As for security issues, China has been partially successful in pinning India to the subcontinent owing to the latter's brawl with Pakistan; opposing India's entry into the NSG and the UNSC; creating discord between India and her neighbours; making sure that India adheres to the "one China policy" and does not internationalise Tibet and Xinjiang etc. issues despite of her raising Kashmir for Pakistan in the UN and not showing Kashmir as an Indian territory in its maps. India's likely embrace with the US, strengthening of the Quad and the Indo-Pacific strategy has long been in the strategic calculus of China, therefore, India trying to make it inclusive has no takers in China.

17

Disruptions of Global Supply Chains and India's Options

The disruption in global supply chains in wake of COVID-19 and the bloody clashes at Galwan has given rise to two sentiments in India.

The first is the *swadeshi* 'movement', which has been there for quite some time. This has been orchestrated by organisations like the Swadeshi Jagran Manch (SJM) with a "boycott made in China" agenda. The agenda has taken roots in public minds, especially after the Galwan standoff in which twenty of our bravehearts made the supreme sacrifice. Since 25 May, 2020, the SJM has launched the "Swadeshi Self-Reliance Campaign" with a five-point program. The very first point is the boycott of Chinese products. This can also be reflected in a government order declaring 42 Chinese Apps as dangerous, followed by the launch of 'Remove China App' developed by One Touch AppLabs, and finally banning 59 Chinese apps including TikTok, share it, Mi Video Call, UC Browser etc. TikTok, which has the largest consumer base outside China, has estimated a loss of US$ 6 billion after the ban. India has made it clear that if there is bloodshed at the border, it cannot be business as usual. Chinese analysts like Yuan Jirong, a former correspondent of *People's Daily* in India, do believe that the ban and the border standoff in Galwan cannot not be treated as isolated events, however, maintain that it is also owing to the "rise of Hindu nationalism, and India's mentality and ambition to become a major power." According to him, India is "evolving from a regional troublemaker to a regional strategic competitor of China," a popular discourse making rounds in academic as well as media writings in China.

The second is the dream of making India an alternative global supply chain destination. As COVID-19 triggered a debate on the decoupling of supply chains from China, India changed its FDI policy on 17 April 2020 to protect Indian companies from "opportunistic takeovers and acquisitions, implying that India abolished the automatic route that does not require government and Reserve Bank of India's permission. Many in India linked the policy change to the People's Bank of China increasing its stake in India's largest private credit institution, the Indian Housing Development Finance Corporation from 0.8 per cent to 1.01 per cent. China immediately rebutted the Indian move, deemed it "discriminatory" and demanded rectification. Draphant, a Chinese start up that assists Chinese investment in India, in a study argued that "although the policy is aimed at India's neighbours on the surface, only China has made significant investments in India. In essence, the policy is aimed at Chinese companies. The policy change involves a variety of Chinese direct or indirect investment behaviours in India." India deems these as initial responses to China's posturing at the border, there may be more in the offing.

India emerging as the next supply chain destination is rather hyped and exaggerated. It took China 40 years to develop its supply chain cluster with the support of its detractors such as the US and Japan. It may take many more decades for India to realise the same, but shutting doors to Chinese investment may further prolong it. Going by Moody's Investor Services, the prospects do not look optimistic, for India's sovereign rating has been downgraded to the lowest investment grade of 'BAA3' from 'BAA2' on 1 June 2020. The agency also changed the outlook from 'stable' to 'negative'. The US-China decoupling is bound to happen in some sectors but don't forget that China is the third largest importer of the US goods. If China cannot replace the US as the main security provider in the Asia Pacific, in the same vein, the US cannot replace China as the main supplier of manufactured goods. On the other hand, China too has intensified the relocation of its labour-intensive manufacturing supply chains to other countries, especially developing countries. Countries like Vietnam, Cambodia, Myanmar and Thailand in Southeast Asia and India and Bangladesh in South Asia are the biggest beneficiaries. Since the focus of most of the governments for the period 2021-2025 will be the health of their economies, trade and investment cooperation between India and China will be crucial, albeit would be determined by the benevolent or malevolent nature of their relationship.

Chinese investment in India has risen up exponentially. It has crossed the US$ 8 billion mark, of which US$ 5billion was pumped by Chinese companies into Indian starts ups, mostly in the "Digital India" project. Alibaba, Shunwei Capital, Fosun Tencent and Xiaomi are the largest investors pumping money into consumer, food-tech, logistics, retail, artificial intelligence, Internet of Things and fintech etc. sectors. Chinese brands such as Xiaomi, Vivo, Oppo, and Huawei have captured 72 per cent of India's market share. Other industries such as energy and pharmaceuticals have also witnessed deep penetration from China. China's investment in this sector, nonetheless, will face stiff competition from local giants like Reliance Jio, for tech bigwigs such as Google, Facebook, Intel and Qualcom have shown great interest in it. Facebook, Google, KKR and Vista have invested US$ 5.8 billion, US$ 4.5 billion, US$ 1.5 billion and US$ 1.5 billion each in Jio. Jio apart from having the above market share of the Chinese in mind, will also participate in the bidding of the 5G spectrum, thus keeping Huawei out of India. Huawei has already announced that they are reducing 50 per cent of their employees in India. Chinese media was abuzz with the news of India launching a US$ 6.65 billion plan on June 2, targeting five global smartphone manufacturers, encouraging them to invest in or expand their smartphone production lines in India. In addition, two other plans will help India produce smartphones and parts worth US$ 133 billion by 2025. There are speculations that these moves, which are part of the *Atamnirbhar* (self-reliance) Bharat program, will gradually push Chinese companies out of the Indian market. Nevertheless, other supply chains in sectors such as electronics, home appliances, optical fibre cable, solar cells etc. will continue to be dominated by the Chinese in the foreseeable future.

Sectors that will continue to be interdependent in the short and medium term are pharma, fertilisers, energy and automobiles. Although COVID-19 exposed India's excessive dependence on active pharmaceutical ingredients (APIs) from China, cooperation in this sector has emerged as one having huge complementarities. According to the Trade Promotion Council of India (TCPI), India imports 53 APIs and critical key starting materials (KSMs) from China accounting for 70 per cent of its API requirements. According to a report in the *Economic Times*, the total pharmaceutical and organic chemical imports from China are close to US$ 10 billion, of which bulk drug imports are more than US$ 2.5 billion in value as per a report by Haitong Securities. Indian companies such as Laurus, Granules India, Solara Active Pharma were listed as having significant exposure. Even though the government is thinking of building new pharma parks, the low cost of the API and medical equipment from China will continue to attract the Indian pharma sector. Not only this, 25,000 Indian students studying medicine in China on competitive fee structures adds another dimension.

Energy and automobile sectors are other promising areas where policy coordination can be initiated. India targets to increase the share of manufacturing in its GDP to 25 per cent, which looks difficult to achieve given that growth has contracted by 1 per cent in the July-September quarter of 2019-20 from the 6.9 per cent expansion a year ago. China's MG Motors started selling cars in India in 2019, though the company has not fully made its promised investment of US$ 650 million in India. Great Wall Motors has not yet started production in India, but in February said it plans to invest US$ 1 billion in the next few years. Since COVID-19 and tensions at the border have thrown in many uncertainties, they are likely to withhold their decision to go ahead with the investment. Irrespective of these negative sentiments, there is still scope for cooperation.

As regards India's options, a hard decoupling from China by any nation is impossible. Therefore, India must identify sectors where investment could be attracted with active consultation and policy coordination. China's investment in "Digital India" happened because it is a growing sector and hassle free compared to other sectors where issues related to labour laws and land acquisition are problematic. While safeguarding big data remains a worrisome proposition, India also needs to worry about lower labour productivity, higher land and industrial electricity costs, higher capital costs, higher logistics and compliance costs, a sudden policy change, delays in the performance of government contracts, costly legal procedures and so on, which are visible bottlenecks for attracting investment.

Therefore, when it comes to factors and resource costs of land, labour, capital, raw materials and electricity, India needs to take measures to make these competitive. The price of industrial electricity is too high, which limits the development of enterprises. India lacks world-class infrastructure, especially in logistics, which is necessary for the rapid movement of goods in and out of India and a necessary condition for international production networks. Logistics costs in India account for 13-15 per cent of the product cost, compared with a global average of 6 per cent. High logistics costs increase operating costs and hinder the competitiveness of the industry. It is possible to create our own supply chain clusters, provided India acts now, identifies sectors, makes a 27 years' roadmap and executes it in letter and spirit. If acted upon I am sure that at the 100th anniversary of India's independence, we would be a different India.

II

PEOPLE-TO-PEOPLE RELATIONS

1

India-China High Level Mechanism on People-to-People Exchanges

The first ever India-China High Level Mechanism on Cultural and People-to-People Exchanges was inaugurated on 21st December 2018 by Foreign Minister Sushma Swaraj and her counterpart and State Councilor Wang Yi in New Delhi. The mechanism is a product of the "Wuhan Spirit" and the consensus reached between Prime Minister Narendra Modi and Chinese President Xi Jinping during the unofficial Wuhan Summit in April. The summit marked the rebalancing of India-China relations after a dangerous 73 days' military confrontation at Doklam in the wake of China blocking India's entry into the Nuclear Supplier Group and a UN ban on the JeM chief Masood Azhar.

Why is there a need for such a mechanism at the highest level? At the outset, it was the unhindered circulation of ideas, technology, objects and people that enriched the Indian and Chinese civilisations. Whether it was the birth of Chinese Buddhism or the dissemination of ancient India's and Central Asian polities' astronomy, literature, music, languages into China or technologies such as sugar making, paper manufacturing, steel smelting, silk, porcelain, tea etc, travelling from China to India and other countries, the circulation of ideas enriched knowledge systems across the world beyond doubt. Moreover, this happened owing to the unimpeded flow of people. The sutra translation industry for example, created in China, had people from India, and many Central Asian polities. Most importantly, these were the people who were responsible for creating the entire repository of Buddhist literature in China and Northeast Asia, which in fact preserved many of the sutras that have been lost in India. Therefore, it was 'learning from civilisations' rather than Huntington's thesis of the 'clash of civilisations' that was at the core of these exchanges. Presently, even though there is a flow of one million people between India and China, there is a tremendous scope for taking these exchanges to new heights, especially in the fields of trade, tourism and education.

Second, the Chinese and Indian studies in each other's countries need to be encouraged and strengthened so as capacities are built across government and private sectors for better understanding. One may ask, how many China experts India has produced since independence? Though some measures were taken in the wake of the border conflict, and a decade back when an act of Parliament to establish new central universities was passed in 2009, however, before and post this Act, there are only around 20 universities in India offering Chinese language courses, most of them only certificate and diploma including Delhi University where courses were started in 1964. Now compare it with the state of affairs of Chinese learning in the US. According to the 2017 National K-12 Foreign Language Enrollment Survey Report, as many as 227,086 students were enrolled in Chinese language courses ranging from kindergarten to grade 12. It is projected that the number will go up to one million by the year 2020. These numbers, however, do not include college and university students, if included the numbers will go past the three hundred thousand mark. In recent years, though the number of Chinese universities offering courses in Hindi have gone up to around 12, it is still not good enough given the large populations of India and China. Furthermore, the student exchange between India and China is highly asymmetrical. Most of the Indian students studying in the Chinese universities (around 20,000) are in the field of medicine, whereas the presence of Chinese students in Indian universities is miniscule (2,000). Jawaharlal Nehru University, one of the premier institutes of the country hosts no more than 25 Chinese students.

The biggest hurdle is the non-recognition of each other's degrees besides many other bottlenecks like accommodating and accepting each other's credit systems. The removal of these very bottlenecks will enhance the flow of students, joint research and seminars between the two countries on the one hand and the understanding of each other on the other.

Third, both India and China being members of many multilateral forums such as the BRICS and the SCO have signed many important people-to-people exchange mechanisms. For example, a comprehensive Action Plan for the Implementation of the *Agreement between the Governments of the BRICS States on Cooperation in the Field of Culture (2017-2021)* was signed in 2017. The action plan envisages the establishment of a BRICS alliance of art museums, national galleries, libraries, media and publishing industries. Besides, the plan encourages international cultural and art festivals, joint programs on archaeological research, cooperation across creative and commercial sectors including performing arts, visual arts, audiovisual, music, gastronomy, fashion, literature, yoga, animation and games, new media, cultural and creative merchandise development, and the training of the people engaged in these fields. The plan is indeed very ambitious; however, similar action plans are required to be taken at bilateral level and may yield more results. The increased presence of media personnel and objective reporting by both sides may add to a better understanding of each other.

Third, the bonding between researchers and the publishing industry is an area that has not been accorded due importance. After all, how many books from China and vice versa are being translated and disseminated in each other's countries? Remember, it was the translators from India, China and Central Asian countries that built a huge repository of Buddhist literature in China and were responsible for changing the entire socio-cultural landscape of east Asia in ancient times. I believe that was a movement, a similar movement is required to turn the relationship into a strong and benevolent one. The mutual translation of classics and contemporary works memorandum signed between India and China, which I am coordinating, is a very good example. The memorandum envisages the translation of 25 representative Chinese books and authors into Hindi and vice-versa. Some of the books include Confucian Classics in the form of *Four Books, Journey to the West during Great Tang, The Romance of Three Kingdoms, Dream of the Red Mansion, The Scholars*, and the works of modern and contemporary writers such as Ba Jin, Mao Dun, Lao She, Moyan, Jia Pingwa, A Lai etc.

Fourth, tourism and pilgrimage will reinvent the bonding and nostalgia that existed between the civilisations in history. It was by way of these pilgrimages and journeys that the spiritual and material civilisations of Asia and elsewhere benefitted immensely from each other. A multilayered approach as regards building better bonding by way of establishing sister municipalities, city, and provinces needs to be expanded. At present, there are just 14 sister cities agreements between India and China, seven more are likely to be signed soon. These measures would be conducive to laying a solid foundation for connectivity, trade and commerce, and above all a robust bilateral relation.

Finally, people-to-people dialogue must be accompanied by the resolution of thorny issues, which calls for abandoning the Cold War mentality and zero-sum games between the two. Both must negotiate mutual, equal and sustainable security as envisaged in some of the confidence building mechanisms. Both India and China need to be mindful of the fact that the bilateral security boundary is not just limited to the border issue, but has sprawled into various other fields such as maritime, river water, cybersecurity, counter terrorism and various other non-traditional securities. In the view of this, both need to establish new dialogue mechanisms while substantiating or replacing older ones. Both must agree that the India-China relationship is one of the most important relationships that will shape the future international order.

2

WHY CIVILISATIONAL DIALOGUE?

If we look at the history of mankind, of the four oldest civilisations of Mesopotamia, Egypt, India and China, the latter two are in Asia and are interestingly still living civilisations. With the Greek and Roman civilisations, these formed four distinct cultures, the Islamic, Indian, Chinese and Western cultures. Contrary to Huntington's thesis of the 'Clash of civilisations', these systems engaged in inter-civilisational dialogue by way of what president Xi Jinping emphasised on the free flow of commodities, capital, technology and personnel and mutual learning in his recent keynote address during the Second Belt and Road Forum for International Collaboration in Beijing recently. The birth of Chinese Buddhism or the dissemination of ancient India's and Central Asian polities' astronomy, literature, music, languages into China or technologies such as sugar making, paper manufacturing, steel smelting, silk, porcelain, tea etc. travelling from China to other countries enriched knowledge systems across the world beyond doubt. Therefore, civilisational dialogue remains an antidote to protectionism, exclusivism, eurocentrism, and nativism.

In the age of protectionism and exclusivism where peace and harmony is elusive, we may take cues from the inter-civilisational dialogue of yesteryear. For example, president Xi Jinping tells us in *Narrating China's*

Governance: Stories in Xi Jinping's Speeches that during the golden period of the Chinese civilisation, i.e. the Tang Dynasty. of all its foreign ministers 29 were foreigners, while the number of foreigners serving as officials was as high as 3,000. There is a detailed analysis of Tang's prosperity and openness in the *Study in History* by Wang Guowei which states, "In the South China Sea, there are merchant ships from the Arab Empire. In Chang'an, there are Zoroastrian temples built by Persians. Foreigners flock here like they are returning home because the Tang Dynasty is in the middle of its heyday". Similar evidences have been found by archaeologists in Quanzhou, Dali, Lopnor etc. places, least to talk about the living example of these exchanges at the Mogao Grottoes of Dunhuang or various nodal points connecting the ancient Silk Road. Therefore, it is of little surprise that Xi Jinping has been invoking the Spirit of Chinese culture as well as the 'Silk Road Spirit' which he says favors peace and cooperation, openness and inclusiveness, mutual learning and mutual benefits. The story of Kasyapa Matanga and Dharmaraksa, two eminent monks from India, arriving in Luoyang, China in 67 AD where they translated the *Sutra of Forty-two Chapters*, the first ever Chinese translation of Buddhist scriptures; stories of the white horse carrying Buddhist scriptures to China and scholar-monk Xuanzang's pilgrimage to the west, and, the great Chinese navigator Zheng He's seven voyages into the Indian Ocean who irrespective of having brute force never seized an inch of foreign land are fine examples of this dialogue. The unearthing of 20 pieces of Roman and West Asian colored glaze from the underground palace of Famen Temple Pagoda in 1987, tells the same story of unimpeded civilisational exchange. Therefore, as rightly said by Xi Jinping, "civilisations have become richer and more colorful through exchanges and mutual learning."

It could be discerned that whether the Western civilisation represented by the Greco-Roman cultural system or the Oriental civilisations represented by the Islamic, Chinese and Indian cultural systems, there was mutual learning and common development. It was owing to the inclusivism of the Orient that the Indian and Chinese civilisations produced more than 50 per cent of the world GDP and maintained that for around 1700 years since our common era. However, relying on military conquests and plunder, the Western civilisations unified the world markets, and the world got assimilated into this system, hence some precepts of the western cultural system penetrated deep into different cultural systems of the world, essentially enriching civilisations. This influence is manifested in each and every aspect, not just in the politico-economic aspects but each and every thing bears the mark of the West. In the literary aspect as well, there came to be the 'world literature', and from this literary form, the entire world was unified. It was equally evident in the fields of science, technology, philosophy, arts etc. Therefore, the influence of the Western civilisations is not necessarily bad as argued by Ji Xianlin. The exchange between two or more cultures, produces a phenomenon which is uniquely complex, there is exchange, there is confluence, there is assimilation, there is disintegration, there is struggle, there is resistance, there is absorption, and there is rejection. History evolves continuously, and the process of the fusion of cultures also carries on consistently.

In this context, China being one of the oldest civilisations is the only living civilisation that has seen unprecedented continuity in the last five millennia, and traditional culture has become part of the Chinese people's genes. Imagine the evolution of the Chinese epistemology from Confucius to Sun Yatsen and then after the liberation from Mao Zedong to Xi Jinping! The kind of value system that has evolved has the indelible imprints of sagacious personalities throughout the dynastic history of China. Qinhua University professor, Chen Lai has attempted to list the characteristics and values of the Chinese civilisation as: morality more important than law, this life more important than the afterlife, community more important than the individual, the spiritual more important than the material, responsibility more important than rights, the wellbeing of the people more important than democracy, order more important than freedom, and harmony more valuable than struggle. Besides, other values such as benevolence, righteousness, courtesy, wisdom, honesty, loyalty, and filial piety that evolved in the course of the historical development of China, and have been enshrined in the *Four Books* and *Five Classics* of the Confucianism are part and parcel of the value system. Undoubtedly, there is also the foreign import that China willingly absorbed if it enriched its civilisation.

It is pointless to argue about who will dominate whom, however, it should be argued how much we know about ourselves and other civilisations. Questions must be asked about whether we have understood the wisdom of the sagacious people of the past and whether what we have inherited in the form of our cultural genes and value systems have formed the fundamental principles of the civilisational dialogue or not. Whether or not the circulatory movement of ideas, technologies, goods and people have been understood or not. In order to understand this, we must go back to history and explore. Some examples such as the technique of making sugar and paper may be helpful in answering some of the questions as to how sugar in India is called *misri* and *cheeni* at the same time, thus indicating the route from India to China and then to Egypt and finally back to India.

While the dialogue of civilisations is the only answer for building communities of a shared future, nonetheless, various steps need to be taken by participants. First and foremost, civilisational studies need to be encouraged. Implying that studies such as Chinese, Indian or any other need to be strengthened. Multilingual translation studies for disseminating the cultural capital of one country to another need to be undertaken. In this regard, the mutual translation project between India and China is an example. People-to-people exchange is the pillar of all dialogues. Had it not been for the scholar-monks from India and China, today we would not have had Chinese Buddhism, and least to talk about the entire repository of Buddhist literature in East Asia. In the present context, the flow of people between the civilisations is extremely skewed, I believe that there is a huge scope to strengthen and broaden its scope. There is a need to establish new and strengthen existing dialogue mechanisms, and more importantly, there is a need to institutionalise these mechanisms so as a better understanding is created for a better future.

3

INDIA AND CHINA NEED A CIVILISATIONAL REBALANCING

In April 2018 when Prime Minister Narendra Modi and President Xi Jinping met for an informal summit in Wuhan, I remember President Xi through the help of an interpreter telling Prime Minister Modi the time period of the bronze statue of that "antlered crane" as 433 BC discovered from the tomb of Marquis Yi of Zeng of the Spring and Autumn Period. A little later Prime Minister Modi was seen striking the famous 64 *bianzhong* or chime bells discovered from the same tomb. It is in these bells that dates have been inscribed, exactly showing that the artifacts are 2400 years old. Now, how many in India and China know that during the time under reference, the civilisational dialogue between India and China was already in place, and that traces of it could be discovered in the textual tradition of China?

The Spring and Autumn Period was the time when Chinese Silk handicrafts had already entered India. India's *Arthasastra* mentions *kauseyam cinapattasca cinabhumijah* (cocoons and fabrics are the products of China), and that Greek and Roman businessmen sailed to India a long time ago and bought Chinese Silk in the Indian markets. The line "What characteristics does the moon have, that it perishes and rises again? What is that good thing it has? Isn't it that rabbit in its belly" in Qu Yuan's narrative poem *Heaven Questioned* of 4th Century BC is believed to have come from the Indian legend of 'rabbit on the moon'. These are the findings of the great Chinese scholar Ji Xianlin on whom the Government of India conferred the Padma Bhushan in 2018 for his contribution towards Indology. Professor Ji is of the view that the line "God releasing his disc and decapitating Yin from Yang" is the depiction of the *Samudra Manthan* story in which Indra decapitates Rahu and Ketu.

In 122BC when Han envoy Zhang Qian returned to the Han Court from the Western Regions, he reported to Han Emperor Wu about the discovery of a great country called *Shendu* (India), and that the traders of Shendu would transport Sichuan silk to *Daxia* country (present day Afghanistan) implying that the Southern Silk Route was the earliest trade route between India and China. From the 1st century AD onward when Buddhism was disseminated into China, this exchange got a fillip and the civilisations of India and China were interconnected, something that was unprecedented in the history of humankind. China's cultural communication and the history of foreign relations would be incomplete without its interface with India and vice-versa for the following reasons.

It was the unhindered circulation of ideas, technology, objects and people that enriched the Indian and Chinese civilisations. Whether it was the birth of Chinese Buddhism or the dissemination of ancient India's and Central Asian polities' astronomy, literature, music, languages into China or technologies such as sugar making from Magadha to China during the Tang Dynasty, paper manufacturing, steel smelting, silk, porcelain, tea etc. travelling from China to India and other countries, this circulation enriched knowledge systems across the world beyond doubt. Moreover, this happened owing to the unimpeded flow of people. The translation industry for example, was created in China, but had people from India, and many Central Asian polities along with hundreds of Chinese scholar monks supporting them. Most importantly, these were the people who were responsible for creating the entire repository of Buddhist literature in China and Northeast Asia, which in fact preserved many of the sutras that have been lost in India. With these sutras, mainstream Hindu literature especially the two epics of India also travelled to China. Another fact, which perhaps neither ordinary Indians nor their Chinese friends would be aware of is that Buddhist and Sanskrit vocabulary made Chinese language richer by over 35,000 words.

During colonial times, even though interactions were interrupted by drastic domestic changes and more importantly by the gradual eastward expansion of western colonialism, the anti-imperialist efflorescence of the Indian and Chinese people manifested itself in a major way as a challenge to the colonial order for the first time during the First War of Indian Independence (1857-59) in India and the Taiping Uprising (1850-1864) in China, as for the first time Indian soldiers stationed in China switched over to the Taipings and fought shoulder to shoulder against the imperialists and the Qing government. The accounts left by soldiers such as Gadadhar Singh, who participated in the Boxer Rebellion in 1901 sympathised with the Chinese people and castigated the British for their wrongdoing in his memoir *Cheen mein terah maas* (13 months in China). It was due to the synergy between the cultures and the plight of India and China that the nationalists and revolutionaries of India and China developed deep mutual contacts and friendship amidst their anti-imperialist struggle. The supporters of Balgangadhar Tilak, the leader of militant nationalists in India, carried out activities like Shivaji's commemorative meetings as far as Tokyo in order to make the Indian voice of anti-imperialism felt outside India. These activities had the active support of Chinese nationalists such as Zhang Taiyan and Sun Yat-Sen. Sun Yat-Sen developed strong links with various Indian nationalists and revolutionaries and by using his good offices, introduced them to leading Japanese personages thus enabling them to carry out their anti-British activities unhindered. Nationalists like Surendermohan Bose, Rash Behari Bose, M.N. Roy, Barakatullah, Lala Lajpat Rai and many other outstanding pioneers of the Indian freedom movement maintained good contacts and friendship with Sun Yat-Sen. The Ghadar support to the Chinese nationalist government and in turn enlisting the latter's support was the direct outcome of the formation of the First United Front in China between the KMT and CPC. Their activities came to an abrupt end with the collapse of the United Front in 1927, though some individuals continued to be active into 1931 and 1932. During the War of Resistance and the Second World War, so long as China suffered at the hands of the Japanese, the reverberations were felt in India too. India dispatched a medical mission to China in 1938. Dr. Kotnis, a doctor of this mission became a martyr when he died while serving the wounded soldiers of the Eighth Route Army and ordinary Chinese people.

Therefore, from ancient to modern times, the civilisational dialogue between India and China went unhindered. It was 'learning from civilisations' rather than Huntington's thesis of the 'clash of civilisations' that was at the core of these exchanges. The same is being reiterated by the Indian and Chinese leadership recently, the 'Silk Road Spirit' namely *peace and cooperation, openness and inclusiveness, mutual learning and mutual benefits* advocated by President Xi Jinping just illustrates this point. Presently, even though there is a flow of 1.2 million people between India and China, there is a tremendous scope for taking these exchanges to new heights, especially in the field of trade, tourism and education.

As regards trade, as China undergoes economic restructuring, India and China are giving full play to their complementarities. No wonder, today, nearly 2000 Chinese companies have invested in India with an around 10 billion dollar investment surpassing foreign direct investment from the US and Japan, and providing employment opportunities to over 200,000 Indian people. There are worries as regards the trade deficit, nonetheless, China passing laws to allow Indian generic drugs to enter its market will have a positive impact on trade figures. Today, China is a partner with India in its "Digital India" and "Make in India" drive. The entire supply chain as regards labor intensive industries such as mobile telephony, electronics, home appliances etc. have been shifted to India. For example, mobile phone manufacturing clusters in Noida, electronics manufacturing in Chennai, white electrical appliances facilities in Pune, optical fiber industry in Hyderabad, and solar panel manufacturing in Bangalore are some of the examples of China shifting its bases to India. This scope is likely to expand and diversify in other areas as China and the US continue to lock horns in the ongoing trade war. India's agricultural sector, including the food processing industry will certainly reap some of the benefits.

Tourism and pilgrimage will reinvent the bonding and nostalgia that existed between the civilisations in history. It was by way of these pilgrimages and journeys that the spiritual and material civilisations of Asia and elsewhere benefitted immensely from each other. A multilayered approach as regards building better bonding by way of establishing sister municipalities, cities, and provinces needs to be expanded. At present, there are just 21 sister city agreements between India and China. Now, compare it with 214 agreements as regards friendly states and sister cities signed between the US and China that were alien to each other during the entirety of ancient history. India and China have a shared cultural heritage, for example who in India and China will not connect to the frescoes and rock hewn Buddhist iconography of Ajanta and Ellora with Mogao, Yungang, Longmen and Dazu? There is a huge scope for cooperation, for example a Buddhist corridor could be established and further connected to other South Asian countries, say Nepal and Sri Lanka. These measures would be conducive to laying a solid foundation for connectivity, trade and commerce, and above all a robust bilateral relation. In this context, the Dialogue of the Asian Civilisations initiated by China is a welcome step that has brought different Asian countries together; India and China being two of the oldest yet living civilisations must resurrect their age-old association and continue this dialogue.

The bonding between researchers and the publishing industry is an area that has not been accorded due importance. After all, how many books from China and vice versa are being translated and disseminated in each other's countries? Remember, it was the translators from India, China and Central Asian countries that built a huge repository of Buddhist literature in China and were responsible for changing the entire socio-cultural landscape of the east Asia in ancient times. I believe that was a movement, a similar movement is required to turn the relationship into a strong and benevolent one. The mutual translation of the classics and contemporary works memorandum signed between India and China in 2013, which I am coordinating, is a very good example. The memorandum envisages the translation of 25 representative Chinese books and authors into Hindi and vice-versa. Some of the books include *Four Books of Confucianism, Records of the Western Regions during Great Tang, The Romance of Three Kingdoms, Dream of the Red Mansion, The Scholars,* and the works of modern and contemporary writers such as Ba Jin, Mao Dun, Lao She, Mo Yan, Jia

Pingwa, A Lai etc. It is indeed heartening that the renditions of the *Analects, Mencius, Great Learning and The Mean* into Hindi by me, have finally been made available to Indian readers for the first time in the recorded history of two millennia of exchanges between India and China. I hope the project is continued and more works introduced to the readers on either side of the Himalayas. The project not only enhances mutual understanding, but also builds bridges between the scholars, academic institutes and publishing industry of both countries.

In the light of the above, the civilisational rebalancing between India and China is the need of the hour, the rebalancing will not only enable us to understand each other better but also dispel some of the distrust in our relationship that has been looked at through the binary of competition and conflict. I believe, we need to look beyond this binary, and the civilisational rebalancing may just allow us to rise above this paradox.

4

How Lord Ram Reached China?

As the people of India revisit the whole sequence of events of the Ram Janmabhoomi Movement amidst the 'bhoomi pujan' for building the Ram temple in Ayodhya, I deem it as an opportune moment to talk about Ram and *Ramayana* in China, an often-forgotten episode in the Indic civilisational construct, owing to various reasons including knowledge of Chinese as a barrier. Amidst the lingering border standoff, India and China may also reflect on as to what the state of their frontiers was during the time Lord Ram made inroads in the folk traditions of the various nationalities of present day China. The article is based on my forthcoming translated book on India-China literary exchanges.

History of Oriental Literature compiled by professor Yu Longyu and Meng Zhaoyi while introducing *Mahabharata* and *Ramayana*, posit that the epics are "eternal fountains of the Indian literary creation", they "not only are valuable collections of the great literature of the Indian people, but are also priceless treasures of the world." These are not just literary works, but at the same time, are religious, political and ethical texts, and have had an invariable and immeasurable impact on the thought, philosophy, culture, art, customs and social life of the Indian people. When and how did China get to know about them? What was the reception and in what shape and form did the Indian epics exist in China? Here, I will delve into the question of the *Ramayana* alone.

The dissemination of the epic occurred at the same time as the eastward spread of Hinduism and Buddhism. Three Jataka stories – *King Dasharatha, Monkey King,* and *Shambuka* are the earliest and most conclusive texts of the dissemination of the *Ramayana* to China. All narrate the *Ramayana* but in a Buddhist setting; tweaking with the characters, and time and place. The first story is exactly the same except for the 12-year exile of lord Ram. The second story has more variations such as Ram as a Bodhisattva who upon losing his kingdom to his evil uncle, retreated to forests with his queen; Ravan is replaced by a sea dragon who abducts the queen; Sugrib is depicted as a doleful monkey who was also robbed of his kingdom by his uncle; Ashok Vatika is replaced by the Dragon's cave etc. The translation goes back to the 3rd, 5th and 6th centuries. One of the tallest Indologists of China, Professor Ji Xianlin, has done an in-depth study on the digressions from the original *Ramayana* in Buddhist translations.

The earliest Chinese scholar who carried out the most systematic exposition of the relation between the Chinese translation of Buddhist texts and the *Ramayana* is Jin Kemu. According to him, *Collection of Writings about the Six Paramitas* volume 5, translated during the Three Kingdoms (Wu state, 3rd Century AD) tells the story of the *Monkey King*; the same text contains another story titled the *Shambuka Jataka,* which talks about the antecedent reason for lord Ram's father punishing his son (who killed Shambuka), however it does not reveal the result, and the name of the kingdom is not correct either; during the Liang and Chen dynasties (6th century AD), the *Biography of Vasubandhu* translated to Chinese by an Indian monk Paramartha, refers to how a person mistakenly recited the Legend of Ram instead of the sutra." *Buddhacarita* translated during the Northern Liang (5th century), and *Mahavibhasa Sutra* (volume 46) translated by Xuanzang during the Tang Dynasty (7th century) also have references to the *Ramayana*. Xuanzang's *The Great Tang Dynasty Record of the Western Regions* also mentions stories from the *Ramayana* in the *Kingdom of Peshawar* and *Kingdom of Pushkarvati* sections. The *Lankavatara Sutra,* also deals with lord Ram and his enemies. These translations were prevalent mostly among various polities of present-day Xinjiang and highly defragmented polities ruled by the Han Chinese, the route obviously was the Central Asian route.

As regards the dissemination of the epics to Southeast Asian countries, Chinese sources often refer to a 6th century AD stone tablet found in Cambodia that mentions the *Mahabharata*. After the 9th century AD, countries like Thailand, Myanmar, Java, Malaya etc. had already begun translating the *Ramayana* into their native languages one after the other. From Thailand and Myanmar, it quickly reached south and southwest China. It could have also travelled through the Assam-Burma-Yunnan route, which was one of the most important routes between India and China, even older than the Central Asian route. The Dai nationality of China, perhaps was the first to assimilate the *Ramayana* (*Lang ka sip ho* and *Ta Lamma* versions in Dai) in its folk tradition with an almost similar line of characters.

In the words of Ji Xianlin, "The 22 sections of the *Lang ka sip ho*, can be divided by contents into five sections. The main plot of the first four parts is basically similar; the fifth part narrates how Tsau Lamma (Dashratha) chose a queen for his son and fought with Mangkosol. Finally, the two polities forge an alliance and Tsau Lamma gave up the throne for his son Loma (Ram). This episode is mostly a creation of the Dai with stark variations. For example, in the *Lang ka sip ho*, Nangsida (Sita) is said to be the daughter of Dasaratha, and is thrown into a river by him. Tsau Lamma left home secretly, not because of court intrigues and exile. In the Xishuangbanna version of the *Lang ka sip ho*, the aunt of Ravana, not Mareech changes into a golden deer to lure Tsau Lamma. Another digression is that the mother of the ten-headed king was a widow. After harming Nangsida, the ten-headed king put her and his wife together on a raft and let it drift away in the ocean. The waves turned the raft over and pushed it to the shore; the wife came ashore and cursed the ten-headed king every day. Later the wife married a monkey and gave birth to two sons, one of whom was Anuman, who avenged his mother by killing her enemies. Names of the places have been localised, that is to say, names from Yunnan. For example, Anuman threw the Fairy Grass Mountain from heaven into the

Dai region of Yunnan. The war between Tsau Lamma and Mangkosol is also fought in the Dai region of Yunnan.

The Mongol version is mostly similar to the Tibetan version as it was disseminated from Tibet. The Khotanese version of present day Xinjiang, presents Ravana begging for amnesty and agreeing to be lord Ram's subject. When the *Ramayana* was disseminated to China, different nationalities like Han, Dai, Tibetan, Mongol etc., made use of it to serve their different political needs. The Han used it to propagate Buddhism, and often emphasised morality, loyalty and filial piety. The Dai used it to praise the feudal lord system and to sing praises of Buddhism. Tibetans used the Golden Age of Rama to praise local governors.

The direct translation of the two epics into Chinese is something that only happened in recent years. Mi Wenkai's translation is perhaps the first when he rendered the epics in prose in 1950. In 1962, Sun Yong also translated both the epics, however, these were translated from English versions. Ji Xianlin became the first Chinese scholar to translate the *Ramayana* from Sanskrit into Chinese during the height of the Cultural Revolution, risking his life. It took him almost a decade to render this gargantuan epic with 20,000 odes and nearly 90,000 lines in 8 volumes published in 1984. Since then, many Chinese scholars have ventured into *Ramayana* studies. Recognising Professor Ji's contribution to Indology, the government of India, awarded him Padma Bhushan in 2008.

Since Buddhism and Hinduism are born of the same roots, therefore, their influence on each other is inevitable. No wonder, contents related to the two epics, especially the *Ramayana* have been discovered in the numerous Chinese translations of Buddhist texts.

5

Know Yourself, Know Your Enemy

In the wake of the government dropping Chinese as one of the foreign languages to be offered at the secondary level in the final document of the New Education Policy 2020, many questions have been raised about the utility of studying the language of an enemy country; and whether the Chinese are learning Hindi or offering courses in Indology in Chinese universities or not. Since I have been trying to render some of the Chinese classics and work done in China on Indology into Hindi and English in my pastime, I deem it important to let the readers know about the kind of work Chinese scholarship has done on India so far.

In one of the chapters of *The Art of War*, Sun Tse [Zi] says, "If you know the enemy and know yourself, you need not fear the result of a hundred battles. If you know yourself but not the enemy, for every victory gained you will also suffer a defeat. If you know neither the enemy nor yourself, you will succumb in every battle." Now the question arises, how much do we know about China and how much does China know about us? It would be wrong to say that China is not well informed about India, however, the same may not be true for India, for the simple reason that the transmission of objectified Indian cultural capital to China has been going on since the dissemination of Buddhism during the first century AD.

Buddhism acted as a catalyst and we see India's spiritual and literary capital making huge inroads in China in the form of the transmission of the *Ramayana* and *Mahabharata* stories, influences of Buddhist literature on Chinese language, literary genres, art and music, the birth of China's translation studies and much more.

The fine tradition of sutra translation in China has continued; the translation and publication of the *Bhagavad-Gita* in the 1940s, *Upanishads* in the 1950s, Kalidasa's *Abhijnanashakuntala* and *Meghaduta* in the 1950s and 1960s, the *Rāmāyana* from Sanskrit in the 1980s, *Ramcharitmans* in 1988, Rabindranath Tagore's works in 24 volumes in 2000, the complete *Mahābhārata* from Sanskrit in 2005, various editions of *Manusmriti*; *Sursagar* and *Kabir Granthavali* in 2018-19 testifies this. Apart from the scattered translation of the Vedas, it could be said that China has almost translated the entire repository of mainstream Indian literature and philosophy including the *Panchtantra, Kathasagar, Six Philosophical Schools of India*, and *Shankracharya*.

Besides, the Chinese scholarship on India has rendered the works of Indian writers such as Bharatendu Harishchandra, Premchand, Yashpal, Mirza Ghalib, Mohamed Iqbal, Krishan Chander, Jai Shankar Prasad, Jainedra Kumar, Phanishwar Nath Renu, Bankimchandra Chatterjee, Aurobindo, Osho, Chinnaswami Subramania Bharathi, and it may not be possible to list them all here, into Chinese. What is interesting is that Chinese scholars have also studied and rendered in Chinese Indian writings in English. The works of Mulk Raj Anand, R.K. Narayan, Raja Rao, Bhabani Bhattacharya, Manohar Malgonkar, Arun Joshi, Khushwant Singh, Vikram Seth and Anita Desai have been extensively translated and studied. Even though the import of Indian films in China is limited, the translation and dubbing right from Raj Kapoor's *Awaara* to Amir Khan's *Dangal* has gone on unstopped.

It could be discerned that the Chinese scholarship has picked up works written not only in Sanskrit and Hindi, but also in Bengali, Tamil, Urdu and English. No wonder many universities across China are offering Hindi, Tamil, Bengali and Punjabi etc. languages at the undergraduate and postgraduate level. The fine tradition laid down by stalwarts like Ji Xianlin,

Xu Fancheng, Jin Kemu, Huang Baosheng and Liu Anwu has been kept alive by their students such as Wang Shuying, Jin Dinghan, Xue Keqiao, Yu Longyu and Jiang Jingkui who in turn have trained a formidable team of young Indologists spread across China. Obviously, such capacity building is not possible without policy formulation, funding and support from the top.

Conversely, it is very bewildering that despite having an equally enormous and unrivalled time line, a miniscule amount of Chinese cultural capital was translated and transmitted into India. The Chinese *Classic of Odes* is at least 2,700 years' old, and even Tang poems and Song lyrics are as old as 1,400-1,000 years, however, in India, we don't find a trace of any renditions. The only thing we gather is that eminent scholar monk, Xuanzang did translate the Taoist classic, *Daodejing* into Sanskrit, but alas the translation has been lost. *Four Books* and *Five Classics* encompassing the essence of Confucian philosophy were produced before Qin Shihuang unified China in 221 BC, but none were translated by Indian scholars.

The West that had no contacts unlike India had with China, also translated and transmitted *Four Books* and *Five Classics* into western languages mostly during the Ming (1368-1644) and Qing dynasty (1644-1911) with the arrival of the missionaries. In 1594, Matteo Ricci (1552-1610), an Italian missionary translated extensive parts of the *Four Books* into Latin but didn't publish it. He also developed the first system for Romanizing Chinese. Almost a century later (1687) Prosper Intorcetta, Christian Herdtrich, Franqois Rougemont, and Philippe Couplet published the first Latin version. The first English translation of the *Analects* was by Randal Taylor in 1691 from a French edition titled *Confucius' Virtue and Chinese Philosophy* translated from Chinese by Philippe Couplet and Pierre Savouet. The Russian edition by Yakov Volkov of the *Four Books* appeared in 1729. Following this, during the 19th century there have been various editions in English and other European languages. The most notable is James Legge's translation of Four Books (1861) titled as *The Chinese Classics*, and translation of *The Analects* by L. Giles (1875-1958) and Arthur Waley (1889-1966) into English (1938). As far as the Indian scene is concerned, it took us over 2,000 years to produce the first translation of the *Four Books* (The Analects, Mencius, The Great Learning, and The Mean) by none other than this author into Hindi. The Confucian classics are just a fraction of the huge repository of Chinese classics and contemporary works.

Now, if we compare China's research and translation of Indian classics, medieval, modern and contemporary works, India's performance is abysmal. This also mirrors the state of China studies in India. India, as such, initiated serious China studies after the 1962 conflict with China. However, the approach has been somewhat ad-hoc, cosmetic and the element of the Chinese language in it has been neglected throughout. Take for example the then Human Resources Minister, Kapil Sibal's statement in 2010 that India will introduce Chinese as a foreign language in secondary education. He also promised to develop a pool of Indian expertise for the task. As usual, it remained a nonstarter, therefore, the present government not mentioning the same in the New Education Policy 2020 has no real value. The government looking into the MoUs the Indian universities have signed with their Chinese counterparts perhaps besides the agreements with Hanban or Confucius Headquarter are equally irrelevant as no exchange is happening owing to hard and soft infrastructure constraints in government universities.

China has opened up degree courses in Hindi at 16 Chinese universities across China. Most of the programmes are run by the so-called foreign studies universities, except for Peking University and the PLA Institute of International Relations. Besides, many think tanks and research Institutes across China, are engaged in various facets of India studies, all scholars may not be versed in Hindi, but are well versed in English. Since China produces only an iota of research work in English, therefore, the knowledge of Chinese must be a prerequisite for any serious research on China.

Finally, I believe that irrespective of India's benevolent or malevolent relationship with China, we must enhance our understanding about China. Without building capacities in Chinese language, our understanding is bound to be shallow. India must lay emphasis on integrating discipline with area studies. Open up borderland studies with strong Chinese language capabilities in union territories and provinces such as Ladakh, Himachal, Uttrakhand, Arunachal and Assam on the one hand, and strengthen existing Chinese studies programmes across India on the other. In view of this, we must chalk out a long-term strategy for the development and growth of China studies in India.

6

INFLUENCE OF SANSKRIT ON CHINESE LANGUAGE

Prussian philosopher and linguist, Wilhelm von Humboldt has remarked in his classic study published in 1836 of human language entitled "On Language: *On the Diversity of Human Language Construction and its Influence on the Mental Development of Human Species*" that "Chinese and Sanskrit are considered to be the two poles that go into two extremes" as far as grammatical formations and sound systems are concerned. If that is the case how come Chinese absorbed thousands of words and concepts from Sanskrit?

It was made possible by the mammoth sutra translation project in China, an undertaking of the Chinese monarchs. In the beginning, sutras were translated by individuals, however, by the time of Fujian (337–385) of Former Qin, and Yaoxing (366–416) of Later Qin, translation was gradually brought under the fold of royal patronage, and by the time of Tang Dynasty, it entered the period of great prosperity. Chinese scholars have classified the translation of Buddhist sutras into four stages. During the first stage (A.D. 148-316) scholar-monks like An Shigao, Lokakṣema, Yan Fodiao, Zhiqian, Kang Senghui, and Dharmarakṣa reigned supreme. The second stage (A.D. 317-617) was dominated by people like Dao'an,

Kumarajiva, Faxian and Paramārtha and others. The third stage (A.D. 618-906) that covers the reign of the Tang Dynasty is considered the heyday of sutra translation. The most outstanding translators include Xuan Zang, Yi Jing, and Amoghavajra. During the fourth stage (A.D. 954-1111) there was sporadic translation as the climax was long over. The *Kaiyuan Era Catalogue of Buddhist Canons* and *Zhenyuan New Buddhist Catalogue* records that in a span of 734 years starting from the 10th year of the Yongping Era in the Han Dynasty (67 A.D.) to the 16th year of Zhenyuan Era in the Tang Dynasty (800 A.D.), in all 185 prominent translators translated 2412 sutras running into 7352 fascicles.

The sutra translation also resulted in the creation of innumerable new images such as Vimalkirti, Guanyin (Avalokitesvara), and Mulian (Maudgalyayana) and associated sutras unfamiliar to Indian Buddhism on the one hand and the dissemination of various thought systems of India and Central Asian polities such as astronomy, literature, music, theatre, languages etc. to China on the other. To cite an example, *A Dictionary of Buddhism* compiled by Japanese scholars lists more than 35,000 entries of Sanskrit in the Chinese language. According to professor Yu Longyu and Liu Zhaohua. "These entries are not coined by the compiler, but created by various master translators through Han, Jin, and Tang dynasties, and added to the Chinese language as a new component. Every vocabulary is a concept and it could be said that 35,000 new concepts have been added to the Chinese language."

Liang Qichao (1873-1929) was perhaps the first Chinese scholar to pay attention to the influence of Buddhist literature on the Chinese language. According to him, in the early days, translators, in addition to the transliteration of proper nouns, retained old names as far as the abstract language was concerned. He calls it the "Lokakṣema School". As regards the so-called terminology, they were not very particular about it, which meant that it remained similar to its embryonic stage. As the translation progressed, it was felt that the old language and the new meaning were incompatible, and the usage was inevitably inconsistent and distorted. Therefore, people endeavoured to create new vocabulary. The translation of Dao'an and Yan Cong is a reference point; Xuan Zang advocated '*Five* Untranslatable Situations', Zan Ning propounded 'Six cases of new translation' in the process. They discarded the usage of Chinese words and used new vocabulary in its place; for example, 'tathātā 真如, avidyā 无明, dharmadhatu 法界, sattva 众生, bhāva 缘缘, vipāka 果报, etc.; or they retained the Sanskrit pronunciation and transformed it into a popular phrase, for example nirvana 涅槃, prajñā 般若, yoga 瑜伽, dhyāna 禅那, kṣaṇa 刹那, yojana 由旬, etc.

It is visible from the new vocabulary listed above that monosyllabic Chinese of the pre-Qin period paved the way for disyllabic and polysyllabic words. Hu Chirui's *Comparative Study of 'Lunheng' and the vocabulary in Eastern Han Dynasty Buddhist Scriptures* has established this fact. Hu's conclusion is that "The vocabulary used in *Lunheng* is more or less same as the pre-Qin classics, whereas the vocabulary in Buddhist classics has more similarities with the vocabulary used in the Wei and Jin Dynasties. The source of vocabulary change in medieval and modern times can be traced back to the Eastern Han Dynasty Buddhist scriptures. Zhou Junxun's *Study on the Vocabulary of Wei Jin Southern and Northern Dynasties Mystery Tales and Supernatural Novellas* also establishes this fact. He collated around 200,000 words from the tales of mystery and supernatural novellas and discovered that of 4,372 polyphonic words, 2,215 were from the previous dynasties and 2,157 were newly generated. The newly created words were mainly polysyllabic, and the proportion of single and new words was as high as 1:11. It can be said that at this time, Chinese mainly produced new words based on polyphony, expanding their vocabulary and satisfying the need to express new things and new concepts.

How did they create this? This was made possible through sat-samāsāh of Sanskrit. *Karmadhāraya* used to form words such as ālayavijñāna 藏识 or "All-encompassing foundation consciousness"; used *Tatpuruṣā* when one component is related to another, for example *rudraakṣa* 眼根 Rudra-eye; *Bahuvrîhi* used for denoting a referent by specifying certain characteristics or qualities the referent possesses, for example, Buddha 觉者 or the enlightened one; *Dvandva* in which multiple individual nouns are concatenated to form an agglomerated compound word in which the conjunction 'and' has been elided to form a new word with a distinct semantic field, for example, life and death 生灭, like and dislike 厌欣, etc.; *Avyayibhāva*, an indeclinable, to which another word is added so that the new compound also becomes indeclinable, for example, *athāśakti* (immense power). Wei Chengsi maintains in his book, *Chinese Buddhist Culture* that even during the modern period these principles have been used to create countless new words in Chinese, such as "generator" 发电机, "death" 死亡, "hard" 坚硬, "something" 东西, "size" 大小, etc.

Prof. Yu Longyu and Liu Zhaohua maintain in their study *History of Sino-Foreign Literary Exchange: India and China* volume that there should be at least three points to note as to why this happened: First, the Sanskrit vocabulary that had no corresponding Chinese words forced the translators to create new words such as reincarnation, life and death, karma, panchsheela, eight tribulations, etc. Second, a large number of newly translated words, along with the spread of Buddhism, became popular in day-to-day sutra recitation and became part of the Chinese vocabulary. Third, with the popularity of Sanskrit translations in China, its word formation principle was also accepted by the Chinese and became part of China's inherent word formation. Today, everyone understands new words like UFOs, aliens, "five stresses four points of beauty", low-carbon economy and so on, but no one will say that the words formation principle is the one which was used by the masters of sutra translation. The internalised influence is silent and leaves no traces. Some of the everyday language developed in the course of sutra translation, such as "convenience" 方便 and "spend" 花 which are essentially *upāya* and *sādhya* in Sanskrit respectively. In modern Chinese the word "convenience" has been further expanded to "when convenient" 趁便, "free ride" 便车, "notes" 便条, "for people's convenience" 便民, "memo" 便笺, "simple" 简便, "casual clothes" 便服, "Cheap" 便宜 and so on. Many other words such as 世界 from *loka*, 不可思议 from *acintya* also follow this principle. Besides there are innumerable idioms and sayings that have enriched the Chinese language. A dictionary titled *The Wisdom of Buddhism in Idioms* has many such entries. Furthermore, many Indologists such as Chen Yinke (1890-1969) believe that the four tones in the Chinese language were created in the process of sutra recitation. According to him these are based on the three tones—Udāttd, Svarita and Anudātta of the Vedas. Xu Dishan (1893-1941) an eminent translator and folklorist confirms this when he says, the sounds of Sanskrit are either long or short, voiced or voiceless, and cannot be mixed up, unlike the Chinese ancient sounds. Therefore, people in the Six Dynasties (A.D. 220-589), added four tones to the Chinese. The emergence of four tones and the yongming genre that was basically same as the Sanskrit verse, exerted a direct influence on Tang poetry. No wonder there are striking similarities between Indian and Chinese poetics.

The influence of Sanskrit through Buddhism on Chinese language and literature is an irrefutable truth. Apart from the above-mentioned vocabulary system, this sprawls into the permeation of Indian fables, folktales, literary genres, themes, images, and aesthetics into Chinese literature. These nonetheless have become inherent to Chinese culture, and without academic investigation, it is difficult for ordinary people to know their Indian blood.

This article has been compiled on the basis of author's forthcoming translation of Yu Longyu and Liu Zhaohua's work titled "China and India: Dialogue of Civilisations."

7

Xu Fancheng:
A Chinese Yogi in India

Imagine you being sent by a government and there is a regime change soon after your departure, which is followed by a bitter class struggle, cleansing of the bourgeoisie and confiscation of properties of landlords! Imagine if you have to spend decades away from your home and return only in your old age!

Xu Fancheng's (1909-2000) destiny was somewhat similar. He was sent by the Nationalist Government of China to Visva-Bharati University at the end of the War of Resistance Against Japan in 1945 to teach Chinese. Four years later, Chiang Kai-shek's government fell and so dried the source of funding to Xu. Whether on his own volition or for the fear of reprisal, Xu stayed back in India and returned to China in 1978 at the age of 70. A scholar of par excellence, who majored in philosophy from Heidelberg University, Germany, attained highest standards in Sanskrit and Indology he was remembered only after his return to China and acknowledged only recently. The class struggle had ended with the demise of Mao Zedong and his Cultural Revolution (1966-76) and China was at the cusp of unfolding an unprecedented reform and open door policy.

True to the traditions of Indian yogis, Xu wandered in India for search of knowledge and fulfilment which he found in Banaras to start with, where he mastered Sanskrit in Aurobindo Ashram, Pondicherry where he stayed for the next 27 years and gave full play to his expertise in Indian, Chinese and Western civilisations. It was in Banaras that he translated works like the *Bhagavad-Gita* and Kalidasa's *Meghduta*; and in Aurobindo Ashram the *Upanishads* from Sanskrit to Chinese, the first Chinese to perform such a feat. His numerous works on the Indian, Chinese and Western civilisations are collected in 16 volumes of the *Collected Works of Xu Fancheng* published by Shanghai Joint Publishing Company in 2006. In the post Mao era, as China embarked on the international stage to spread its soft power, people like Xu Fancheng became relevant.

It was perhaps in the course of his teaching in Visva-Bharati that he authored books like *Quintessence of Philological Studies* and *Confucianism Explained* in English for his foreign audience. Xu was an out and out Confucianist. He had a deep understanding of the development of Confucianism throughout the dynastic history of China – the Axial Age, state philosophy of the Han and its revival during the Song by the "Five Masters." These according to Xu are Zhou Dunyi, the author of *Book of Zhou Zitong*; two of Zhou Dunyi's students—Chen Hao (1032-1085) and Chen Yi (1033-1107) brothers; Zhang Zai (1020-1077); and Zhu Xi (1130-1200).

No wonder, Xu also considered Zhou Dunyi as his teacher and chose to translate *Book of Zhou Zitong* written by Zhou Dunyi in English. He compared Zhou Dunyi with Sri Aurobindo, his spiritual guru, for he believed that Aurobindo was the true inheritor of mainstream Indian culture and studies of *Vedas*, *Upanishads*, and *Bhagavad-Gita*. Xu believed that the Chinese nation could survive and preserve its culture because of its character that has an indelible imprint of Confucianism. He believed India too will rise like a phoenix from the ashes and have a great future because of its strong civilisational character. In his words, "While evaluating the true value of a nation, one should not confine one's vision only to the present, a person should not only look back to its long history, but also to its infinite future.... A nation might be neglected temporarily, but the glory of its past and its contribution to mankind cannot be written off. Acknowledging the past, signifies the hope for a great future. After the baptism of fire, the sight of the phoenix rising from its ashes is much more magnificent than before."

It was perhaps for his understanding of the Indian and Chinese civilisations that he tried to find a connecting link between the philosophies of the two. According to him, the *Bhagavad-Gita* is compatible with Confucianism, conforms to Buddhism and leads to Daoism. In the preface of the translated edition of the *Bhagavad-Gita*, after expounding these facets, Xu Fancheng lamented that post Xuanzang (602-664) and Yijing (635-713), China gradually regressed as far as its understanding of India is concerned; China hardly knew that besides Buddhism, this nation had its own fundamental laws and principles. In the same vein, India also failed to understand that besides Buddhism, China too had its own fundamental laws and principles. He recognised the fact that China's research on India had fallen far behind in modern times, and therefore, resolved to change this situation through his own efforts. In his words, "If, from now on, we continue to collect and translate Indian classics, we will positively have a better reservoir of scriptures than the Buddhist or Taoist canon." True to the efforts of Xu Fancheng, today China has rendered almost the entire repository of mainstream India's classic, modern and contemporary works. Beside Xu, the credit must also go to other gentle academic giants of Indology in China like Jin Kemu, Ji Xianlin, Huang Baosheng, Liu Anwu, Jin Dinghan, Wang Shuying, Wang Bangwei, Yu Longyu and the younger experts led by Jiang Jingkui.

Xu Fancheng has compared Indian culture to a tropical forest, which he said abounds in invaluable woods, vines and weeds wherever the eyes meet. However, in the midst of *mithyā-drishti* it becomes difficult to find the right path. Therefore, he says setting his hands to the *Bhagavad-Gita* was like finding a treasure. Besides translating the *Bhagavad-Gita* and the *Upanishads*, Xu also translated Aurobindo's works such as *Essays on the Gita, Foundation of Yoga, Essay on Yoga 1: Yoga, a Holy profession, Essay on Yoga 2: Integral Yoga, Essay on Yoga 3: Sacred Love Yoga, Essay on Yoga 4: Yoga of Self-perfection, Collected Books on Yoga. The Theory of Sacred Life*, a masterpiece running into more than 800,000 words. Most of the Chinese works published by Mr. Xu in the 1960s were from Ko Tam Sing's printing press in Hong Kong. On the last page of the published book was noted "Chinese Section of Sri Aurobindo Ashram in Pondicherry, South India" or just "The Chinese Section." Starting from 1970, Sri Aurobindo Society Singapore took over the printing and composition of Mr. Xu's works in Chinese.

In the year 2000, when Mr. Xu departed from this world, the newsletter of Sri Aurobindo Society, Singapore published a special issue (Vol 14, September 2000) to commemorate Mr. Xu Fancheng. This issue has now become the main source of information on Xu's 27 years in Aurobindo ashram. The Society also planned and organised an exhibition on his paintings in his memory. In 2002, when Patel Nandlal, editor in Chief of the newsletter of Sri Aurobindo Society, Singapore visited China, he donated more than 5000 copies of Xu's works published in Singapore to the Chinese Academy of Social Sciences.

As far as Indian studies in China are concerned, Xu Fancheng, Ji Xianlin and Jin Kemu are the three pillars of the study of Sanskrit in modern China. As regards the academic evaluation of Xu Fancheng, Ji Xianlin and Jin Kemu, Lu Yang posits that "Mr. Xu is a very special person in the galaxy of modern intellectuals. Many of his accomplishments in humanities are beyond the reach of his peers. One of his strengths was that his mastery in Chinese and Western classics far exceeded that of Mr. Ji Xianlin, and was more systematic than that of Mr. Jin Kemu." During the 2010 Shanghai World Expo, Xu's name was entered in the records of Pondicherry Exhibition Hall along with Sri Aurobindo and St. Mother mirroring his indispensable role in the Sino-Indian cultural exchange. The introduction read: "Though very few Chinese know, the city of Pondicherry in fact has played a prominent role in cultural exchanges between India and China in modern times. This is due to the influence of a Chinese scholar, who lived in Pondicherry for 27 years. His name was Xu Fancheng, also called the 'Modern Xuanzang'.

This article has been compiled on the basis of the author's forthcoming translation of Yu Longyu and Liu Zhaohua's work titled "China and India: Dialogue of Civilisations."

8

HANUMAN AND SUN WUKONG:
INTEGRATION OF THE CHINESE AND INDIAN LITERARY IMAGES

Lu Xun has pointed out in his *A Brief History of Chinese Fiction* that "Since the Wei (386-534) and Jin (266-420) dynasties, with the gradual translation of Buddhist sutras, Tianzhu (Indian) fables also spread to China. The literati loved mysteries hidden in these tales and used them consciously or unconsciously in their writings, and these gradually became Chinese products." Nevertheless, no matter how Sinicized they became, like other images such as Vimalakirti, Avalokitesvara, and Maudgalyayana, the Indian blood in them remains irrefutable. In the line of these images, the image of Tang Seng (Xuan Zang) and Sun Wukong (the monkey king) in the Ming Dynasty (1368-1644) vintage novel, *Journey to the West* remains one of the most popular images in China.

The story of the *Journey to the West* is based on Xuan Zang's epic pilgrimage to India in search of Buddhist Sutras, however, the main protagonist in the novel is Sun Wukong, who saves the scholar monk from various dangers throughout his journey. It was Lu Xun who initiated the debate about the origins of Sun Wukong, and the debate has continued till date. Lu Xun believed that Sun Wukong evolved from a water goblin (Huai river monster, Wu Zhiqi) in Chinese mythology. In his *A Brief History of Chinese Fiction,* he says, "Since the Song and Yuan dynasties, the saying has been widely circulated amongst people and scholars...it was not until the Ming vintage *Journey to the West* by Wu Cheng'en that this supernatural image was transformed into a fast-moving figure in the form of Sun Wukong, as a result, the water goblin mythology was completely buried." Soon after Lu Xun's proposition, in 1923, Hu Shi in his textual research on the *Journey to the West* refuted Lu Xun's point of view and said that "I have always suspected that this magical monkey is not a domestic product, but an Indian import. Perhaps even the myth Wu Zhiqi is also created and influenced by India.... Therefore, I rely on the guidance of Dr. Baror A. von Staël Holstein who argues that in the *Ramayana* there is a Hanuman, which is probably the real image of the monkey king, Sun Wukong."

Following these arguments, an intense debate followed in China on the identity of Sun Wukong. Cai Tieying, author of the *Epiphany and Immortality: A Biography of Cheng'en* has summarised this debate into following theories. The first is the "Local product theory" attributed to Lu Xun that primarily focuses on exploring the influence of China's cultural traditions on Sun Wukong and refutes that the *Ramayana* had influenced the formation of Sun Wukong. It is supported by scholars such as Wu Xiaoling, Liu Yuchen, Xiao Xiangkai and Li Guming etc. The second is the "Foreign import theory" attributed to Hu Shi, which draws parallels between the *Journey to the West* and the *Ramayana,* and looks for similarities in the characterisation of Sun Wukong and Hanuman. Those who argue in this favour are, Zhao Guohua, Chen Shaojun, Lian Guangwen and others. The third is the "Hybrid theory" which argues that the image of Sun Wukong cannot exclude local as well as foreign influence. The scholars who support such a view are Cai Guoliang and Xiao Bing etc. The fourth is the "Buddhist Canon theory" propounded by Japanese scholars, who believe that Sun Wukong is mainly derived from the monkey-shaped gods in Buddhist scriptures as well as some of the disciples of Xuan Zang. There are not many responses from mainland Chinese scholars as regards this theory.

Of all these theories, the "Hybrid theory" has gained currency in China.

Professor Yu Longyu posits in the *Indian Classics and Chinese Texts: Indian Writers and Chinese Culture* that Ji Xianlin is the most famous representatives of the "Hybrid theory". According to Ji, "We can't refute the relationship between Sun Wukong and Nala and Hanuman of the *Ramayana*. However, at the same time, it cannot be denied that Chinese authors have further developed Sun Wukong, and have innovatively, combined the Indian monkeys with China's Wu Zhiqi. With their powerful imagination and refinement, they have created the brave and bold, lively and artistic image of Sun Wukong, which is loved by the people." Prof. Yu has argued that if we look at Ji Xianlin's works such as *Ramayana: A Preliminary Study*, it belongs to the "Foreign import theory" but is strikingly different from the one proposed by Hu Shi. However, on the whole, it belongs to the hybrid theory.

The latest masterpiece supporting the hybrid theory is Liu Anwu's book *Comparative Studies of Indian and Chinese Literature*. After the three pillars (Jin Kemu, Xu Fancheng and Ji Xianlin) of Indian studies in China, Liu Anwu could be considered as the fourth pillar. He was also trained in Sanskrit and Hindi and has been regarded as an authority on Premchand studies in China. In the book, Prof. Liu has dedicated two chapters titled "Rescuing the kidnapped wife – Rama's story in the *Journey to the West*", and "A Comparison of the Curse Mantra and other Mantras – Hindu Mythology and *Journey to the West*" to prove his point by referring to a mass of original sources. He has established that various descriptions of Sun Wukong in the *Journey to the West* are very consistent or similar to the Rama story in the Buddhist sutras and the great epic *Ramayana* itself. According to him, "When you look at these descriptions independently and individually, you don't necessarily think that they are borrowed from somewhere, but believe that they are created in parallel. But seeing holistically, you will have a second thought about them."

Professor Liu Anwu is of the view that the formation of the *Journey to the West* passed through several stages and saw versions such as *Story of the Tripitaka Master Xuan Zang going on Pilgrimage for the Buddhist Sutras*, *Storytelling Text of Journey to the West* and *Storytelling of Tripitaka Master Xuan Zang's Journey to the West*. Hence, Wu Cheng'en comprehensively polished and recreated the mythical novel *Journey to the West*. He undoubtedly epitomised the novel, but in addition, there are many unsung authors who were generally familiar with Buddhism and the pilgrimage story. As the *Ramayana* is a household name in India, those who had gone from China to India certainly must have heard this story, similarly the Indians who had come to China also must have told the story to their audience.

He argues that after the 7th century AD, Buddhism gradually declined in India and was almost extinct in the 13th century. What is disseminated to Southeast Asia is a mix of Buddhism and Indian culture. This situation will inevitably have its impact on the southeast coast of China, Buddhist and Indian temples in Quanzhou is its testimony. During the Tang, Song and Yuan dynasties, Guangzhou, Quanzhou, Mingzhou, and Yangzhou were the world's busiest international business hubs that were frequented by merchants, sailors, and monks from India and other parts of Asia. The story of Rama must have been the subject of their pastime; therefore, it was natural for the story including that of Hanuman to spread on the southeast coast of China. According to him, the Chinese people have always underscored the importance of textual tradition but ignored the oral tradition, therefore, they must pay attention to the influence of the oral tradition on the literature of southeast coast of China, and even need to study the spread of the *Ramayana* in Southeast Asia. For example, Ji Xianlin's study of Ramayana's circulation in China's Dai nationality is constructed on the basis of oral tradition. He suggests Zhang Yu'an and Xiao Xiaorui's *The Story of Rama and Southeast Asian Literature*, a book having more than 400,000 characters as a great reference book. Since Wu Cheng'en's *Journey to the West* is in folk style, however, it has undoubtedly turned the oral into textual literary form. In short, Sun Wukong is the crystallisation of the integration of Chinese and Indian literary images in the long process of cultural exchanges. It is a hybrid of the Chinese and Indian civilisations.

This article has been compiled on the basis of the author's forthcoming translation of Yu Longyu and Liu Zhaohua's work titled "China and India: Dialogue of Civilisations."

III

INDIA AND THE US

1

INDIA-US DEFENCE PARTNERSHIP:
WHY IS IT NOT AN EMBRACE?

The three day visit of the US Defence Secretary, Ashton Carter to India between 10th and 12th April 2016 culminated with the signing of the Logistics Exchange Memorandum of Agreement (LEMOA), a variant of the logistics support agreement (LSA) that the US has with its NATO allies. This agreement 'in principle' sheds the traditional ambivalence of India, unfolding the pragmatic Modi-fied security paradigm in India's foreign policy. The 'paradigm shift' didn't happen overnight, for the US had proposed the LSA during the UPA's time too.

Two other components of the foundational agreements are the Communications Interoperability and Security Memorandum of Agreement (CISMOA) and Basic Exchange and Cooperation Agreement (BECA). However, the then Manmohan Singh government remained sceptical of inking it for the fear of losing the element of 'strategic autonomy' in its foreign policy, as well as its 'non-aligned' posture. In 2005, both signed the New Framework for the India-U.S. Defence Relationship (renewed in 2015 for another 10 years), and in 2012 the Defence Technology and Trade Initiative (DTTI). As soon as the Modi government came into power, it started to push these initiatives of the UPA regime with more vigour and assertiveness. Indian Defence Minister Manohar Parrikar during his US visit in 2015 hinted that India may reconsider its stand on the foundational agreements. Therefore, the signing of the LEMOA should not be seen as a surprise.

The gradual yet steep strategic engagement with the US shows that India is willing to deepen defence cooperation by elevating dialogue on joint research and development on its own terms keeping in view its national interests. The converging strategic interests between India and the US perhaps take into cognizance the asymmetric comprehensive national strength between India and China, and also the deep rooted contradictions between the two on bilateral, regional and global issues. The Modi government is aware that given this asymmetry with China, it would be difficult to expect concessions, be it the border, cross-border terrorism or China's forays into the Indian Ocean Region (IOR). It is perhaps owing to these contradictions and China's 'all weather' military cooperation with Pakistan including the PLA's projects in the Indian claimed Pakistan Occupied Kashmir (POK), that the Modi government has issued statements in tandem with the US, Japan and Vietnam on the freedom of navigation in the South China Sea (SCS) much to the displeasure of China even though India has not agreed to the US request for 'joint patrols' in the SCS.

Second, through deepening cooperation with the US, India eyes high technology, indigenising defence technologies by way of co-development and co-production, building a solid Defence Industrial Base, reducing dependence on foreign weapon systems, and boosting defence exports etc. For example, both sides have been exploring the possibilities of cooperation on aircraft carrier design and operations, jet engine technology, and fighter aircraft etc. For such technological cooperation to materialise, the US had insisted on signing the foundational agreements. Nevertheless, it remains to be seen how India will respond to LEMOA's implementation in real time conflicts where both countries would be involved. Of course, the question remains a hypothetical one before the actual agreement is concluded.

Third, though some in India believe that it is a message to our 'neighbours', they are also quick to assert that by doing so India is not allying with the US. Even if India is increasingly aware that the maritime security boundaries of both India and China have expanded and stretched from the Pacific to the Indian Ocean, India will not be averse to selectively cooperating with China on the Maritime Silk Road (MSR) to invite investments.

On the sidelines of the Maritime India Summit, 2016, Modi released his pet project, the National Perspective Plan of the Sagarmala Programme, which aims to modernise India's ports and integrate them with Special Economic Zones, Port based Smart Cities, Industrial Parks, Warehouses, Logistics Parks and Transport Corridors. I believe there is a tremendous scope for bilateral cooperation between India and China on these projects.

The Modi government is of the belief that expanding cooperation with the US and countries in the Asia Pacific on the one hand and aggressive economic engagement with China on the other will ultimately help India alter some of the contradictions with China on the bilateral, regional and global levels to India's favour.

Finally, India would jeopardise its relations with China, if it acts like a front state of the US. In the same vein, if the US would like to offset China's geopolitical pull in the region and globe by way of India confronting China, certainly the US is mistaken, for India is too large to play second fiddle to the US. Nonetheless, India has seen an invaluable geopolitical strategic space for itself in the Indo-Pacific and is attempting to capitalise on it. It is in this background that if at all India would like to be a 'swing power' between China and the US, she needs to be a swing power as far as cooperation and healthy competition is concerned not confrontation and conflict, which is neither in India's interest nor in the interest of China and the US.

2

INDIA-US LEMOA:
A STRATEGIC MASTER STROKE OR A BLUNDER?

India and the US had reached an agreement 'in principle' on signing the Logistics Exchange Memorandum of Agreement (LEMOA), a variant of the logistics support agreement (LSA) that the US has signed with its NATO allies during the three day visit of the US Defence Secretary, Ashton Carter to India between 10th and 12th April 2016. The support for signing such an agreement was reaffirmed by Prime Minister Modi during his US visit in June this year. The agreement was officially signed yesterday during the Indian Defence Minister, Manohar Parrikar's US visit between 29th August and 1st September. The agreement will allow India and the US to use each other's military bases for supplies, maintenance and refuelling.

Security analysts have formulated varied perspectives as regards the LEMOA. Some have argued that China has pushed India into the US' lap, as it remains insensitive towards India's sensitivities as regards the border resolution, cross border terrorism, India's sensitivities in the disputed region of Pakistan Occupied Kashmir, China's assertiveness in the Indian Ocean, and so on and so forth. Thus, unnecessarily forcing India to be a link in the US 'pivot to Asia', which India may not have desired to be so.

There are others who believe that the signing of the agreement is essentially good for India, for India needs to shed its foreign policy ambivalence or non-alignment of yesteryear that did no good to protect India's national interests. The agreement will boost India's capabilities and enable it to project power beyond the region. They argue that as Indian interests sprawl across the continents, India would be in a better position to protect these with the aid of a new instrument. Also, since India aspires to be a 'net security provider' in the region, the agreement is a big leap in that direction. Moreover, they argue that LEMOA is essentially different from the LSA the US has signed with the NATO countries, for access to each other's bases will be under a book-debit payment system and transactions cleared on a case-to-case basis, and there is a provision whereby India can deny the US the use of its facilities for military operations if such operations run counter to India's interests.

Yet another view adheres to the viewpoint that LEMOA is a 'sell out' as far as India's 'strategic autonomy' is concerned. Since there are astronomical asymmetries in India's economic as well military power vis-à-vis the US, India will have to play the role of a second fiddle to the US. It will be reduced to a mere chess piece in the larger canvass of the US' security interests in the region and beyond. These analysts envision the footprints of US soldiers on Indian soil as has been the case with US troops and their bases around the globe. They believe India is bound to jeopardise its relations with Russia and China on count of the realignment of its policies with the US. Therefore, India's involvement in the US actions against these nations in the region and beyond would be disastrous for India.

This author believes that the signing of LEMOA is India's trade-off for getting access to US high technology. It was this trade off that saw India concluding a civil nuclear deal with the US, that saw India on board the Missile Technology Control Regime (MTCR), and it is the same trade off India is counting on to enter the Nuclear Suppliers Group (NSG). India will certainly push the US for the same during the forthcoming Strategic and Commercial Dialogue to be held in New Delhi in days ahead where we will see the US Secretary of State, John Kerry and Commerce Secretary, Penny Pritzker leading a powerful delegation.

Second, as India goes on building a solid Defence Industrial Base, it would be happy to forge a closer security cooperation with not only the US but other western countries too so as dependence on foreign weapon systems is drastically reduced. It is in this context that I see an increased level of closely knitted security cooperation between India and the US. However, India would certainly draw a red line as regards getting involved in real time conflicts. The Modi government knows it requires economic cooperation with China as much as it requires security cooperation with the US.

Finally, both India and China need to be sensitive towards each other's sensitivities, be accommodative of each other's core interests, and continue to work towards shaping the new international order as envisaged by forums such as BRICS, SCO and the G20. For a country like India, and many other emerging economies, there remain huge asymmetries in their power and economic structures vis-à-vis the developed economies, therefore, it becomes pertinent for these to bide their time, and become partners in each other's development by aligning their developmental strategies. The higher economic stakes in each other's economic systems may offset many of the security prejudices of the day.

3

James Mattis' India Visit:
Deepening India-US Defense Cooperation

The September 26-28, 2017 India visit of Jim Mattis, the US Secretary of Defense, was the first high level visit under the Trump administration. He had extensive talks with his counterpart Nirmala Sitharaman, National Security Advisor Ajit Doval, as well as Prime Minister Narendra Modi. Before leaving for India, the Pentagon in a briefing had said that the "United States views India as a valued and influential partner, with broad mutual interests extending well beyond South Asia." From his joint press conference with Sitharaman, it could be discerned that there is a convergence of issues between India and the US ranging from bilateral defense cooperation to the Indo-Pacific to Afghanistan. It may be recalled that in a bid to strengthen bilateral defense and security cooperation, the Obama administration had designated India as a 'Major Defense Partner.' Will Mattis take this partnership to the next level? Will President Donald Trump's 'America First' be a rider to some of the potential technology transfers to India?

Defense Partnership

Ever since the signing of the New Framework for the India-U.S. Defense Relationship in 2005, which was renewed for another ten years in 2015, and the Defense Technology and Trade Initiative (DTTI) in 2012, India-US defense ties have expanded exponentially. In 2016 defense trade reached US$ 15 billion, making India the largest buyer of US equipment. The US supplied India with 3 C-130 Hercules, 10 C-17 Globemaster, and 12 P-8 Poseidon aircraft, and 22 AH-64 Apache and 15 CH-47 Chinook helicopters. Deals have been signed to supply 145 M777 Howitzer guns to India, and there are talks of selling 70 F-16 Block combat aircraft and predator drones.

Notwithstanding the procurement list, New Delhi knows that mere acquisition will not work, if India has to modernise its armed forces and create its own defense industrial complex. The time looks opportune as many US defense companies have shown interest in investing in India. Lockheed Martin has signed a deal with Tata to manufacture F-16s in India. Since the Modi Government has offered preferential policies to foreign companies as regards its 'Make in India' initiative, there are possibilities of a technology transfer. This could also be gleaned from the press statement of Ms Sitharaman, when she said, "I appreciated Secretary Mattis' willingness to share further cutting-edge platforms which would enhance India's defense preparedness to meet current and emerging threats. Secretary Mattis and I agreed that we need to expand on the progress already made by encouraging co-production and co-development efforts."

However, in the face of president Trump's 'America First' campaign, the transfer could be difficult. For example, two components of the foundational agreements – the Communications Interoperability and Security Memorandum of Agreement (CISMOA) and Basic Exchange and Cooperation Agreement (BECA) which the US was keen to sign with India during the Obama administration might never be signed under the Trump administration. Similarly, projects under the US-India Defense Technology and Trade Initiative (DTTI) may not see light at the end of the tunnel owing to inherent contradictions between India as a 'Major Defense Partner' and 'Trump wanting to 'make America great again'! Whether we blame it on bureaucracy or the trust deficit between India and the US, procrastination and to be able to identify the areas of cooperation, especially joint production demonstrates that it is a difficult goal to achieve.

Indo-Pacific

With the rise of China, its reclamation of the islands in the South China Sea of which the US was a helpless moot spectator, its forays and building of soft and hard infrastructure in the Indian Ocean, the Indo-Pacific has emerged as one of the most important theatres of contest between various powers. It is the China factor in this area, which has brought together the US, India, Japan and possibly Australia. The inclusion of Japan in the Malabar naval exercises, and probably Australia in the future shows the evolution of new contours in the region. As expected, India and the US reiterated freedom of navigation, over flight and unimpeded lawful commerce. Secretary Mattis resonated it by saying that "a peaceful and prosperous future in the Indo-Pacific region is based on a strong rules-based international order and a shared commitment to international law, to a peaceful resolution of disputes and respect for territorial integrity." While appreciating India's 'stabilising role in the Indian Ocean' the US deems it fit for India to have "a vital role to play in supporting Southeast Asia's regional institutions, particularly in ASEAN and in building partner capacity across the region."

Here again, irrespective of India and the US terming cooperation in maritime security as a lynchpin of their strategic partnership, progress is slow. It appears that the response is in reaction to China's creations of hard and soft infrastructure in the Indo-Pacific, from the South China Sea to Gwadar to Djibouti in the form of various free trade agreements and port developments. The Indo-Japanese Asia-Africa Growth Corridor, the revival of the 'New Silk Road' and the Indo-Pacific Economic Corridor linking South and Southeast Asia thought to be counters to China's 'Belt and Road' initiative are shrouded in uncertainties, for lack of political will and economic support.

Afghanistan Issue

The unfolding of the Trump administration's Afghanistan policy in which he has asked India to play bigger role along with the US beefing up its military presence is currently under way. While sending Indian forces to Afghanistan has been completely ruled out by the Indian Defense Minister, in the spirit of the 2011 Strategic Partnership Agreement, and the recently issued Joint Statement on the 2nd meeting of the Strategic Partnership Council between India and Afghanistan, it could be gleaned that India remains committed to building capacities in Afghanistan. It ranges from training the Afghan army and police in India to building infrastructure in the war-torn country. Both have agreed to take up 116 High Impact Community Development Projects to be implemented in 31 provinces of Afghanistan, including in the areas of education, health, agriculture, irrigation, drinking water, renewable energy, flood control, micro-hydropower, sports infrastructure, and administrative infrastructure.

Under the US$ 3 billion grant-in aid assistance from India, some of the new projects included in the joint statement are the Shahtoot dam and drinking water project for Kabul, low cost housing for returning Afghan refugees in Nangarhar Province, road connectivity to Band-e-Amir in Bamyan Province, water supply network for Charikar city in Parwan Province, establishment of a Gypsum board manufacturing plant in Kabul, and the construction of a polyclinic in Mazar-e-Sharif. These developments demonstrate that India's engagement in Afghanistan would be on India's own terms, albeit it would leverage its ties with Iran and Russia in building a better security environment in the region.

Undoubtedly, India-US relations are on an upward trajectory as far as defense cooperation is concerned. However, there remain uncertainties, and we must not forget US president Donald Trump accusing India demanding billions of dollars for compliance with the Paris Climate Change Accord. He has already accused Indians for robbing jobs from the US. Will the transfer of technology not rob these jobs? On the issue of Afghanistan too, India needs to watch out for the SCO action plan. Once Afghanistan is brought to the SCO folds, the hope for a regional solution will be on the table.

4

INDIA-US 2+2 DIALOGUE AND CHINA

The new India-US 2+2 dialogue slated to be held on 6 September 2018 will replace the earlier India-US Strategic and Commercial Dialogue established in 2010 and 2015 respectively. The new ministerial dialogue involving the foreign and defense secretaries/ministers of both countries is aimed at enhancing strategic coordination and maintaining peace and stability in the Indo-Pacific region, a construct that has been increasingly used by governments and strategic communities alike, but has evoked strong reactions from China.

The much-awaited dialogue was unilaterally postponed twice last year in April and July by the US owing to "unavoidable reasons." Chinese scholarship on India at that time speculated that the real reason behind the US decision was India's oil and arms imports from Iran and Russia respectively. They also cited Trump's displeasure with India, and India imposing up to 100 per cent tariffs on imports from the United States in retaliation to US tariffs.

Long Xingchun, director of the Indian Research Center at Xihua Normal University and a senior research fellow at the Chahar Institute, had opined in *Cankao Xiaoxi*, a widely-circulated newspaper that there was a long-standing deep rooted mistrust between India and the US. On the one hand the US is wielding the stick of "protectionism" against India, and on the other by unfolding its "Indo-Pacific" strategy, the US wants India to make a choice between China and the US. Given the choice, China is more "reliable" argues the Chinese academia. Modi's pronouncements on the Indo-Pacific during the Shangri-La Dialogue and the Wuhan unofficial summit have been interpreted in this context. Nevertheless, in India many believed that the real reason was US Secretary of State, Mike Pompeo's North Korea visit, as the denuclearisation of North was at the top of Trump's agenda. Nikki Haley, US envoy to the United Nations had then clarified that the postponement was not due to tensions in bilateral relations.

China must be watching the proceedings of the new dialogue with keen interest as the US officials prior to the US Secretary of State, Mike Pompeo and Secretary of Defense, James Mattis' India visit, have underscored the "China focus" of these talks. Randall G. Schriver, Assistant Secretary of Defense for Asian and Pacific Security Affairs while speaking at an event at the Carnegie Endowment for International Peace said that "China and how to respond to it will be front and center" of the dialogue. He did raise India's purchase of S-400 missiles from Russia and ruled out any waiver albeit he did talk about the US providing India alternate platforms. He also talked about China's Belt and Road Initiative (BRI) and the militarisation of the South China Sea, and said that we need to have an alternative and the US is talking with India. It is interesting to note that Zhang Jun, China's assistant foreign minister said on 27th August that India was a natural partner in the ancient Silk Road and remains in the Belt and Road Initiative. He also tried to address India's concerns about the China Pakistan Economic Corridor (CPEC) when he said that it was a pure economic initiative and does not alter China's position on Kashmir. In fact, China's investment in the disputed territories was one of the reasons as to why India did not participate in the BRI Forum hosted by President Xi Jinping.

Notwithstanding the India-China reset during the Wuhan Summit, India is moving closer to the US as regards security cooperation. India has been granted "major defense partner" status by the US and has been the signatory of the Logistics Exchange Memorandum of Agreement (LEMOA) a variant of the logistics support agreement (LSA) that the US has with its NATO allies. It is believed that the "partnership" will be further strengthened by signing another foundational agreement, the Communications Compatibility and Security Agreement (COMCASA) during the dialogue, which will allow India to operate on high-end secured communication equipment on platforms such as C-130 J, C-17, P-8I aircraft, and Apache and Chinook helicopters procured or to be procured by India from the US. Other deals in the pipeline are a US$ 1 billion purchase of 24-multi-role Sikorsky-Lockheed Martin helicopters for the Indian Navy, US$ 1 billion National Advanced Surface to Air Missile System-II (NASAMS-II), and US$ 2-3 billion unmanned Guardian drones. The tri-service military exercises and anti-terror exercises are also on anvil. The Indo-Pacific certainly would be an important issue.

Professor Zhang Guihong of the Institute of International Studies, Fudan University says that China on the one hand needs to strengthen its economic engagement with India, while on the other allay India's security concerns as regards the Kashmir issue, as well as China's relations with Pakistan and other smaller states in South Asia. In the same vein, India needs to address China's security concerns as regards the Tibet, Taiwan and East Turkistan etc. issues. It appears that both India and China remains skeptical of each other's moves, the Doklam confrontation that almost triggered another war between the two is a reference point. Therefore, close India-US defense cooperation is certainly going to ruffle many feathers in the power corridors in Zhongnanhai, India would be jeopardizing its relations with China, if it acts as a front state of the US. In the same vein, if the US would like to offset China's geopolitical pull in the region and globe by way of India confronting China, the US is certainly mistaken. Nonetheless, China also needs to be sensitive towards India's concerns and try not to push India into the US embrace.

5

CHINA SARCASTIC AND SUSPICIOUS ABOUT DONALD TRUMP'S INDIA VISIT

The kind of flattery, Donald Trump indulged in during his 2-day state visit to India from 24th to 25th February 2020 is unprecedented. Even though he found it difficult to pronounce names such as Sachin Tendulkar and Vivekananda, nonetheless, he exhibited confidence and managed to force his over 125,000-strong audience in Motera stadium to cheer for him after uttering every single sentence. The situation on the ground may not reflect the optics, however, although it would be wrong to conclude that India-US relations have not made headways. The India-US strategic partnership has been elevated to a "Comprehensive Global Partnership" that has sprawled into deepening cooperation in defense, energy, counterterrorism, trade and technology, homeland and regional security including the Indo-Pacific. The very fact that 5 US presidents visited India in the last two decades compared to only 3 between 1959 and 2000 demonstrates that the rise of China and the repositioning of the strategic global objectives of the US has made such a difference. How has China reacted to president Trumps India visit?

Even though China has waged an all-out 'people's war' against COVID-19, however, the state media and scholarship have paid very close attention to President Trump's India visit. China's *Xinhua* News Agency pronounces it as "more rhetoric than reality" and "much ado about nothing." First and foremost, some of the Chinese scholars indicate that Trump did not accord India priority even if India extended him an invitation as soon as he entered the White House in 2017; in 2018, India wished to invite him as the guest of honor for its 2019 Republic Day parade, however, Trump kept India on the tenterhooks until as late as November and then chose China, Japan, and South Korea instead, forcing India to invite South African President Cyril Ramaphosa on a very short notice. This visit took place because of the forthcoming US election in which 4 million Indian origin voters could make some difference, assert the Chinese scholars.

Second, China believes that Trump has been successful in "giving away less and getting more" from India which have been reflected in a number of areas. The analysts argue that the main objective of Trump's India visit was to sell arms. The US$ 3 billion deal that Trump said will "provide India with some of the best and most feared military equipment" has not gone well with the Chinese. A piece published by Tencent says, "To say that the US-made helicopters are not the best in the world is a bit unfair, but to say they are most feared is totally nonsense, for these are all tactical weapons devoid of any strategic significance in the battlefield. Though the Apache helicopters look beautiful, the US has discovered from their deployment in Bosnia and Herzegovina in the 1990s that they were highly inefficient and extremely vulnerable to local shoulder-fired anti-aircraft missiles; the 21 anti-submarine helicopters are rather more effective. In contrast, the Obama administration's approval to sell P-8A anti-submarine aircraft and C-17 strategic transport aircraft to India was the real big deal." Furthermore, the article ridicules India's purchase under the circumstances when she confessed to Trump that "90 million of her people were without electricity!" In contrast, as early as the end of the Ninth Five-Year Plan (1996-2000), China realised the first major electrification of rural areas and transformation of the first large-scale urban and rural power grid thus making electricity accessible to 97 per cent of its population."

Third, Chinese analysts believe that there are structural contradictions between India and the US as far as trade is concerned. Even if there is so much hype about the friendship, both failed to sign a limited trade deal.

Trump didn't even spare India as far as the trade war is concerned and accused the country of having the "highest tariffs in the world" levelling it as the "tariff king." If this wasn't all, the US President also complained that the outsourcing of services by American companies had led India to steal American jobs argues one scholar. He says, "there have been several trade related frictions between the US and India since 2018. In June 2019, the US announced the abolition of India's Generalised System of Preferences, or GSP, forcing India to retaliate by imposing up to 120 per cent duties on 28 US products, further exacerbating bilateral trade tensions. However, the scholar believes that the US remains optimistic about India's economic development prospects, and the normalisation of US-India economic and trade relations is conducive to US companies having a larger pie of the Indian market. Another article in Sohu.com reveals that even if India and the US talks about cyber security cooperation, however, the market predicts that India is likely to choose HUAWEI technology and equipment based on cost over other players such as Nokia and Ericsson, predicts the article.

Fourth, what has worried China most is the US wooing of India in its Indo-Pacific strategy and Blue Dot Initiative that aims to bring governments, the private sector and civil society together to promote "high quality, trusted standards for global infrastructure development against China's Belt and Road Initiative. Chinese scholars have started to pronounce the "US-Japan-India-Australia" Quad as the mainstay of the Indo-Pacific Strategy, the main objective of which they say is to contain the rise of China. One article says that at this point in time, "India needs the "tiger skin" so as it can have a backup when it plays against a bigger and much stronger country, even if it has a lot of symbolic significance." At the same time, there are others who believe that India is reluctant to act as a pawn of the US, Modi knows that in the hour of crisis such as 2017 Doklam, "the West didn't come forth with any substantial help." The Chinese commentators are silent on the US's support for India's entry into the NSG and adding the Haqqani Network and TTP to the terror list, but are quick to tweet that the Indian audience at Motera stadium went from "Cheers to Chill" when Trump declared that "Our relationship with Pakistan is a very good one." Some others reported that Trump's visit was greeted with violent riots between Hindus and Muslims in Delhi and between the Maoists and police in Madhya Pradesh.

In conclusion, there has been sarcasm as well as paranoia about the convergence of Indian and the US interests, especially the security ties and interoperability of the defense platforms of the two countries. However, China believes that owing to the asymmetrical relationship between India and the US, the latter will not give in much. As regards India, China believes, it will not mind taking a free ride, but will not compromise its strategic autonomy.

6

QUAD 2.0 WILL NOT 'DISSIPATE LIKE SEA FOAM'

The first ever highest level Quadrilateral Security Dialogue (Quad) Summit held on 12 March 2021, followed by a joint statement that calls for a "free, open, inclusive, healthy" Indo-Pacific region "anchored by democratic values, and unconstrained by coercion", addressing "shared challenges, including in cyber space, critical technologies, counterterrorism, quality infrastructure investment, and humanitarian-assistance and disaster-relief as well as maritime domains," promoting/a "free, open/rules-based order, rooted in/international law to advance/ security and prosperity and counter threats to both/in the Indo-Pacific and beyond" has undoubtedly upset China. This can be noticed in the statements emanating from the Chinese strategic community, media and politicians alike. Setting up a vaccine expert working group, working group for critical and emerging technology, and a climate working group were some of the tangible results, besides the institutionalisation of the dialogue mechanism at the highest level. How has China reacted to the Quad, the summits and how does it wish to mitigate the challenges posed by it? Let's examine some of the views aired by the Chinese scholarship on the Quad.

First, Quad 2.0 has gained traction and is more resilient than Quad 1.0. The origin of the Quad could be traced back to cooperation between the US, Japan, India and Australia in the aftermath of the 2004 Indian

Ocean tsunami. The cooperation fructified in the first ever security dialogue in 2007; this was also the year when the then Japanese Prime Minister, Shinzo Abe talked about the "confluence of two oceans" (Indian and Pacific Ocean) while addressing Indian Parliament. Five years later, he propounded the idea of "Asia's democratic security diamond". Abe argued, "I envisage a strategy whereby Australia, India, Japan, and the US state of Hawaii form a diamond to safeguard the maritime commons stretching from the Indian Ocean region to the western Pacific. I am prepared to invest, to the greatest possible extent, Japan's capabilities in this security diamond." Most Chinese scholars, including Chen Qinghong, a researcher at China's Institute of Contemporary International Relations (CICIR), argue that the Quad 1.0 "collapsed within a year of its establishment" but since the first meeting of senior officials of the Quad in November 2017, it has gained traction. The flurry of activities such as Quad's upgradation to the foreign minister level dialogue on the sidelines of the UN General Assembly in 2019; the US Think Tank, Centre for Strategic and International Studies (CSIS) releasing a report on the Quad in March 2020; the bilateral, trilateral and "2+2" dialogue mechanisms between the Quad members; and the first virtual summit of the Quad leaders on 12 March has been held responsible for the new version named as Quad 2.0 by Chinese scholars.

Two, Quad 2.0 is aimed at containing and diluting China's influence in the region. Even if the first ever Joint Statement (2021) refrains from naming China, but the Chinese strategic community, especially since 2017, has been vocal in pronouncing the Quad as anti-China, with the aim to "contain the rise of China". Besides the above-mentioned mechanisms between the Quad countries, they are quick to point to the security cooperation between the Quad nations. Researchers Chen Qinghong of the CICIR and Zhang Jie of the Institute of Asia-Pacific and Global Strategy, Chinese Academy of Social Sciences refer to the first ever military exercises between the Indian and Japanese air and ground forces in Agra (2018) and Mizoram (2019) respectively, Malabar naval exercise, and signing of a series of logistic support agreements among the Quad as security pacts aimed at "diluting China's influence" in the region.

Since Quad 2.0 is more resilient than 1.0, therefore, its future development is bound to have a significant impact on the development and evolution of regional security architecture, argues Chen Qinghong of the CICIR. According to Liu A'ming, a researcher at the Institute of International Studies, Shanghai Academy of Social Sciences, the "upgraded version of Quad has a clearer goal, which is to confront China. This is clearly different from the Quad of ten years ago". The "Quad signals unity among the four in their foreign policy approaches, which in turn strengthens the leadership of the United States". In fact, "no country in Asia is willing to confront China strategically. They are all tempted and coerced by the United States" according to an op-ed titled "The United States can't afford to build and even pull the cart of 'Mini Asian NATO'!" by *Huanqiu Shibao* on 14 March. According to the op-ed, "the United States has lost its way, and its only remaining sense of strategic direction is how to destroy China".

Three, "democratic values" have become the ideological foundation of the Quad. This is the thing perhaps feared by China the most, as it may give rise to an ideological cold war as was witnessed between the US and the Soviet Union. The Trump administration did try to differentiate between the Communist Party of China and the Chinese people during the last leg of his regime, and it appears that the Joe Biden administration is continuing with the same policy. According to Liu A'ming, ideology wasn't at the centre of the debate during Quad 1.0, but has taken precedence in Quad 2.0. China is apprehensive that the "alliance of democracies" will be expanded further. According to Chen Qinghong, no doubt the Quad is "not going to be an exclusive club" but the expansion will be based on "common values and interests". Prime Minister Narendra Modi's Shangri-La statement (2018) that "We choose the side of principles and values, of peace and progress, not one side of a divide or the other" has been interpreted by the scholar in this context. He says that there is a consensus on this in the Quad, but it remains to be seen whether expansion will change the Quad from four to five or six or the Quad+ approach. On the other hand, ASEAN+3+3 version has also been put forth to diminish China's "charm offensive" and "dilute its influence in Southeast Asia". According to Chinese scholars, when China proposed ASEAN+3 to the East Asia Summit, Japan and other countries actively promoted inclusion of Australia, New Zealand and India to join the East Asia Summit.

Four, the Quad is an inalienable part of the US "Indo-Pacific Strategy".

Chinese scholars argue that the range of issues under discussion among the Quad countries have expanded into various domains. It is not only limited to the "free and open Indo-Pacific" (FOIP), North Korean nuclear issue and the South China Sea, as has been the case during its earlier version, but also include "the importance of good governance in strengthening the rule-based order"; promotion of "openness, transparency, and the development of high-quality infrastructure based on international standards", and coordination with other regional forums such as ASEAN, and the Indian Ocean Rim Association (IORA) etc. A mention is made of some cooperation in infrastructure projects in the "Indo-Pacific" region initiated by the Quad. For example, Australia, New Zealand, Japan, and the United States have jointly announced the construction of a power grid in Papua New Guinea; at the Pacific Business Forum in Bangkok (2019), Japan, Australia and the US launched the "Blue Dot Network" that will serve as a global evaluation and certification system for roads, ports and bridges, with the focus on the Indo-Pacific region. This is certainly being looked at as a counter to President Xi Jinping's project of the century, the "Belt and Road Initiative" that has been aggressively opposed by India owing to China's insensitivity to India's territorial concerns in Pakistan Occupied Kashmir.

Five, China's burgeoning economic and military muscle has alarmed the US and its allies. Chinese scholars assert that not only China didn't become a "western style democracy" but has increasingly defended its maritime rights and sovereignty. Some of the "decisive actions," according to researcher Chen of the CICIR, include a series of countermeasures against Japan's "nationalisation" of Senkaku in 2012; imposition of Air Defence Identification Zone (ADIZ) in the East China Sea in 2013, reclamation of islands and reefs in Spratly in 2014, and thwarting of India's "infringement in the Doklam" in 2017. They have argued that Doklam was instrumental in India's rethinking on the Quad, if that is the case then, Galwan could be regarded as instrumental in India lodging both the Quad and Indo-Pacific Strategy in its military and foreign policy matrix. Conversely, they posit that the United States is aware of the fact that it is "difficult to contain China with its own strength" therefore, deliberately draws on the strength of its allies and partners.

Six, formation of an "Asian NATO" will be an uphill task, with India the weakest link. Although there are academicians in China who believe that Quad will vanish soon, for they argue that China is the largest trading partner of all the four Quad nations. Zhou Bo of the Centre for International Security and Strategy (CISS), Tsinghua University, aired such views in a recent debate on the Central Global Television Network (CGTN) of China. Moreover, since the threat perceptions are different, formation of an "Asian version of NATO" is by no means an easy task, argues Zhang Jie. These assumptions resonate Chinese Foreign Minister, Wang Yi pronouncing Quad as a "headline grabbing" idea that will "dissipate like sea foam" during a press briefing on the "Two Sessions" in March 2018. Most of the Chinese scholars deem India as the "weakest link" in the Quad. India's intervention in the South China Sea and the East China Sea is mainly limited to the level of diplomacy and public opinion, according to Zhang Jie. In fact, the scholar says that this applies to all the Quad members at this stage, hence the possibility of forming a substantive alliance in the short term is unlikely. However, they also agree that "to some extent, the breadth and depth of Quad's development depends on India's attitude" and that Quad will be instrumental in enhancing India's military strength.

Finally, as a way out, the Chinese are banking on their strong trade ties with the ASEAN, and hope that the grouping will not accommodate the Quad. China hopes that the ASEAN will seek a balance between the economic benefits from China and the security provided by the United States. Therefore, "maintaining economic influence and limiting conflicts within a controllable range" has been stated as one of the goals of China's diplomacy. Zhang Jie recommends that China must manage well strategic competition with the US, avoid challenging the existing interest structure at global level excessively, circumvent the balancing tendencies of small and medium-sized countries at the regional level, and avoid the formation of military and economic bloc confrontation in the region. As for India and Japan, China believes it should be able to strengthen normal relations with both countries, for strategic confrontation with China is considered as "an unbearable burden" for both of them.

IV
CHINA AND THE US

1

CHINA'S "SHARP POWER" AND THE HEGEMONIC CONTEST

During the 40 years of reforms and opening up, developed economies such as the United States, Europe, Japan, Taiwan, Hong Kong and South Korea etc. reaped hefty dividends in China. These economies literally turned China into 'the factory' of the world by transferring technology and investing huge sums in various sectors, meanwhile ignoring the so-called "human rights" record, suppression of political pluralism and freedom of speech inside China. They also hoped that their integration with authoritarian China would bring in the so called "peaceful transition" in China, which will eventually follow the democratic path followed by most of the countries as prophesised by Fukuyama.

However, after four decades of hyper globalisation, China has turned the tables on these very developed economies. China, rather than treading the Soviet path of disintegration, triumphantly emerged as the second largest economy of the world with a US$ 13 trillion GDP, and increasingly challenged the American hegemony in its vicinity and beyond. With ever-expanding economic muscle, China is exporting capital, technology, as well as labour and capturing markets across the continents. It is filling all possible vacuums left over by the US abdication from competition in the economic, strategic and above all in the realm of ideas. Slowly and steadily graduating from the ideas of building "spiritual civilisation" advocated by Deng Xiaoping, to Hu Jintao's "harmonious world" where the promotion of Chinese culture is an important component, to Xi Jinping's concepts like "cultural soft power" and "Core Socialist Values" which heavily draw from the Chinese traditional value system, have been promoted inside and outside China with great enthusiasm.

The "soft power" exercised by authoritarian regimes is categorised as "sharp power" by Christopher Walker and Jessica Ludwig of the National Endowment for Democracy. They have argued that China relying on the instruments of authoritarian influence by way of co-option and manipulation are applied to targets in media, academia, and the policy community. The "sharp power" they say "pierces, penetrates, or perforates the political and information environments in targeted countries," and enables the authoritarian regimes to cut, razor-like, into the fabric of a society, stoking and amplifying existing divisions. Joseph Nye who coined the word "soft power" in the year 1990, pushes the argument even further by comparing "sharp power" with that of hard power when he says that in the context of "sharp power", the deceptive use of information for hostile purposes, is a type of hard power. However, at the same time he says that "the distinction between the two is difficult to discern."

One of the instruments that has been often cited is the establishment of over 500 Confucius Institutes and over 1000 Confucius Classrooms all over the world by China. Second, as Chinese media is spreading its wings all over the world, the supremacy of Western media is increasingly being challenged. For example, Xinhua has 180 news bureaus globally, China Central Television (CCTV) has over 70 foreign bureaus, broadcasting to 171 countries and regions in six UN official languages, the world's second biggest radio station after the BBC, broadcasts in 64 languages from 32 foreign bureaus, major Chinese newspapers such as *People's Daily*, *China Daily* etc. cover 5.5 billion people in over 200 countries. The academic collaborations, thousands of scholarships offered by China to foreign students, sending Chinese cultural troupes abroad etc. have been allegedly "taking advantage of the openness of democratic systems while denying the same to others inside China. Making headways into joint publications such as *Encyclopaedia of India and China Cultural Contacts*, the goal of which according to some critics is not scholarship but to advance political goals and portray a benign image of China. This may not be true of other projects such as the mutual translation of 25 each classical and contemporary literary works from Chinese into Hindi and Indian literary works into Chinese.

China, obviously has rubbished the concept of "sharp power" and has argued that it is essentially the reproduction of the "China threat theory" and the United States' excessive concern about their global leadership. The US and the Soviet Union employed their "sharp power" throughout the Cold War. Moreover, who doesn't use sophisticated tools for international influence? The quantum computing and artificial intelligence that has been employed to boost trade, marketisation, security, and war games by China of late has emerged as another area for supremacy. It has been reported that China's theft of intellectual property rights has cost American companies over one trillion dollars and the US is considering punitive measures. Added to this the trade deficit of US$ 275 billion with China owing to China not giving access to American companies such as Google, Facebook, Twitter, Instagram, and many others in pharmaceutical, insurance etc. sectors have made the US and western countries believe that China has increasingly raised barriers to external, political, cultural and economic influences at home, while simultaneously taking advantage of the openness and democratic systems of abroad.

2

THE MARGINALISATION OF CHINA IN THE KOREAN CRISIS

A four hour long working dinner between the North Korean leader, Kim Jong Un and South Korean president Moon Jae-in's envoys Chung Eui-yong, national security adviser, and Suh Hoon, National Intelligence Service director on 5th March 2018 resulted in prospective summits between Kim Jong-un and South Korean president on the one hand, and between Kim and Trump on the other, perhaps in April and May respectively. Though Trump apprised president Xi Jinping over phone about it, and Ministry of Foreign Affairs Spokesperson, Geng Shuang welcomed the development reiterating that 'China will continue to play a positive role" as regards resolving the denuclearisation issue through dialogue, however, there is a feeling in Beijing that its trusted ally, the North has circumvented Beijing and left it in the lurch. The role of China that has been instrumental in hosting the six party talks as a 'mediator' in Beijing has been undermined.

Social media inside China is abuzz with all sort of speculations and pointing fingers towards China's failure to see through the 'opportunism' of the North as well as 'misjudging' the situation. Wang Mingyuan, editor of the *Reforms Internal Reference* has pointed to the 'selfishness' and 'unilateralism' of Korea throughout history that resulted in the downfall of the Ming and Qing dynasties, incurring irreparable costs including the loss of territories, for example Taiwan in the wake of the Sino-Japanese War of 1894 over the Korean issue. As recently as in the year 2000, the North also circumvented China when the former sent Jao Ming-lu, the second in command in North Korea to the US and issued a North Korea-US Joint Statement. According to him, North is doing this, because it is attempting to breakaway from its security reliance on China. Some others believe that ever since China actively cooperated with the US to sanction the North, the sanctions played a key role in changing North Korea's attitude. However, after the North and the United States started to establish direct contacts, the role that China can play will be very limited, for it stands totally 'marginalised'. China's current affairs analyst, Deng Yuwen, and Zhang Bohui from Hong Kong Lingnan University hold such views.

A Sudden twist in the events has caught China in a very precarious situation. On the one hand she has been participating in sanctions, which has already invited the displeasure of its ally; on the other, it has also maintained the momentum of humanitarian supplies inside North Korea, for China doesn't wish to see the collapse of the North least to talk about Korean unification and the US chipping in as a security provider. It has been reported by North Korea's media that their supreme leader wishes to "write a new history of national reunification." As a matter of fact, the security guarantee remains the precondition for the denuclearisation of the peninsula. If consensus builds around the issue, North Korea abandoning China as a security guarantor should not come as a surprise.

From North Korea's point of view, it perhaps has completed a stage of missile and nuclear tests, thus wanting to come out of the present predicament, especially in the wake of sanctions. If this is the thinking in Pyongyang, the environment can deteriorate instantly. From the perspective of South Korea, the present president certainly would like to have improved relations with the North, however, since the US remains its security provider, it needs to take the US in confidence. Either way, it is a problem for China. If nothing comes out of the prospective summits, and if the North sticks its gun to possess nuclear weapons, China not only will have to accept the reality, but also the reality of others in the vicinity going nuclear. If the US emerges as the security guarantor in the wake of the US-North Korea normalisation of ties, China's image as a 'mediator' will further be diminished. And the last thing China would wish to happen is the unification of two Koreas. For the time being, the best China can expect is to be part of the dialogue whether quadrilateral or the resumption of six parties. Undoubtedly, the task is uphill and the road long and uneven, but sometimes unconventional leaders are capable of producing miracles.

3

CHINA, US, WAR CLOUDS OVER NORTH KOREA AND INDIA'S PREDICAMENT

According to Chinese diplomats, Donald Trump is far easier to do business with compared to Obama. This has been confirmed by Trump himself in an exclusive interview to Maria Bartiromo of Fox Business before calling Chinese president Xi Jinping on April 11, 2017. In the interview, Trump talked about his meetings with president Xi, and revealed that he had a very, very good meeting with the latter and liked him. He talked about a certain chemistry and understanding between them, and said that Xi was the one with whom he can get along very well. More importantly, when asked about trade and currency, Trump's reply was that 'the first thing I brought up was North Korea. I said you've got to help us with North Korea, because we can't allow it...I told him that if China helps the US on the issue, China will do better in trade with the US.' While enjoying his chocolate cake dessert, Xi was briefed by Trump about the US firing 59 missiles in Syria. Trump revealed that Xi Jinping's response was 'it's ok.' 'I believe he is O.K. with it, he was O.K....I think he understood the message and I understood what he was saying to me.' No wonder Chinese diplomats told me they were at ease with doing business with Trump.

Now as North Korea condemns the missile attack on Syria as an 'unforgiveable act of aggression' and gets ready for its sixth nuclear test, the US in a 'show of force' has dispatched the USS Carl Vinson carrier strike group to the Korean Peninsula which has created a lot of hue and cry in China. North Korea on its part has justified its 'self-defensive and pre-emptive strike capabilities with the nuclear force at the core.' What are the reactions and responses coming from China?

In the wake of the Trump-Xi meeting and Wednesday's phone call between the two leaders, Chinese analysts argue that as long as China's and Russia's interests are taken care of, this may be an opportunity to 'reboot' China's ties with North Korea. First and foremost, the present leadership in North Korea must step down, the new leadership must accept denuclearisation, however, the US must not unify the country. Furthermore, the US and South Korean armies must not cross the 38th parallel. Even if there are surgical strikes inside North Korea by a small force, they also must retreat to the south of the parallel immediately. In order to secure its interests, China must simultaneously send its ground forces and navy to the North, thus reinforcing the above interests. If the US brushes aside these interests, conflict with the US cannot be ruled out.

Some in China also fear the convergence of Russian and American interests in the Korean peninsula for pinning down China, however, given the present equations, they believe this kind of convergence is ruled out. On the other hand, the possibility of an anti-US Sino-Russian alliance of the 1950s is also ruled out. What conspired between Trump and Xi on the morning of the 12th is not known except Xi telling him that China wishes to resolve the crisis through peaceful means, however, Chinese are of the view that China will not go to war with the US over North Korea. In the face of this consensus, some argues that Kim Jong Un in order to save his skin, must compromise, for war rhetoric will not work. Nevertheless, in official circles, China has been warning the US with consequences of the strikes in its backyard, and that North Korea is not Syria, the former has the capabilities to counter attack.

As far as India is concerned, though it has no stakes in the Korean Peninsula, however, the consensus which Trump has reached with China, is not just on the Korean crisis but a whole gamut of the US-China relationship. It is an open secret that whenever the US and China have reached such a consensus, China has exerted more pressure on India; one may recall the Chinese pronouncements in the wake of India's nuclear explosions in 1998.

Coming closer to the US as regards its security dilemmas, has always been a strategic temptation for the Indian leadership. This temptation was incrementally and discreetly elevated by the UPA II regime in India, however, the Modi government seems to have gone overboard; siding with the US on the South China Sea issue and the signing of the 'vision statement' is the manifestation of this. India's political relationship with China presently is at its lowest ebb, how far the US will protect Indian interests at the regional as well as international level is anyone's guess. In the wake of the Dalai Lama's Tawang visit, China has threatened India to take necessary steps to protects its 'territorial integrity.'

As far as India's relations with China are concerned, India has been high on rhetoric, whereas border infrastructure is in shambles. Someone has pointed that Kautilya's 'duel policy' and 'war by counsel' provided in his classic, *Arthshastra* will provide some clues to deal with China, however, I have been arguing that both will not work unless, India's domestic drivers are strong. India must seriously rebalance its relationship with both the US and China at the earliest and make a choice between strategic temptation and strategic opportunity.

4

BEHIND THE US-CHINA TRADE WAR

Irrespective of 45 US trade associations, representing retail, technology, agriculture and other consumer-product industries urging the White House not to go ahead with imposing tariffs on Chinese imports, US President Donald Trump on Thursday signed a presidential memorandum that could impose tariffs on up to US$ 60 billion of imports from China. The scare of the trade war began to take its toll on the global stock indices. China quickly denounced the punitive measures that it said were based on outdated US trade laws put in place during the Cold War era to protect domestic industries. It accused the Trump administration of "unilateralism", "zero-sum mentality" and endangering the "rule based global trading system." China's Ministry of Foreign Affairs spokesperson, Hua Chunying said on 21 March 2018: "The Chinese side does not want to fight a trade war with anyone, but if someone forces us to fight, one, we will not be scared, and two, we will not be shy. If the United States takes action that harms China's interests, China will certainly take firm and necessary action." China retaliated by imposing 15 per cent import tariffs on 120 types of US products, 25 per cent on another eight categories of products totalling around US$ 3 billion.

There are various voices making rounds in China. The mainstream viewpoint is that the US-China economy is hugely intertwined, moreover, US trade with China has created 2.6 million job for the Americans, which someone has interpreted as China saving around US$ 850 for each American household. Another argument given by nationalistic Chinese voices is that China could sell the US treasury bonds that it holds. The third argument is that China will stop importing US$ 15 billion worth of soybean from the US, including the orders it places to Boeing so on and so forth. Some Chinese analysts have pronounced these as dangerously harmful for Chinese interests as the efficacy of the same is doubtful. For example, the amount of US$ 850 is merely 1 per cent of the average annual income of US citizens; the very withdrawal of the Chinese treasury bonds that account for just 7 per cent of the total treasury bonds, will end up depreciating their value by 40 to 50 per cent or even more, and moreover the orders placed by China to Boeing are insignificant in the face of an average 500 aircraft sold by the company annually. Conversely most of the imports from the US to China are high-tech products including the spares of the much flaunted C919 passenger Jet. There are other voices that call for greater openness, market access to American products and services on equal footing, however, they do not form part of the mainstream opinion.

It is the latter opinion in China that has made western countries feel that the very thinking that the integration with authoritarian regimes would inevitably change or bring in peaceful transition in such regimes has basically been proven wrong. However, after four decades of integration with the global economy, China has turned the tables on these very developed economies. It has become the second largest economy of the world with US$ 13 trillion GDP, and is increasingly challenging American hegemony through so called "sharp power" pronounced by Christopher Walker and Jessica Ludwig of the National Endowment for Democracy. It is filling all possible vacuums left over by the US abdication from competition in the economic, strategic and above all in the realm of ideas. The quantum computing and artificial intelligence that has been employed to boost trade, marketisation, security, and war games by China of late has emerged as another area in the battle of supremacy.

Therefore, the so-called theft of intellectual property rights by China, the trade deficit of US$ 275 billion with China, China increasingly raising barriers to external, political, cultural and economic influences at home, while simultaneously taking advantage of the openness and democratic systems of foreign countries may be true at the surface, however, underneath everyone including the Americans know that China has emerged as a challenger to the established hegemon and disrupted the latter's 'established norms' of the international order. Both may cry foul over trade, and China may drag the US to the WTO, but the protracted contest over trade, politics, as well as the ideology in the backdrop of China's and Xi Jinping's rise has just started.

5

US-China Trade War Kicks Off

On 6th July 2018, the bulk carrier Peak Pegasus, laden with US soybean was desperately trying to make it to Dalian Port in Northeast China before the 12 pm deadline to evade tit for tat 25 per cent levies. As the US imposed deadline came into effect, China accused the US of violating WTO rules and thus setting off "the largest trade war in economic history, demonstrating a typical hegemonic attitude against the rules of world trade."

In fact, the fears of a US-China trade war loomed large early this year in March when US president Donald Trump signed a presidential memorandum that would impose tariffs on up to US$ 60 billion of imports from China. In April, the US barred ZTE, one of the largest telecom companies in China from purchasing components from American companies for 7 years for trading with Iran and North Korea. A deal whereby ZTE has agreed to pay a US$ 1 billion fine to the US and embed a US selected compliance team in the company for a period of 10 years has given the Chinese giant a reprieve. Both sides were hoping for a similar breakthrough on the 2nd and 3rd June trade talks, however, the talks failed as the US stuck to its guns that China must import more from the US but failed to assure China that it will not impose duties on the Chinese exports.

On 15th June, the US announced 25 per cent tariffs on 1102 Chinese products amounting to US$ 50 billion, of which the first batch of US$ 34 billion it said would come into effect on 6th July at 12.01 P.M. Chinese time. China retaliated immediately by imposing duties on 629 US products worth US$ 50 billion mostly covering agro, automobiles and aquatic products. It reserved the right to impose similar duties on chemical, pharma and energy products perhaps for the second batch of tariffs. China also claimed that about 59 per cent of the US$ 34 billion of the products that have been levied duties against by the US are produced by foreign-invested enterprises in China. The US was undeterred, on 18th June, it ordered its trade representative to further identify Chinese products worth US$ 200 billion for further levies. It threatened that if China retaliated, the US will impose additional duties of 10 per cent. The worth of goods from China was further raised to US$ 500 billion, covering almost the entire value of Chinese exports to the US.

Why is the US initiating a trade war with China? On the surface, the Trump administration has accused China of the so-called theft of intellectual property rights, taking advantage of the openness and democratic systems of foreign countries, subsidising its enterprises, raising barriers to external, political, cultural and economic influences at home, thus causing the US a trade deficit of US$ 375 billion, however, underneath everyone including the Americans know that China has emerged as a challenger to the established hegemon and disrupted the latter's 'established norms' of international order. In the last 40 years of reforms, China has indeed raised its stakes in the global economy; it has become the second largest economy in the world, its GDP of around US$ 14 trillion accounting for around 15 per cent of the global economy. It is projected that if China is able to maintain its present growth rate, it will dislodge the US as the largest economy by 2027. No wonder, the national security strategy of the US in December 2017 labeled China as a "strategic competitor" from a "potential competitor" a decade back. At that time, Trump had accused China of "economic aggression," a revisionist power trying to "shape a world antithetical to US values and interests".

China is filling all possible vacuums left over by the US abdication from competition in the economic, strategic and above all in the realm of ideas. The quantum computing and artificial intelligence that has been employed to boost trade, marketisation, security, and war games by China of late has emerged as another area for the battle of supremacy. If we read the 19th Party Congress Report of president Xi Jinping, we will find that China has identified Made in China 2025, the Belt and Road initiative, 5G network, financial technology and the use of Chinese currency, the RMB as core areas by way of which China would assert global leadership in the realms of technology, cyberspace, geopolitics and economics. It is in this context that the hegemonic contest between the US and China whether trade or otherwise would be a protracted one.

What could be expected from China? The best China could do at moment would be "talk a bit and fight a bit" for realising a bipolar world. To this end, it will reduce import duties on many products. For example, on 31st May 2018, China reduced tariffs for 1,449 products from most-favored nations, mostly member countries of the World Trade Organisation. Duties on marine products and Soybean have been slashed to as low as 2 per cent and 0 per cent respectively. It will continue to forge better trade partnerships with the Asia-Pacific region, Eurasia, especially the Belt and Road countries, the European Union and depreciate the RMB to boost exports to these countries and regions.

6

US-CHINA ECONOMIC WAR GETS COLDER

As US president Donald Trump and Chinese president Xi Jinping sat down to have dinner at a Buenos Aires hotel on 1 December 2018 at the sidelines of the G20 Summit, Huawei's chief financial officer (CFO) Ms. Meng Wanzhou, daughter of Huawei founder, Ren Zhengfei was being detained at Vancouver airport for selling US origin products to Iran through Skycom, a so called "hidden" subsidiary of Huawei thus violating US sanctions. Though she was granted bail she will be subjected to physical and electronic surveillance, and certainly is the "hostage" of the economic cold war between the US and China.

The case is similar to the US probing ZTE, another telecom giant of China trading US products with Iran. ZTE paid almost US$ 2 billion to settle the deal. As the US lobby to put pressure on its allies to proscribe Chinese companies amidst the escalating trade war, Chinese telecom giants like Huawei, ZTE and more recently the likes of Fujian Jinhua Integrated Circuit Co. Ltd. are facing heat in the Western world. For example, the BT of United Kingdom has announced that it will not use Huawei equipment for its 5G networks, Huawei equipment from existing 3G and 4G networks would also be removed. Many other countries including New Zealand and Australia are following suit.

In the wake of the US-China trade war, multilateral forums are increasingly becoming platforms for US-China duels, as was witnessed during the recently concluded APEC Summit in Papua New Guinea, where the leaders failed to reach a consensus on the final communiqué. Tensions soared as the US Vice President, Mike Pence criticised China for its policies and practices related to technology transfer, intellectual property and innovation, and said that the US "will not change course until China changes its ways." President Xi Jinping in turn refuted these in his keynote address; China, rather accused the US of protectionism, unilateralism, disruption and for creating uncertainties.

It was speculated that the recently concluded G20 would also be used to score points by the US and China, for on 26 November, in an interview with the *Wall Street Journal*, the US President had threatened that if the trade deal is not reached, the US will go ahead with punitive tariffs on US$ 200 billions of Chinese imports. Notwithstanding the rhetoric, a temporary 90 day truce was agreed upon. The US made it clear that if at the end of this period of time, the parties are unable to reach an agreement, the 10 per cent tariffs will be raised to 25 per cent. It was reported that China has agreed to import substantial amounts of agricultural, energy, industrial, and other products from the US to reduce the trade imbalance between the two. Both sides were under pressure to strike a deal as US stocks and the Chinese currency fell by around 10 per cent.

Notwithstanding the truce, will it stop the economic and political cold war between the two? The tariff is not the only elephant in the room. Undoubtedly, as admitted by the US, China has emerged as the "strategic competitor" the single largest disruptor of the international order established by the US. The "Made in China 2025", by way of which China would like to achieve 40 per cent "self-sufficiency" by 2020, and 70 per cent "self-sufficiency" by 2025 in core components and critical materials in a wide range of industries, including aerospace equipment and telecommunications etc. has rattled the US to its core. China has already made huge headways in artificial intelligence, robotics and quantum computing. The US is doing every bit to stop the export of cutting edge technologies to the Chinese companies. Early this April it banned its companies from doing business with the Chinese telecom giant ZTE, albeit a bailout deal was reached, and more recently on 29 October 2018 the US Commerce Department announced that US companies would require a special licence to export all commodities, software and technology to the Fujian Jinhua Integrated Circuit. The order was passed in the aftermath of the US chip giant Micron accusing the Fujian based company for intellectual property thefts. This is how protectionist measures by the US have been linked to national security. The US believes that any competition from China would be unfair, for the latter takes advantage of the openness and democratic systems of foreign countries, subsidises its own enterprises, and raises barriers to external, political, cultural and economic influences at home.

Both sides have portrayed the deal reached in Buenos Aires very differently. If the US talked tough and mentioned the 90-day truce as a second chance for China, conversely the Chinese official media did not make a mention of the truce period, it rather talked about a trade agreement and cooperation between the two and that both sides will gradually work towards decreasing the trade imbalance. It is clear that both countries are prepared for a long haul as the economic cold war gets murkier with the passage of time.

7

CHINA AND THE INDO-PACIFIC

Chinese academics like others have also attributed the coinage of the Indo-Pacific construct to Cdr. Gurpreet S Khurana who first explained it as a concept in an academic paper titled "Security of Sea Lines: Prospects for India-Japan Cooperation" published in the January issue of the *Strategic Analysis* in 2007. The construct referred to a maritime space stretching from the littorals of East Africa and West Asia, across the Indian Ocean and western Pacific Ocean, to the littorals of East Asia. The term didn't find much currency in Chinese discourse even if it was referred to by Japanese Prime Minister, Shinzo Abe during his Speech to Indian parliamentarians in the same year, for they believed that India was out of the Asia-Pacific construct. Irrespective of Chinese reservations, the construct has been readily accepted by the Indian strategic community and national leadership alike for the very thinking of the Chinese.

China started to feel discomfort as the construct started to appear in the official discourses of governments. It appeared in *Defending Australia and its National Interests*, a defense White Paper issued by the Australian Government on 13 May 2013, where the term was referred to as many as 56 times. The White paper referred to it as a new "strategic arc" and "system" with US ally Japan remaining a "major power" and India playing an "increasingly influential role." The White paper called for a stable, prosperous Indo-Pacific and a rules-based global order. In June 2013, the idea of the Indo-Pacific Economic Corridor was conceptualised during the US-India Strategic Dialogue of 2013 in New Delhi. The Joint Statement that was issued at the end of the dialogue reaffirmed India and United States' shared vision for peace and stability in Asia and in the Indian and Pacific Oceans.

Both "reaffirmed the importance of maritime security, unimpeded commerce and freedom of navigation, and the peaceful resolution of maritime disputes in accordance with international law." In the Joint statement issued during Prime Minister Narendra Modi's US visit in June 2017, India and the US pledged to promote stability across the Indo-Pacific region, increasing free and fair trade, and strengthening energy linkages. Similar statements emanated from the first and second quadrilateral talks between Japan, India, United States and Australia in 2017 and 2018, however, the construct of Indo-Pacific must not be confused with the formation of the "Quad." More recently, during the Indo-Pacific Business Forum held in Washington, the Trump Administration announced US$ 113.5 million in immediate funding to seed new strategic initiatives in areas such as enhancing US private investment, improving digital connectivity and cybersecurity, promoting sustainable infrastructure development, and strengthening energy security and access.

References to a "Free and open Indo-Pacific" have often been interpreted as countering China's assertiveness in the South-China Sea and the Indian Ocean Region with willing and able US allies in the region. Since the US has deemed China as a "coercive", "revisionist" power following "predatory" economic policies, and India is being projected as a "lynchpin" in the US strategy, China has denounced the Indo-Pacific Strategy as a containment theory aimed at diminishing China's geopolitical and economic influence. Undoubtedly, the Indo-Pacific Strategy is the outcome of the shift in the balance of power shifting from the West to East. It has been estimated that by 2050 the region will account for over 80 per cent of global GDP.

Earlier in May, when the US renamed its Pacific Command (PACOM) as US Indo-Pacific Command (USIPC), China reacted strongly in an editorial published by the Chinese edition of the *Global Times* saying that the "two long-term goals of the United States' Indo-Pacific Strategy is the mutual strategic depletion of China and India." It compared the Strategy to "a big pit" that will bury both the rise of China and India. Other Chinese scholars like Yang Rui and Wang Shida from the Communication University of China and China Institute of Contemporary International Relations posit that India will continue to readjust its policies to best serve the Indo-Pacific Strategy so as to realise the "dream of becoming a great power", meanwhile, counter China's "Belt and Road Initiative" and "balance China's rise" by joining the US and other countries. Li Haidong, a professor at the China Foreign Affairs University's Institute of International Relations says that the main purposes of the Indo-Pacific strategy by the US is to establish an Indo-Pacific geopolitical order that targets China on the one hand, and formulates a trade rule centered on itself on the other.

As regards the US injecting US$ 113.5 million in the region, Chinese academics see the security in command shifting to economy in command in the Indo-Pacific but are still skeptical of the US and its allies committing investment in the region. Ma Xiaolin, a professor at the Beijing Foreign Studies University has snubbed it as the "economic edition" of the Indo-Pacific accompanying its "military edition" in the region, the main motive of which remains to counter China's "Belt and Road Initiative." Prof. Ma has pronounced it as a "barking dogs seldom bite" phenomenon. According to him since the Indo-Pacific region overlaps with China's "21st Century Maritime Silk Road", Southeast and South Asian countries are eagerly wanting to board the "Belt and Road" ship and improve their lot. China's strong economic ties with ASEAN irrespective of its disputes with various member states in the South China Sea will make it difficult for the Southeast Asian and smaller South Asian countries to forgo their interests believe the Chinese scholars.

As far as India is concerned, they still question India's relevance in Indo-Pacific strategy. In the words of Zhang Feng, an adjunct professor at the National Institute for South China Sea Studies, India, undoubtedly is an Indian Ocean country. When did it become a "Pacific country" and an "Indo-Pacific" country? According to him, India's primary concerns lies in the Indian Ocean, therefore, its strategy is the "Indian Ocean Strategy" not the "Indo-Pacific Strategy"; it is merely because the confluence of its "Act East Policy" and Southeast Asia that it has endorsed the Indo-Pacific Strategy. He argues that the bottlenecks in India's strategic capability have limited India's investment in the South China Sea and Pacific region. He believes that India rejoining the Quad was the outcome of its malevolent relations with China before and during the Doklam confrontation. Post Doklam truce, especially after the Modi-Xi unofficial summit in Wuhan, China appears to be very positive about what Prime Minister Modi spoke at the Shangri-la Dialogue.

Was it the rebalancing of the India-China relations at the unofficial summit or India being sensitive towards the Chinese sensitivities or the differing perceptions on the Indo-Pacific and India's own vision of SAGAR, standing for Security and Growth for All in the Region that Prime Minister Modi made it clear during his speech at the Shangri-la dialogue that "India does not see the Indo-Pacific Region as a strategy or as a club of limited members. Nor as a grouping that seeks to dominate. And by no means do we consider it as directed against any country." India's vision for the Indo-Pacific according to the Chinese is a positive one. And, why not when the "six elements" such as openness, inclusivity, common prosperity and security, globalisation and connectivity except for "freedom of navigation" largely conforms to the Chinese notion of the new type of international relations paradigm. The Indo-Pacific Strategy certainly is not limited to the Quad as it has already incorporated Mongolia and Indonesia, many more may join. Meanwhile, the shelving of the Varghese report titled 'An India Economic Strategy to 2035: Navigating from Potential to Delivery' by Australia perhaps owing to the China factor where China's ambition to become the predominant power has been cited as a concern for both China and Australia could be a setback. Integrating security, economic, and development investments in the Indo-Pacific could be a difficult task for even the allies and partners of the US, and China may have the last laugh.

8

Donald Trump's Asia Policy:
Will it be a 'Fight a Bit and Talk a Bit' Strategy?

The electoral victory of Donald Trump at the outset could be attributed to the momentous changes in the global economic and political architecture on the one hand and a populist revolt against the globalisation and immigration that perhaps divided the US along racial, religious, gender and class lines unprecedented in the entire history of the US on the other. Added to this was the erosion of US power under pro establishment forces or the so called old hands in governance.

All these reasons are accompanied by an inherent fear of China's rise, be it China's vehement advocacy about 'unhindered multilateral trade' thereby taking leadership of re-globalising the world through the Belt and Road initiative or its drubbing to the Philippines, a close military ally of the US, and finally winning it over on the issue of the South China Sea irrespective of the US 'pivot to Asia' or reconnaissance sorties by US fighter jets over the South China Sea. It was under such international and domestic undercurrents that the US public chose a hot-headed, offensive and anti establishment unorthodox leader in the form of Donald Trump, who according to them would restore the fast eroding American exceptionalism and prestige. Will Trump deliver? What are going to be his foreign policy priorities, especially in the Asia Pacific?

Though it is too early to predict the 'unpredictable' Trump, however, the writing on the wall is clearer if we go through his election rhetoric and what his advisors have been indicating. It seems drifting towards unilateralism or at minimum towards a new kind of uni-multipolarity where the US would be in the core with its allies extending it diplomatic, economic and military support for its initiatives.

Undoubtedly, some allies like Turkey and the Philippines and may be some others may pull out of such a structural arrangement but the US may find new allies in the region. The new structural change is likely to begin with retrenchment, de-escalation in some theatres as well as measured escalation in others depending on US economic growth and prospects.

As regards retrenchment, the Trump administration is likely to concentrate on domestic issues such as job creation, tax cuts and infrastructural development, to this end the US will aggressively develop shale oil, clean coal, and other energy production to reinvigorate its national economy. His immigration policy is likely to be moderate contrary to his election rhetoric such as building a wall between the US and Mexico. Toeing unilateralism at the international front, the US will pull out of alliances such as the Trans-Pacific Partnership (TPP) but initiate bilateral trade agreements, as China has been doing for some time, and secure better deals for the US. Here again contrary to his election rhetoric that once in power, he will declare China as a currency manipulator, he is likely to initiate a moderate approach to negotiate better trade deals with China. Trump is aware that if pushed to the wall, China may hit back by cancelling contracts with leading US manufacturers like Boeing and others.

As far as de-escalation is concerned, the Trump administration would gradually pull out from morasses like Af-Pak, the Middle East and to some extent the Asia Pacific. In the Af-Pak region Trump would cease to be a cash cow of the region as has been the case for decades. In the Middle East it may rope in Russia for stabilising the situation but will face resistance from both Russia and China on scrapping the Iran nuclear deal. As regards lifting the nuclear blanket from Japan and Korea, it may be a ploy to coerce China to force North Korea to roll back its nuclear program or at maximum freeze it at its current level; the US knows that more than a nuclear North Korea China would not like to see a nuclear South Korea and Japan.

This in other words could be regarded as measured escalation by the US in the Asia Pacific. Receiving a congratulatory phone call from Taiwanese leader Tsai Ing-wen could also be seen in this regard that has ruffled quite a few feathers across power corridors in China and US alike. The call is unprecedented since the signing of the 'Three Communiqués' with China, so much so that it was deemed an act of 'in experience' in the matters of foreign policy on the part of Trump. On the contrary, this is a conscious policy decision by way of which Trump has hit China hard where it hurts. Rather than expecting him to render an apology and play by international rules, Trump hit back even harder by tweeting: "Did China ask us if it was OK to devalue their currency (making it hard for our companies to compete), heavily tax our products going into their country (the US doesn't tax them) or to build a massive military complex in the middle of the South China Sea? I don't think so!" He may further escalate the issue to test China's nerves by negotiating a free trade area (FTA) as well as selling more weaponry to Taiwan. China on the contrary, is not likely to make a fuss out of the president-elect's 'irresponsible remarks' however, but will wait and watch until he resumes the office on January 20 next year. China will definitely draw a bottom line on the issue and hold the US responsible for consequences if this line is crossed.

India which has been described as an 'indispensible partner' by the Obama administration is likely to be indispensible during Trump regime as well. However, Trump tightening a noose around China, will throw challenges to India's foreign policy approaches in the region and beyond. While India has moved closer to the US as regards security cooperation, he is aware that China remains indispensible for India's economic rise. It is here, we really need to calibrate our foreign policy well. If India would like to gain at China's expense, this is not only reflective of poor thinking but will also put India's relations with China at jeopardy. Ultimately one and all issues have to be resolved bilaterally not with the help of an off shore balancer. Finally, even though we will find a lot of structural changes in the global political and economic architecture under Trump, irrespective of the wind of US unilateralism under Trump, existing multilateral mechanisms will stay in place or even be strengthened as we have seen in the case of BRICS New Development Bank (NDB) and the Asia Infrastructure Investment Bank (AIIB). The contest for supremacy between the established and the emerging superpower will go unhindered, and we are likely to witness a protracted *data tantan* or a fighting and talking alternatively strategy, not necessarily the use of force by both the sides.

9

TRUMP-XI SUMMIT IN FLORIDA:
CAN THE US AVOID THUCYDIDES TRAP?

In April, when Chinese president Xi Jinping meets the US president Donald Trump probably in his Florida mansion, Xi will reiterate China's advocacy of the 'New type of major power relationship' and that this is the only way out to avoid Thucydides Trap for sure. However, the question that would be asked is, will Trump be convinced? Can he avoid Thucydides Trap for the US?

In September 2015, in an article, Graham T. Allison, a Harvard professor wrote in the *Atlantic Daily* that the 'defining question about the global order for this generation is whether China and the United States can escape Thucydides' Trap.' The Greek historian Thucydides had argued in *The History of the Peloponnesian War* that the cause of the war was the rise of Athens and the fear it caused in Sparta. It is in this context, Allison on the basis of a study conducted by his team at Harvard Belfer Centre for Science and International Affairs argued that in 12 of 16 cases over the past 500 years, the fear and injury to honour resulted in a bloody war.

Now Athens of today, China has indeed risen exponentially in almost every sphere, causing a sort of paranoia in the US, where leading China experts including David Shambaugh in a recent lecture in JNU have termed

China a free rider and an extremely coercive power. It is no denying the fact that China has aspired to be rich and powerful. The grand strategies that have culminated into two centenary goals – one, on the eve of the foundation of the Communist Party of China in 1921, when China is likely to comprehensively usher itself in as a well-off society, and two, on the eve of the founding of the People's Republic in 1949, when China is likely to usher itself in as a moderately developed country, are demonstrative of the fact that China undoubtedly would like to be a super power, and if it fails to become one, the Chinese dream or the great mission of China's rejuvenation will remain unaccomplished.

The decades of Japanese recession did maintain and sustain US exceptionalism for a certain time, but will China recede into recession? If the current statistics are to be believed, it is unlikely.

Though there are strategic temptations to fall into Thucydides' trap, China has consciously avoided the trap so far by advocating its 'peaceful rise' which was modified into 'peaceful development' in 2006. Simultaneously, China during the 1990s under Jiang Zemin advocated 'a new security concept' cantered at 'mutual trust, mutual benefits, equality cooperation and coordination' and a partnership with countries that was 'non-aligned', non-conflictual, and not directed towards any other country.' The last three were further elaborated and incorporated into a 'new type of major power relationship' in an article on China's peaceful rise in the *Study Times* brought out by the CPC Party School. It was perhaps during the second round of China's strategic and economic dialogue in 2005 that China's state counsellor, Dai Bingguo officially spelled out that the 'new type of major power relationship' between China and the US should be built on the basis of 'mutual respect, harmonious coexistence, and win-win cooperation.' In early 2012 the then vice president of China, Xi Jinping during his visit to the US expounded that both China and the US must endeavour to build a new 21st century type of major power relationship. The above contents of the 'new type of major power relationship' were incorporated by Hu Jintao in his speech during the fourth round of the China-US security and economic dialogue in May 2012 and a few months later by the 18th Party Congress of the CPC.

Now this concept of relationship proposed by China has never been accepted by the US albeit a few American officials including Condoleezza Rice and more recently US Secretary of State Rex Tillerson did refer to a 'new type of major power relationship' occasionally. China knows that the US has not accepted this model of relationship in reality. Why has the US not accepted it? Will Donald Trump reconcile with the Chinese notion? It appears that the US including Trump will continue to shun the 'new type of major power relationship' advocated by China for the following reasons.

At the outset, as argued by eminent Chinese scholar Yan Xuetong, the US will never consider China fit for an equal footing in the Asia Pacific as well as globally. If it does, its strategic relationship with some of its allies say Japan and South Korea will necessarily be 'downgraded.' And moreover, since the new type of major power relationship calls for 'mutual respect' the honour and hubris of US hegemony will not deem China fit for that respect. From China's perspective, the rationale behind this new type of relationship is to avoid the kind of conflict the bipolar world witnessed during the Cold War, and try to learn from the relationship the US and the UK established after World War II. However, this is not possible; as the focal point of China's new type relationship is 'peaceful strategic competition' rather than 'comprehensive strategic cooperation' that resulted between the US and the UK. Secondly, China desires to take the relationship to the G2 level, and jointly share power with the US in Asia Pacific as well as the world on an equal footing. If not at minimum to have a relatively longer period of peaceful coexistence so that the asymmetric military gap with the US is narrowed down. Meanwhile, if the US doesn't subscribe to this, China would explore the idea of building a 'community of shared future for the mankind' in the Asia Pacific, Eurasia and Africa an antidote to US security alliances.

Undoubtedly, massive economic growth will enable China to surpass the US GDP in a couple of years, and its military arsenal including naval capabilities would be enhanced to the level matching or surpassing the US exactly the way Germany trounced the UK in every sphere during the Second World War.

Indeed, by the way of peaceful strategic competition, China has trounced the US as a major trading nation across the continents albeit it still needs to strive hard to become a global market. It has also infuriated the US by challenging the Bretton Woods institutions of global governance, and has established its own ones such as the Asia Infrastructure Investment Bank, New Development Bank of the BRICS, the Shanghai Cooperation Organisation Development Bank; this is not all, China also drew many US allies lining up for the membership of these institutions. Nonetheless, China has argued that it is supplementing existing institutions and sharing greater responsibility in global governance. Furthermore, if Donald Trump has made the Trans Pacific Partnership and the Pivot to Asia the first and second causalities of his regime, and reprimanded its allies for not sharing the costs of global security with the US, China on the contrary is balancing globally by way of its 'Belt and Road' initiative on the one hand and expanding BRICS and SCO etc. institutions lead by it on the other. Through 'Belt and Road' initiative it has assumed the leadership of globalisation, unimpeded trade, and people-to-people exchanges on an unprecedented scale across the continents. No wonder, upon Xi's return in Beijing, he would be hosting over 20 heads of states from the Belt and Road countries in mid-May, thus putting China at the Centre of geopolitics as well as geo-economics in the face of US retrenchment and protectionism.

One of the ways to avoid the Thucydides trap for the US would be an economic slowdown or an economic hard landing of China, but if the current statistics are to be believed, it is unlikely. The Chinese economy registered 6.8 per cent growth last year and is poised to grow at 6.5 per cent this year. It still remains an engine of global growth and contributes over 30 per cent to the global economy annually. The Belt and Road Initiative, which has participation of over 65 countries as of now, will certainly push or sustain this growth in times to come. Germany trounced the UK in terms of its TERRESTRIAL MILITARY only. In terms of its power projection capabilities and air force, it could be said to be roughly equal to the UK. However, Germany's navy was far smaller to that of the UK – in the early 20th century, a necessity for a great power. More importantly, Germany's industrial capacity and access to resources was far lower than the UK's.

History reminds us how Japan, Germany and the US behaved when they built massive military capabilities relying on strong economic credentials. Will a country of 1.4 billion behave differently? *'Taoguang Yanghui'* or 'bide your time and hide your capabilities' of the yesteryears has long been abandoned by China under Xi Jinping. China's assertiveness in the South China Sea may not lead to a war contrary to the predictions of Trump's chief strategist Steve Bannon, however, many other flashpoints in the vicinity such as Taiwan, Senkaku, North Korea, even rivalry between India and China or any unthinkable trivial issue could provide a spark for a larger conflict between the established super power and the one which is signalling its arrival at the global scene. The onus is on the US side to accept the 'new type of major power relationship.' China has carefully crafted this notion since the 1990s, if Trump accepts the notion, the US may avoid the Thucydides trap, however, it will also hasten China realising its super power ambition, albeit at the cost of injuring the hegemonic pride, honour and hubris of the US in the same way as Athenians did to the Spartans in Greek history. Will the US accept such an injury?

V

MULTILATERALISM

1
India's Entry into the Shanghai Cooperation Organisation:
A Boost to Regional Stability?

As India and Pakistan set to become formal members of the Shanghai Cooperation Organisation (SCO) during its forthcoming summit on 8th June 2017 in Astana, Kazakhstan, there are lot of anxieties as regards the SCO turning into a battleground for settling scores owing to their animosities over the question of Kashmir and diametrically opposite approaches towards counter terrorism. While the Indian Prime Minister, Narendra Modi has thanked Russian President Vladimir Putin for his 'active help' in supporting India's entry into the SCO, China on 1 June, cautioned both India and Pakistan to 'strictly follow the SCO Charter, the idea of good neighbourliness, uphold the SCO spirit, improve their relations and inject new impetus to the development of the SCO.' Indeed, since the SCO is a cohesive political, economic and military bloc contrary to the loose grouping of the BRICS, and perhaps the most successful multilateral organisation in Eurasia and the world; the inclusion of new members certainly offers opportunities as well as challenges.

First and foremost, as China's GDP surpasses the combined total of all the members, it offers immense opportunities for member states to benefit at bilateral and multilateral levels. As of now, the SCO was limited to China, Russia and Central Asia, the inclusion of India and Pakistan will extend the reach of multilateralism to South Asia, thus expanding its diplomatic, economic, cultural, and security boundaries. The inclusion of more dialogue partners as members, and perhaps further expansion into the Middle East and Europe, will turn the bloc into a real Eurasian organisation, and Eurasia into a 'Super continent' as advocated by Professor Feng DaHsuan, Advisor to Rector, Macau University. Even if China and Russia remains dominant economic players in the region, India believes there is enough space for its strategic and economic interests in the region that would be welcomed by both Russia and the Central Asian Republics (CARs). Its connectivity projects in Chabahar in Iran and in energy security in Central Asia, and the International North-South Transport Corridor (NSTC) are points of reference where policy could be coordinated.

Moreover, since regional and trans-regional connectivity, expansion of trade, investment and commerce are top priorities of China in Eurasia and beyond, and since the mechanism of the 'Belt and Road' is an important instrument in realising the policy goals, which in turn have been supported by the SCO members, the new entrants, especially India who boycotted the Beijing Belt and Road Summit in May, may have second thoughts on the same, as it initiates a close policy dialogue with incumbent and new members. China has pledged that in coming years, it will construct 4000 kilometres of railways and 10,000 kilometres of highways in the region. It would make sense if India's connectivity projects, especially NSTC, which has remained a non-starter so far could be docked to similar Chinese CARs, and Russian projects in the region. It was here in Astana in 2013 that President Xi Jinping floated the idea of building the 'Silk Road Economic Belt.' Since then around 70 countries and scores of organisations have joined the Chinese initiative.

Second, in the long run, the SCO may provide an opportunity to resolve outstanding issues between India and Pakistan on the one hand, and India and China on the other. It may be remembered that in 1996 when Russia, China, Kazakhstan, Kyrgyzstan, and Tajikistan established the 'Shanghai Five', the idea was to resolve border disputes, and downsize military forces along the borders. The resolution of border disputes has undoubtedly resulted in greater connectivity and economic cooperation between the member states. However, ultimately borders need to be settled bilaterally, but the SCO will certainly ameliorate the environment to a certain extent, as there would be frequent meetings between heads of the states. There are apprehensions too, that Pakistan may attempt to internationalise the Kashmir issue through the SCO, but good sense will prevail and the platform will not be used for settling scores on certain issues, especially when the SCO has no such mandate to do so.

Third, since fighting terrorism, separatism, and extremism is another important goal of the SCO ever since its formation in 2001, and during the Tashkent Summit in 2004 a Regional Anti-Terrorist Structure was officially inaugurated in Tashkent, I believe the expansion of the SCO would entail a more coordinated approach on terrorism. Sharing of intelligence, counter terrorism operations and combat experience etc. of various countries will come handy. The large-scale Peace Mission military exercises of the SCO, which have gained importance in the backdrop of the Islamic State spillover into the region, will provide the new entrants, especially India a rare opportunity to engage with the PLA and Pakistan army at the same time. Since the exercises promote interoperability, mutual trust and transparency, it may help to ease up some of the paranoia about the PLA in India on the one hand yet bring the Indian army face to face with the personnel, technological and integrated command capabilities of the PLA on the other. Nevertheless, since perceptions on cross border terrorism between India and Pakistan are diametrically opposite – if India believes that Pakistan differentiates between good and bad terrorists and uses the 'good' terrorists as assets against India, conversely, Pakistan believes India is fomenting trouble in Baluchistan, cooperation especially between the duo would be difficult, and both including China will look at the issues from their own strategic interest. Therefore, to expect any breakthrough on issues like Massod Azhar will be a far cry.

Fourth, since most SCO members have huge stakes in Afghanistan's security, political and economic stability, they need to devise a magic formula, for the security situation in Afghanistan has been worsening, tensions between Pakistan and Afghanistan are escalating, peace with the Taliban that again owing to diametrically opposite perspectives between some member countries is elusive, and the Islamic State has been expanding its reach in the region exponentially, thus endangering the regional peace and stability. Trade and connectivity remains the best bet in the restive region that will yield better results than foreign doles, and enable the country to stand on its own feet. However, here again, the Quadrilateral Traffic in Transit Agreement (QTTA) between China, Pakistan, Kirghizstan and Kazakhstan that has been docked with the China-Pakistan Economic Corridor (CPEC) will further test India's diplomatic manoeuvrability with the CARs, as India has voiced its opposition to the CPEC. Since regional integration form the bulwark of the 'Belt and Road' as well as the SCO, it remains to be seen how these complex issues are handled within the SCO.

Finally, in order to have better results, the SCO members in the true spirits of its Charter, need to coordinate their policies, integrate their developmental strategies, and pool resources to tap into the vast potentials in the region. For India and Pakistan, the SCO will provide an excellent platform for dialogue and constructive cooperation, and hopefully they should be able to narrow down their differences on some areas if not all. As India seeks greater engagement with the CARs through the SCO, it needs to set its footprints on the ground firmly, as of now its remains a non-player in the region with less than US$ 1 billion of trade compared to China's over US$ 50 billion trade with the CARs.

2

BRICS:
The Driver of Global Growth and Governance?

Notwithstanding the 'imaginary' foundation of BRICS and challenges the grouping is facing internally and externally, it's 10 year short journey has indeed achieved remarkable growth and is increasingly being seen as a major economic grouping contributing tremendously to global economic growth and governance.

BRICS Achievements

With the establishment of mechanisms like the stock exchanges of the BRICS emerging markets (2011), agreements to promote trade in local currencies (2012), BRICS University League (2013), BRICS New Development Bank (2014), BRICS Contingency Reserve Arrangement (2015), BRIC first Regional Center of the New Development Bank in South Africa (2017) etc. have demonstrated that BRICS has emerged as a fine example of multilateralism. It has also demonstrated the desire of emerging economies to assume greater responsibilities in global financial governance albeit it's power of discourse remains limited as it holds only 13 per cent and 15 per cent of voting rights in the World Bank and the International Monetary Fund respectively. It was agreed during the 8th summit in Goa, India that an independent BRICS Rating Agency would be established to transform global financial architecture based on the principles of fairness and equity. It is believed that the West led agencies such as S&P, Fitch and Moody's that account for 90 per cent of the rating market are biased against developing countries. For example in May 2017, Moody's ratings agency downgraded China's credit score, warning that economy-wide debt is expected to rise as potential economic growth slows over the coming years. Both India and China had slammed Moody's 'inappropriate methodologies' at that time.

On the economic front, BRICS has become an important engine of global economic growth. If we see its performance since inception, we will find that the grouping's GDP share in the world economy rose from 12 per cent in 2006 to 23 per cent in 2016; the proportion of total trade increased from 11 per cent to 16 per cent; and the proportion of foreign investment increased from 7 per cent to 12 per cent. Today BRICS contribution to global economic growth is more than 50 per cent. Notwithstanding these impressive figures, BRICS intra trade has been abysmal at around US$ 250 billion. During the last BRICS summit in Goa, Prime Minister Modi called for doubling this figure by 2020, however, it appears a far cry given the asymmetries and reluctance of aligning their development strategies.

9th BRICS Summit in Xiamen, Fujian

Xiamen is one of the earliest SEZs of China. The city of 3.80 million people with over US$ 13,000 per capita is one of the 'pivot cities' for the construction of the Belt and Road Initiative. Together with two more pivot cities in Fujian, namely Fuzhou and Quanzhou, the pivots add US$ 224 billion and US$ 400 billion to the GDP of Fujian province, where Xi Jinping spent 18 years of his career. No wonder it is one of the 'pilot free trade zones of China, a 'demonstration district for cross-strait emerging industries and modern service cooperation,' an international shipping centre in southeast China, a regional financial service centre and trading centre of the two sides of the Taiwan straits. Of late, Fujian has taken the lead in declaring three important projects funded by the China-ASEAN Maritime Cooperation Fund: China-ASEAN Marine Products Exchange, China-ASEAN Maritime University, and China-ASEAN Marine Cooperation

Center respectively. In 2016, the province's total import and export trade with the BRICS amounted to 67.9 billion yuan, accounting for 6.6 per cent of the province's total foreign trade. Fujian boasts of well-developed tertiary industries, Yama Ribbon manufacturing, if the sources are to be believed, has decided to invest around US$ 30 million in Andhra Pradesh.

Globalisation vs. De-globalisation

The retrenchment of the West led by the US; fissures in the Western alliance; doubts over the success of the European Union following BREXIT and economic slumps in most countries, and the refugee crisis etc. issues in the West have increasingly made these countries protectionist, so much so the US has pulled out of the Paris Climate Change Agreement. On the contrary BRICS including many developing countries have remained committed to globalisation and connectivity initiatives in the region and beyond albeit some members are reeling under economic stagnation. However, BRICS remains committed to the Paris Climate Change Agreement as well as multilateralism. In the face of such a scenario, BRICS faces new opportunities but entails greater responsibilities too. Since all BRICS countries have initiated their own connectivity projects, it remains to be seen if some unanimity is reached on some of these, for it is projected that these will essentially push economic growth in the region as well as the world.

South-South Cooperation

It is evident that the developing countries would like to break free from the subservient role they had with the industrialised economies and forge stronger economic and political relations among themselves, which are based on mutual respect, equality and win-win cooperation. The establishment of BRICS and its affiliated institutions such as the BRICS New Development Bank (NDB) and Contingency Reserve Fund should be seen in this light. China's connectivity initiative appears to offer such a model for cooperation, which is seen as less exploitative and more relevant to mutual development. No wonder, over 70 countries are on board China's BRI initiative, albeit some smaller BRICS countries have apprehensions about the ultimate goals of connectivity. Nonetheless, it is fact that the

BRICS countries, especially China have been instrumental in south-south finance flows; today China's policy banks lend more capital than any other bank in the world. Cooperation has resulted in foreign direct investment, trade, transfer of technology especially in mining, energy, infrastructure etc. sectors. Therefore, South-South Cooperation will be one of the major themes of the summit. It was with this thinking that China floated the notion of BRICS+ aimed at expanding the BRICS 'friends circle' thus giving a fillip to South-South cooperation.

Counter Terrorism

BRICS countries remain committed to combatting terrorism in any shape and form, and believe that there is a need to expand practical cooperation in intelligence sharing, capacity building, and providing security to their sprawling interests abroad. In this context a Counter-Terrorism Working Group was established during the 8th summit in Goa and held its first meeting. The group agreed to expand counter terrorism cooperation further to include measures for denying terrorists access to finance and terror hardware such as equipment, arms and ammunition. The second meeting was held in Beijing on 17th May 2017 and conducted extensive discussions on the issue affecting the region and beyond. India has been urging the BRICS nations to back its efforts for the adoption of a comprehensive convention on terrorism at the UN and shed the ambiguity on 'good' and 'bad' terrorists.

Combating Global Warming

At a time when President Donald Trump is withdrawing the US from multilateral arrangements such as the Paris climate agreement the BRICS countries have repeatedly expressed their commitment towards the Paris deal and the emission cuts they have undertaken for combating global warming. No one denies the fact that the combined population of 3 billion people and a GDP of US$ 16 trillion will have a huge impact on global emissions; however, can BRICS initiate joint research and development into new energy technologies? It has been expressed by some BRICS countries like Russia and Brazil that they do not want to be seen as exporters of their natural wealth.

People-to-People Exchange

As regards the people-to-people exchanges between the BRICS nations, I believe, even if there are various exchanges such as cultural festivals, media and film exchanges, BRICS scholarships etc. programs, however, there is a huge scope to strengthen and broaden the scope of these exchanges. The establishment of the BRICS University League is an excellent example. There is a need to institutionalise these mechanisms and establish even more at various levels. China has initiated various scholarships, seminars and workshops in this regards thus providing opportunities to people from all walks of life, while it could do more owing to its economic size, other members too need to initiate similar programs whatever the scale may be.

The Way Ahead

It is owing to robust economic growth in India and China that BRICS has been able to contribute to global economic growth and governance. I believe the slide in India's economic growth to 5.7 per cent is a temporary phenomenon owing to its adjustment to demonetisation and the Goods and Services Tax. The weak economic indicators will certainly impact the bilateral, regional and global posturing of a country or grouping. It is owing to strong domestic drivers that emerging economies would be able to support ideas such as a global infrastructure hub and global infrastructure fund mooted by the 2014 G20 Brisbane summit and the World Bank. China has supported such moves and has rendered support for the same through the 'Belt and Road' initiative, the AIIB, the Silk Road Fund etc. mechanisms. In order to build capacities India, China and Russia owing to their geographical proximity could be instrumental in driving regional growth, prosperity and stability provided they align their development strategies. Needless to say, they need to take a holistic and long-term view of their relations as well as the global shift from the Atlantic to the Pacific. BRICS will cease to exist if India and China cannot hold together. Perhaps this was one of the reasons that paved way for the disengagement at Doklam. It is up to the member countries whether they would like to have a benevolent or malevolent relationship, and determine the future of BRICS.

3

COMMUNITY OF SHARED FUTURE:
WIN-WIN PARTNERSHIP TO BENEFIT BOTH INDIA AND CHINA

The concept of building a community of shared future for the mankind was propounded by president Xi Jinping in October 2013 when he said at the conclusion of the Central Meeting on the Works of Foreign Affairs that China must integrate the Chinese dream with the desire of the people of neighbouring countries for a good life and with prospects for regional development, and let the awareness of a community of shared future take roots in neighbouring countries. He reiterated it the following year while addressing the Central National Security Commission and added the feature of common security to it. Gradually the concept was further elaborated and substantiated during various speeches he delivered in China and beyond. For example, his speech at the General debate of the 70th Session of the UN General Assembly at the UN Headquarters in New York, the US on 28th September 2015 systematically sheds light on the scope and substance of this concept. During the 19th Party Congress where Xi Jinping delivered a marathon three and a half hour speech, the community of shared future was included in one of the 14 dimensions of Xi Jinping's Thought on Socialism with Chinese Characteristic. This is an indication that the concept would be matched with actions by China while executing its bilateral, multilateral, regional, and major country economic and foreign policy.

As regards India and China, I will first flag out inter-civilisational exchange, one of the fundamentals of the community of shared future. It was the unhindered circulation of ideas, technology, objects and people that enriched these civilisations. Whether it was the birth of Chinese Buddhism or the dissemination of ancient India's and Central Asian polities' astronomy, literature, music, languages into China or technologies such as sugar making, paper manufacturing, steel smelting, silk, porcelain, tea etc. travelling from China to India and other countries, this circulation enriched knowledge systems across the world beyond doubt. Moreover, this happened owing to the unimpeded flow of the people. The translation industry for example, was created in China, had people from India, and many Central Asian countries. Most importantly, these were the people who were responsible for creating the entire repository of Buddhist literature in China and Northeast Asia, which infact preserved many of the sutras that have been lost in India. Therefore, it was 'learning from civilisations' rather than Fukuyama's thesis of the 'clash of civilisations.' Presently, even though there is a flow of one million people between India and China, however, there is a tremendous scope for taking this exchange to new heights, especially in the field of education.

Second, common prosperity through mutual cooperation, openness, and inclusive and sustainable development is integral to the community of shared future. Accounting for almost 40 per cent of the world population India and China are the 7th and 2nd largest economies of the world respectively. These are like the twin engines of global economic growth, especially China, which is contributing over 30 per cent of present global growth. Both have initiated grandiose development strategies and connectivity initiatives that will integrate these countries with the regional and global economic ecosystems even more closely. For example, 'Made in China 2025', 'Belt and Road Initiative', 'Make in India', 'Digital India', and 'Sagarmala' etc. Now the question arises, can India and China harmonise their development strategies, complement each other and forge a win-win partnership? There are tremendous complementarities in realising and sharing the benefits of fourth industrial revolution too.

China's development experience of the last 40 years, its capital and technology will immensely complement India's labor intensive market, and that it should meanwhile send out some of its most competitive industries such as pharmaceutical and information technology provided there is a principle of reciprocity as regards market access. India tends to benefit more than China as it would be able to build capacities in hard and soft infrastructure that would unleash productive forces and ensure sustainable economic growth. The docking of connectivity initiatives even selective would integrate India more closely to the ASEAN countries, for economic globalisation is a historical and irreversible trend. The circulatory movement of ideas, commodities, technology and people during ancient times has demonstrated that it was never mono dimensional rather a multi vectored, multi nodal and multilateral movement.

Third, the community of shared future calls for peace and security through dialogue. It calls for abandoning the Cold War mentality and the zero-sum game. Meanwhile, it advocates common, comprehensive, cooperative and sustainable security. Both India and China need to be mindful of the fact that the bilateral security boundary is not just limited to the border issue between the two, it has sprawled into various other fields such as maritime, river water, cybersecurity, counter terrorism and various other non-traditional securities. In view of this, both need to establish new dialogue mechanisms while substantiating or replacing older ones. Many of these issues have transcended bilateral dialogue mechanisms and have been discussed at other multilateral forums such as BRICS and the Shanghai Cooperation Organisation (SCO). The peaceful resolution of the Doklam standoff last year exhibits that both would like to resolve crises with peaceful dialogue, minimise differences and broaden cooperation. Nonetheless, the occurrence of such episodes must be avoided at all costs, for these are extremely dangerous and injurious to good neighbourliness.

Finally, building a sound ecosystem equally remains an important element of the community of shared future. India and China being two of the largest consumers of energy are duty bound to build a sound ecology not only for the region but also for the future of humankind. In this context, they must be complemented for adhering to the Paris Agreement irrespective of being at crucial stages of their development. Therefore, cooperation in the energy sector is very crucial. India and China coming together against the so called 'Asian Premium" by the OPEC is a good example. Besides, both could think of building a network of gas and oil pipelines in order to integrate their economies more closely on the one hand, and forge a collaborative partnership in renewable energy and anti-smog technologies where China has made huge forays.

In view of the above, India-China relationship remains one the most important relationships of this century that will determine the future global economic and political architecture. In other words the building of the community of shared future in Asia and beyond, both need to be sensitive towards each other's sensitivities, and nurture and strengthen this relationship for the bright future of Asia as well as the world.

VI

THE BRI

1

Yunnan in the Belt and Road Calculus:
Building Capacities for Sub-regional Economic Cooperation

Right from the initiation of the Greater Mekong Sub-regional economic cooperation plan (GMS) in 1992, the 'Western Development Campaign' initiated in the year 2000 which covered six provinces, five autonomous regions and one municipality across China, and the 'Belt and Road Initiative' (BRI) Action Plan rolled out in early 2015 aiming to connect China with Central Asia, Europe and Africa by land and sea, China has encouraged provinces that are part of these mega projects to promote regional as well as transnational cooperation in areas such as trade and commerce, social and cultural, and non-traditional security etc. domains within China's foreign policy goals. As a member of all these initiatives, Yunnan has become a hub connecting China to Southeast Asia and South Asia. For example Kunming, the capital city of Yunnan would be connected to various transport corridors, the most ambitious of these – the Trans-Asia Railway (TAR) to be completed by 2020, will connect Kunming to Singapore.

By way of the GSM, Yunnan has gradually converted itself as transport, logistic and information hub, thus integrating Yunnan with the northern and southern provinces of China on the one hand and Southeast and South

Asia on the other. The Yunnan Power Grid Corporation earns over a billion dollars in revenues by exporting electricity to Southeast Asian countries. It has also attracted huge investments from many coastal provinces such as Zhejiang, Jiangsu and Guangdong wanting to be part of opportunities that Yunnan brought to various companies from these areas. Moreover, the China-ASEAN Free Trade Area (CAFTA) and various economic corridors including the BCIM were conceived and facilitated by Yunnan. Building a strong ethnic culture, green economy and thoroughfare have been the three major goals of Yunnan. Kunming–Tengchong–Myitkyina–India is one of the highways besides three others that will connect it to Hanoi, Bangkok and Yangon. The route has a total length of about 2,597 km. The China, Myanmar, India, and Bangladesh sections cover 704 km, 504 km, 892 km, and 497 km respectively.

Having laid a network of highways and railways, Yunnan is investing heavily in logistics. During my recent visit facilitated by the International Department of the Central Committee of the Communist Party of China (IDCPC) for a track II dialogue that included delegates from India, Pakistan, Bangladesh, and Myanmar, I happened to have extensive deliberations with academics at the Yunnan Academy of Social Sciences, Party cadres at grass root levels, and entrepreneurs at the Pan Asia Logistics Centre in Wangchong Yunnan Industrial Park. What interested me most was the Pan Asia Logistics Centre built by Yunnan Pan Asia Logistics Group with an investment of US$ 1 billion, completed and operational in less than three years time. The logistics Centre has integrated transportation, storage, loading, handling, packaging, circulation etc. processes with information technology and e-commerce thus cutting logistics costs and improving labor productivity. The Logistics Centre certainly has a long-term futuristic strategy geared towards becoming a bridgehead connecting north-south China, Southeast Asia and South Asia.

Aligning Yunnan's developmental strategies with BRI of the Central Government, it is coordinating policy, planning, allocating resources, and integrating its markets with the countries along the Belt and Road routes.

We were told by the Chairman of the group that by 2020, 8 logistics bases would be built insides Yunnan bordering Southeast Asian and South

Asian countries, smaller bases with an investment of 2 billion RMB and bigger ones with 6 billion RMB. It has been estimated that by 2020, the present annual output of 20 billion RMB would be enhanced to 100 billion accounting for about 10 per cent of China's entire logistics output. The BCIM economic corridor is certainly a part of this calculus, albeit it is not the top priority at moment owing its multilateral strings as was evident with our discussions with the scholars at the Yunnan Academy of Social Sciences.

Nonetheless, despite the skepticism about the progress of the BCIM, it could be discerned that at the sub-regional level, be it bordering Myanmar, Bangladesh or India's northeast, cooperation is difficult to scuttle with the kind of connectivity and capacities that are being built along the border areas of this corridor. This was exactly how despite many Southeast Asian countries harbouring mistrust towards China, it did not stop them from cooperating with and integrating their economies with China. It appears that we have recognised the value of economic corridors but are reluctant to facilitate our bordering areas to tread the path Yunnan has treaded. China on the other hand in tandem with its frontier provinces facilitated integration once it recognised its value by way of implementing facilities such as 24 hour customs clearance and simplified visa regimes etc. These are some of the simpler things that enhanced the competitiveness of China in the region and the world. No wonder last year Yunnan's GDP reached 1.37 trillion RMB, roughly ¼ of India's.

One may argue that it was only when China laid the foundation of a solid domestic infrastructure network that it undertook massive infrastructure integration projects outside the country with an aim to export overcapacity, capital and technology. It is precisely this aspect of the BRI that developing countries could take benefit of, and build their own capacities. India's Northeast, irrespective of being congruous to Myanmar geographically, however has been on 'extreme ends' as far as connectivity is concerned. As a result, the areas have remained closed or semi closed for a long time in history. If India would like to have deeper economic stakes in China's economy, and more importantly if India would like to root out insurgency as well as the backwardness and underdevelopment in the area, it cannot afford to be a bystander to the processes of globalisation unfolding in China's southwest. It is time that we stop looking at the issue with a geopolitical mindset, rather we ought to provide a space for geo-economics, and yes, if there are issues related to security, we must initiate bilateral or multilateral dialogue mechanisms for the same.

2

CHINA'S BELT AND ROAD FORUM:
SHOULD INDIA GET BACK ON BOARD?

Delivering a keynote address to a gathering of 1500 people that included 29 heads of states and officials, entrepreneurs, financiers, academicians and journalists from over 130 countries including figures such as Vladimir Putin, UN Secretary-General Antonio Guterres, World Bank President Jim Yong Kim, and Managing Director of the International Monetary Fund Christine Lagarde etc., Chinese president Xi Jinping reminded people of Zhou Enlai's speech at the Afro-Asian Conference at Bandung in April 1955 that was also represented by the 29 heads of states. If India was the prime mover of the conference in Bandung, China is in the driver's seat as far as the Belt and Road Forum is concerned, and India is conspicuously absent after it boycotted the Forum on the issue of sovereignty.

In his address, Xi Jinping said "China's construction of the Belt and Road Initiative is not to make a new start, but to connect development strategies of different countries and complement each other's advantages ... China is willing to share its development experience with all the rest of the world, but we will not intervene into other nation's internal affairs, export our social system and development model, nor force others to accept them." Reiterating the 'Silk Road Spirit', the Chinese president said,

"Spanning thousands of miles and years, the ancient silk routes embody the spirit of peace and cooperation, openness and inclusiveness, mutual learning and mutual benefit." Reassuring the gathering of China's 'peaceful rise', he said, "We will not follow the old way of geopolitical games during the push for the Belt and Road Initiative, but create a new model of win-win and cooperation. It will not form a small group undermining stability, but is set to build a big family with harmonious co-existence."[1]

If at Bandung, Zhou Enlai was successful in smashing the international blockade by seeking commonalities between nations, in Beijing Xi Jinping has been successful in smashing protectionism and convincing nations about common development, globalisation with Chinese characteristics, and even common security. In order to bulldoze the US$ 1.4 trillion 'project of the century', Xi Jinping pledged US$ 14.49 billion more to the existing US$ 40 billion Silk Road Fund founded in late 2014. The Development Bank of China and the Export-Import Bank of China have pledged to inject US$ 124 billion in the Belt and Road Initiative to support infrastructure, financing and industrial capacity. This is understandable as China's trade volume and investment with the Belt and Road Initiative countries in 2016, exceeded US$ 3 trillion and US$ 50billion respectively.

India which is considered an important country by China along the 'Belt and Road' perhaps went overboard to boycott the Forum. India's dissatisfaction primarily originates from: (1) no policy consultations over the concept and more importantly the Bangladesh China India Myanmar Economic Corridor (BCIM) and the China Pakistan Economic Corridor (CPEC) that form part of the six Belt and Road Initiative economic corridors, especially the CPEC that runs through Pakistan Occupied Kashmir (POK) parts of which are under Chinese jurisdiction. India considers POK as an integral part of Kashmir, the sovereignty of which has been decided by the Instrument of Accession in 1947. India has conveyed to China that there would be no compromise on the core issue of sovereignty in the same way as China has never budged on its 'one China' policy. (2) Since China-Pak relationship is primarily considered as an anti-India axis, it believes that both will further pin down India. Thousands of Chinese soldiers operating in POK territories go beyond the notions of connectivity and unimpeded trade. (3) Contrary to Xi Jinping's overtures at the Forum that there is no geopolitics in the project, India sees it as China's ambition to realise its long-term vision for an Asian regional and world order where given the nature of India-China asymmetrical relationship, and Sino-Pak entente cordiale, India's strategic space would further shrink. In the South Asian context, the 'Indian centric' fragmented integration according to Chinese scholars has provided an opportunity to China to build the 'community of shred future' with neighbouring countries proposed by Xi Jinping in 2014, which since then has been made integral to the construction of 'Belt and Road.' In fact Xi Jinping's reference to 'build a big family with harmonious co-existence' just demonstrates that.

Given the rise of China, these concerns of India are genuine, however, India has rolled out its own connectivity initiatives such as the 'Act East' policy, and the 'Look North' policy that envisages India's economic integration with ASEAN and Central Asia. Projects such as the India-Myanmar Friendship Road link which is part of the greater India-Myanmar-Thailand Trilateral Highway; the Kaladan Multimodal Transit Transport Project; the Mekong-India Corridor, which aims to connect India to Cambodia, Myanmar, Laos, and Vietnam; the development of Sittwe port in southwest Myanmar; the master plan for integrating India's Northeast to ASEAN; India's gas and pipeline projects, and the more recently signed Chabahar port development with Iran has no conflict whatsoever with the similar Belt and Road projects.

Russian president Vladimir Putin in his address at the Belt and Road Forum in Beijing remarked that 'the integration of the Belt and Road Initiative, the Eurasian Economic Union (EEU), the Shanghai Cooperation Organisation (SCO) and ASEAN has laid the groundwork for building a great Eurasian partnership.' In order to reap win-win benefits, it is indeed essential to dock connectivity initiatives; I do not see any reason why India's 'Act East Policy', 'Look North Policy' or any other domestic development strategy such as 'Sagarmala' and 'make in India' cannot be docked with other initiatives such as the BRI, EEU, the US' New Silk Road, and similar Japanese initiatives in the Central Asian region. On the other hand, and more importantly, India would be in a better position to implement the above mentioned projects if its domestic drivers and production capacities are strengthened by aligning its development strategies with those of Chinese initiative, after all the AIIB, of which India is a founding member has shelled out over US$ 100 billion to support BRI projects. India tends to gain rather than lose anything.

The CPEC is just a miniscule project in the scheme of the 'Belt and Road' initiative. It would have been better to enhance India's stake in the territory, had India shown interest in its joint development as the Japanese have shown in the Kuril Islands with Russia. At the same time China's outreach to the Islamic world through Pakistan, and its quest for seeking a way out of the Malacca dilemma is understandable, however, what is incomprehensible is China's silence on policy consultation even if the same is an integral part of the 'five Connectivities' of the entire Initiative. It is a given fact that the China-Pakistan 'all weather' strategic partnership; China wooing smaller South Asian countries, and China's presence in the Indian Ocean Region are some of the reasons for India-China rivalry in the region. However, if there are better consultation mechanisms between the two, some of the mistrust could be done away with.

India's boycott is just a onetime thing, but not the boycott of the entire 'Belt and Road' Initiative. Both India and China need each other, both have been contributing massively for global economic growth. If they join hands, it will bring greater prosperity to their people, to the people of the region as well as the world. The new realities in the global and regional arena have demanded that they make space for each other in the Asia Pacific. In the process, some collision and confrontation is imminent, however, the same could be avoided by way of policy coordination and consultation and more so by establishing dialogue mechanisms at various levels.

NOTE

1. Belt and Road 2017 Summit, South China Morning Post, May 14, 2017 http://www.scmp.com/news/china/diplomacy-defence/article/2094250/your-quick-guide-what-xi-jinping-said-his-belt-and-road

3

Belt and Road Initiative will not Fail

The "Belt and Road Initiative" (BRI) is completing five years on 7th September 2018. It was on the 7th of September, 2013 that the concept was first proposed by President Xi Jinping during his speech at Nazarbayev University, Kazakhstan. A month later, he proposed the 21st Century Maritime Silk Road which envisages building hard and soft infrastructure from the Indo-Pacific to Africa, including transport, energy, water management, communication, earth monitoring, economic and social infrastructure, thus turning the concept into a "Belt and Road" formulation. In 2015, during the Bo'ao Forum for Asia in Sanya, Hainan, China rolled out an action plan that enunciated five major goals of the vision in terms of promoting policy coordination, facilitating connectivity, uninterrupted trade, financial integration and people-to-people exchanges.

China also announced the establishment of a Silk Road Fund with US$ 40 billion, which was increased to US$ 54.40 billions during the Belt and Road Forum for International Cooperation in May 2017 attended by 1500 delegates from across the world. On the occasion, the Development Bank of China and the Export-Import Bank of China pledged to inject US$ 124 billion in the BRI to support infrastructure, financing and industrial capacity. China also signed 76 mega projects, trade cooperation deals with 30 countries, and agreements related to unimpeded trade with 60 countries along the Belt and Road. The newly established Asia Infrastructure Investment Bank (AIIB) and the BRICS New Development Bank (NDB) where China has major stakes were also pronounced as financial institutions supporting the initiative.

There are various arguments put forth by analysts as far as the historicity, geo-economics and geopolitics of the new Silk Road is concerned. Taking stock of the BRI in the last five years, Ning Jizhen, deputy director of the National Development and Reform Commission (NDRC) and director of the National Bureau of Statistics (NBS), revealed on 28 August 2018 that the total trade of China with the BRI countries as of June 2018 had reached US$ 5 trillion. China invested US$ 28.9 billion, and created 240,000 jobs in these countries. Ning Jizhen revealed that as of now, 103 countries and international organisations have signed 118 cooperation agreements with China on the BRI, the implementation rate of these projects according to Ji has reached 95 per cent. The focus has been on the "six economic corridors" of which the China-Pakistan Economic Corridor (CPEC) is the flagship, and work is supposedly progressing smoothly. The construction of the China-Laos Railway, the China-Thai Railway and the Hungary-Serbia Railway have been progressing steadily; construction work on some sections of the Jakarta-Bandung High-speed Railway has been initiated, and the Gwadar Port could be operated to its full capacity. Other rail projects such as Djibouti-Addis Ababa and Mombasa-Nairobi have been completed.

I have pronounced the BRI as China's global rebalancing in terms of geo-economics, geo-civilisation, governance and geopolitics in my latest book *China's Global Rebalancing and the New Silk Road* (Springer 2018), albeit China doesn't subscribe to the element of geopolitics in it. I have argued that the BRI is indispensable to globalisation and the deepening of reforms in China, no wonder the concept has been embraced by many developing countries and China has become the largest trading partner of 25 countries along the route. China's trade with the BRI countries has grown with an average annual growth rate of 1.1 per cent even as world trade has registered negative growth. The initiative is also aimed at civilisational rebalancing and enacting the "Silk Road Spirit" of *peace and cooperation, openness and inclusiveness, mutual learning and mutual benefits.* The BRI is synonymous with the circulatory movements of ideas, technology, commodities and people along the ancient Silk Road that enriched Asian and world civilisations. As regards the educational exchanges, Ning Jizhen said that in 2017, there were more than 300,000 international students from the BRI countries studying in China, while more than 60,000 Chinese students went to study in these countries. It is estimated that by 2020, the number of two-way tourists between China and the BRI countries will exceed 85 million. The BRI remains an antidote to anti-globalisation and protectionism and fundamental to the global industrial chain. The initiative must be seen in tandem with Xi Jinping's advocacy of building a community of shared future for mankind and the Chinese Dream, which are integral to China's, regional as well as global economic development.

Obviously, the Chinese initiative including others such as "Made in China 2025" has invited backlash from some countries, especially the US. They have blamed China for initiating "neocolonial" policies and establishing a "China centric" order. The issue of government debt in some countries has been hyped and the Chinese loans to such countries are portrayed as debt traps. If one believes the data provided by the Asian Development Bank, Asia will require an infrastructure investment of US$ 1.7 trillion by the year 2030, which is roughly about US$ 800 billion per annum. If the West remains non-committal towards investing in the region, people will certainly welcome Chinese investment. For example, the US commitment of investing US$ 113 million in the Indo-Pacific may be a case of too little too late. Nevertheless, some concerns are genuine. Some of the smaller participants of the BRI such as Mongolia, Pakistan, Laos, Sri Lanka, Kyrgyz Republic and Tajikistan are deep in debt. China committing US$ 62 billion for the CPEC may be difficult for Pakistan to service; the example of Sri Lanka been forced to swap over US$ 1 billion for Chinese equity is an example often cited to highlight the "ills" of the BRI. Though the Laos high speed railway may connect China to Thailand the cost is high and Laos may never be able to return the money. Last year, citing "tough financing terms" Pakistan cancelled the US$ 14 billion Diamer-Bhasha Dam project; Nepal and Myanmar followed suit by scrapping a US$ 2.5 billion and US$ 3.6 billion hydroelectricity project respectively. In the same vein, Malaysia too has cancelled the East Coast Rail Link and the Sabah natural gas pipeline projects in August once the new regime under Mahathir Mohamad formed government.

These may be few aberrations amongst the 21,284 projects the Chinese companies contracted in more than 60 countries between 2015 and 2018 worth US$ 410.78 billion. China perhaps has come a long way to understand the political, economic, cultural, environmental and legal risks of the BRI projects. Unlike the initial phase of the BRI, the projects are weighed for every risk and are subjected to asset-liability ratios and return on capital requirements. Moreover, some of the debt issues may have existed before the Chinese investment, therefore, they are not necessarily related to the BRI.

Notwithstanding these aberrations, the BRI remains indispensable to globalisation and will further improve the global supply, value and industrial chain by strengthening interconnectivity between countries and regions. As regards India, though it didn't participate in the BRI Forum for International Cooperation in 2017, however, India's development interests remain intertwined with those of China's. I believe if we answer the following questions, the cooperation on BRI projects could be feasible. One, do we agree that there is a huge disequilibrium in the world economic systems, and that neither India nor China can single handedly offset this imbalance? Together in tandem with other developing countries this could be possible. Two, do we agree that both are committed to globalisation and are opposed to protectionism? I believe both have immensely benefitted from globalisation. Three, do we agree that there is a proliferation of connectivity initiatives taking place across the region and globe, and that both India and China are at the center of these initiatives? Will it make sense if the bilateral or multilateral connectivity initiatives are docked together? Four, do we agree that the security boundary between India and China has been sprawling into various domains on land and oceans, therefore, there is need to establish more dialogue mechanisms? Are not both cooperating on various multilateral forums, especially the Asia Infrastructure Investment Bank and the New Development Bank of the BRICS, which China has said would be the banks funding connectivity initiatives? If the answers to the above questions are in the affirmative, I believe, both India and China need to work on a consultation mechanism as regards their connectivity initiatives and work out modalities for strengthening and deepening cooperation. The connectivity initiatives of both India and China offer tremendous opportunities to have policy coordination in areas such as infrastructure, energy, transport, power, e-commerce, investment and trade. Needless to say, it would be possible if both think of aligning their development strategies while giving a full play to the "Silk Road Spirit".

Undoubtedly, the BRI is here to stay, and would be further integrated to new technologies such as e-commerce, big data, cloud computing and artificial intelligence to enhance the efficiency and efficacy of projects. Meanwhile, we will see China accelerating the construction of free trade pilot zones, cross-border and economic cooperation zones etc. along the Belt and Road countries thus promoting regional economic integration. Can India be a moot spectator to China's global rebalancing?

4

A New Roadmap for the Belt and Road Initiative

The Second Belt and Road Forum for International Cooperation (BRF) was held in Beijing from April 25-27, 2019 with the theme of "Belt and Road Cooperation: Shaping a Brighter Shared Future". The Forum was attended by 37 heads of state and delegates from 150 countries and 90 international organisations around the world. At the end of the conference, it was revealed that 282 deliverables worth US$ 64 billion were signed sprawling into agriculture, science and technology, ecological protection, cultural exchange etc. spheres, thus taking the Belt and Road Initiative (BRI) beyond infrastructure connectivity projects. I was among the few Indians, perhaps the only one from academic circles to attend the forum and had the opportunity to engage in extensive discussions with delegates from other countries.

The Belt and Road Initiative is almost six years old and China has taken stock of the 'project of the century' in terms of its geo-economics as well as politics. One thing which emerged clearly out of President Xi Jinping's speech during the Forum on 26th morning is that China is convinced that the projects signed with 125 countries and 29 international organisations during the first forum in 2017 have "taken roots" along the "six economic corridors" in various countries (newly signed China-Myanmar Economic Corridor (CMEC) maintaining the tally at 6), as China's trade with the BRI countries exceeded US$ 6 trillion, implying that 50 per cent of China's GDP originates from these countries. Not only China, but various countries along the BRI including the participants from new entrant Italy (the first in the G7) and Switzerland etc., echo President Xi Jinping's words that the "BRI is a common road of opportunities, a road towards prosperity." The China club, as many have referred to it, is undoubtedly becoming more and more attractive to countries across the globe.

There was almost unanimity amongst the participants that prior to the Chinese initiative, the US and its allies were the sole providers of global goods, however, when China is willing to provide the same and wanting to make them inclusive by everyone's participation, the question has been asked about the intention behind these. Delegates from South Asia have seen the initiative as a massive opportunity for building capacities and eradicating poverty. China has invested billions of dollars in India's immediate neighbourhood; in Bangladesh infrastructure projects over US$ 10 billion are being executed. Nepal is executing the China-Nepal Transit and Transportation Agreement that will facilitate the building of a connectivity network in terms of roads, rails, air and optical fiber cables along Koshi, Kaligandaki and Karnali etc. corridors. Interestingly, during this forum, of all the 13 bilateral and 16 multilateral agreements with Myanmar, Bangladesh, Sri Lanka, Nepal and Pakistan almost none are in the infrastructure sector. India's official absence from the 2019 forum was conspicuous even though our flag flew high along the BRI countries flags at every venue of the forum. India has been critical of China's insensitivities towards India's core interests in the region, especially China's investment in the Pakistan Occupied Kashmir.

While the "Five Connectivity" and "mutual consultation, joint development contribution, and shared benefits" remain the golden principles of the BRI, however, the BRI-2 has laid emphasis on "high quality development" that would be accompanied by a greater opening up to the outside world, green, clean and sustainable development bringing greater benefits to the people along the BRI countries in terms of poverty alleviation, employment opportunities, and bonding between the people as was demonstrated by President Xi Jinping's speech at the forum. In this regard, he said the projects will adhere to the international norms of bidding, local laws and customs, and transparent financing. Execution of the projects "under the broad day light" spelled that China will monitor the projects for malpractices such as corruption and under the table deals. Second, he emphasised the free flow of commodities, capital, technology and personnel and the mutual learning from civilisations, and said that innovation was the key to productivity and will drive the 4th Industrial Revolution. The "high quality development" perhaps is meant to blunt the Japanese pitch of building "quality infrastructure" in the Asia-Africa Growth Corridor and the Indo-Pacific Region where India is a partner country. The presence of all the ten ASEAN countries and many African and Latin American nations at the forum shows that the Japanese pitch was never a counter to the BRI. Furthermore, the presence of former Japanese Prime Minister Yukio Hatayama and many other delegates from Japan shows that the country has warmed up to the Chinese initiative, and is even proposing joint investment in third countries, which China has welcomed for various reasons including financing projects.

Certainly, if the focus of the first forum was infrastructure development, and the reclamation of the old Silk Road, the BRI-2 has incorporated industrial capacity building, technological cooperation, environmental protection, cultural connections, and legal sensitivities more prominently, thus enhancing the scope of the BRI from Eurasia to other continents. For example, there were many delegates from the Latin American countries, who now felt part of the initiative contrary to their feelings a few years back. No wonder China has been talking less of building the "major country relationship" with the US, rather it is vehemently proposing the idea of "building a community of shared future", for it has been seen as more inclusive and enshrining the components of common development, prosperity and security. This has been referred to at various summits including this one, and is supported by China's commitment to deliver things on the ground. For example, President Xi Jinping flagged out five points as to what China will be offering to the world in coming years. One, China will further open and deepen its reforms and give greater market access to foreign investors (a concern of Indian companies and many from the West has been flagged out.) Two, China supports international cooperation on intellectual property rights (one of the reasons behind the ongoing US-China trade war). Three, China will increase imports of goods and services, will aim at further lowering tariffs and non-trade barriers. To this effect another Import Expo would be held in Shanghai later this year. Four, China will promote international macroeconomic policy Coordination. Five, China will continue to implement the policy of opening up to the outside world. For policy coordination and consultation, as well as to undertake various field research and projects pertaining to various facets of the BRI globally, a Belt and Road Study Network (BRSN) has been established having top scholars from over 60 think-tanks and universities globally.

Finally, as I have argued earlier, the BRI is here to stay. The longevity of the BRI has been ensured by it being incorporated into the constitution of the Communist Party of China and the life-term presidency for Xi Jinping. In other words, this makes it part of Xi Jinping's Thought on Socialism with Chinese characteristics, which makes it an important component of China's development blueprint as well as the dream of rejuvenation of the Chinese nation. As for India, "opposition" or "boycott" to the BRI will not yield any results. India's passive participation in the BRI through the Bangladesh-China-India-Myanmar Economic Corridor (BCIM) has been rendered meaningless, as the corridor has been replaced by the CMEC. The question of sovereignty as regards Pakistan Occupied Kashmir is not new. Did we stop engaging with China or Pakistan on account of this? If not, I believe, it is time for India to rethink on the question of the BRI.

VII
COVID-19

1

Coronavirus:
A 'Black Swan' for China and the World

On 21st January 2019 while addressing hundreds of senior officials from all provinces and autonomous regions at the Communist Party School in Beijing, President Xi Jinping told them that "We must maintain a high degree of vigilance. We must keep our high alert about any 'black swan' incident, and also take steps to prevent any 'grey rhino'". A 'black swan' incident refers to an unforeseen occurrence that typically has extreme consequences, while a 'gray rhino' is an obvious threat that can be ignored. According to the latest figures released by China's Health Commission on Wednesday, 490 people have died and 24,324 people are known to have been infected, mostly in Wuhan. Given the intensity, lethality and speed of its proliferation, the virus is no more a local problem, rather a global concern requiring global solutions.

There appears to be initial laxity on the part of Wuhan authorities in recognising the gravity of the epidemic when the virus was detected in early December 2019 for obvious reasons of 'losing face' to higher authorities and putting lid on a 'negative news', however, it is also a fact that China has demonstrated greater transparency and swiftness compare to the SARS scare in 2003. Critics fail to appreciate the swiftness of the

Chinese government with 11 million residents of Wuhan instantly quarantined and three new hospitals built in 10 days with a capacity of 3500 beds. Undoubtedly, extreme and stringent quarantine measures coupled with the shortage of protective medical equipment have caused panic and frustration amongst the people, nevertheless, the Chinese army taking control of the delivery of basic essential supplies in Wuhan has restored confidence in the people as well as frontline medical personnel.

Though the World Health Organisation has not recommended travel or trade restrictions against China, however, it is also understandable that many bordering countries have sealed their bonders, many have cancelled flights and evacuated their citizens from Wuhan and issued travel advisories to its citizens. India too brought back 647 of its citizens by special flights from Wuhan. The fear of the epidemic has also forced India to cancel all visas to Chinese nationals as people have tested positive for the virus in states such as Kerala, Bihar and Delhi. Kerala has declared coronavirus as a state calamity after three returnees from Wuhan were tested positive. According to the Union health ministry, as of now, there are around 2,815 people across India but mostly from Kerala under community surveillance.

The move to evacuate citizens from Wuhan and the issuance of travel advisories by a few countries has certainly irked China, as it is believed that such measures by countries will flare up an already tense situation. Chinese ambassador to India Mr. Sun Weidong has revealed that Chinese State Councilor and Foreign Minister Wang Yi did tell his counterpart Mr. S. Jaishankar over telephone that "We don't think it is helpful for a certain country to hype up the situation or even create panic." Earlier on 31 January 2020, Hua Chunying, the spokeswoman of the Chinese Ministry of Foreign Affairs accused the United States for spreading panic instead of offering significant assistance to halt the coronavirus outbreak. Such measures including mass quarantine may offer short-term solutions but fall short of finding long-term solutions, as the dissemination of objective and credible information emanating from Wuhan and other affected areas will not be available to the outside world.

Though China has activated all-round emergency response mechanisms at central as well as local levels, and has the resilience and economic means to overcome the hard times, it becomes pertinent for other countries to express their support and sympathy with the Chinese people for two reasons. First, the moral and material support coming from countries across the globe will certainly boost the morale of affected people, and common efforts may lead to certain breakthroughs in combating the disease. In this context, governments and civil societies sending teams of medical experts and aid is a welcome step. Second, if the epidemic persists for a longer period, the reverberations of China's economic loss will be felt across the globe. It will not augur well for the global economy, as China contributes over 30 per cent to global growth. Asia would be affected the worst, as almost 50 per cent of China's GDP is accounted by its economic engagement with the BRI countries. As for India, the kind of investment we have seen from Chinese companies in the last couple of years would be a thing of the past impacting the digital India and make in India drives.

India's connection with the present-day Hubei (the Chu state of ancient times) could be traced back to the 4th Century BC poem of Qu Yuan, where there is a reference to the Sagar Manthan story. Wuhan, the capital city of Hubei is also the place where the Ghadr revolutionaries supported the Chinese revolution and called upon the British Indian government that Indian soldiers must not be used against the Chinese people in the 1920s; it is the same place where Prime Minister Narendra Modi held his first ever unofficial meeting with Chinese President Xi Jinping in 2018, the place where a consensus was reached that India and China will not let their differences become disputes. In the 1920s, when China was struggling to fight the warlords and unify the country, the Hindustan Seva Dal proposed to send a medical mission to China in 1927 to extend the support and sympathy of the Indian people to Chinese people, but could not muster enough money and supplies until 1938 when a subjugated India managed to dispatch a team of five doctors along with an ambulance and supplies to China. Now, when India is in a much better position, can we reenact Dr. Kotnis' international spirit, the spirit of selfless service and the support and sympathy of the Indian people for the Chinese people by dispatching a team of doctors in this hour of crisis?

2

COVID-19 AND THE POLITICS OF COMPENSATION

As the fatalities caused by COVID-19 climb to 228,239 (as on 30 April 2020) around the world and the liberal international order and institutions of global governance established by the western powers fail to serve humanity, the western camp has clamored for seeking hefty compensation from China for "concealing" the outbreak of coronavirus from the outside world. The calls are becoming louder with escalating fatalities and the failure of western countries to contain the virus.

On 4th April, the Henry Jackson Society, a British foreign policy think-tank, advocated that since China has directly breached international healthcare treaty responsibilities, therefore, China should be taken to international courts for £351 billion (US$ 449 billion) in coronavirus compensation. The think tank also claimed that the G7, the world's leading economies, face a bill of £3.2 trillion (US$ 6.3 trillion). This was followed by Germany's largest tabloid, the *Bild* seeking a compensation of 149 billion euros from China. In the US, American lawyer Larry Klayman's Freedom Watch along with Texas company Buzz Photos have filed a US$ 20 trillion lawsuit against Chinese authorities in the US over coronavirus. A Miami-based Berman Law Group has also filed a lawsuit seeking billions of dollars in compensation from China. On 27th April, US President, Donald Trump also clamored saying that he could bill China for the damages caused by the COVID-19 pandemic.

Some developing countries have also joined the chorus seeking compensation. Oby Ezekwesili, a Nigerian chartered accountant wrote in *The Washington Post* on 17th April that "China should immediately announce a complete write-off of the more than US$ 140 billion that its government, banks and contractors extended to countries in Africa between 2000 and 2017. This would provide partial compensation to African countries for the impact that the coronavirus is already having on their economies and people." On 14th April, a Mumbai based Indian lawyer filed a petition in the International Criminal Court (ICC) in the Netherlands seeking a total of US$ 2.5 trillion in damages for India. Similar bills could be raised by other countries in the coming days.

Therefore, is it the '*Gengzinian*' (year 1900) moment for the Western countries when eight of them namely Russia, Germany, France, United Kingdom, Japan, United States, Italy, Belgium, Austria-Hungary, Netherlands, Spain, Portugal, Sweden and Norway forced China to pay millions of dollars to them in the wake of the Boxer Rebellion?

First of all, the very logic for compensation is indefensible in any court of law. One, did China notify the WHO in time? It did so in December, and on 11th January, the Chinese Center for Disease Control and Prevention uploaded the entire genome sequence of five new coronaviruses to the website, sharing its information with the world and the WHO. Did China share the information that human to human transmission of the epidemic was possible? Yes, it did on 20th January when Dr. Zhong Nanshan of the Chinese Academy of Engineering said in a television interview that the virus was human-to-human transmissible. Did China block down the epicenter of pandemic, Wuhan? Yes, it did on 24th January. Did the virus in Europe and the US spread from China? Some in the West have argued that regular direct flights from Wuhan continued to run to London, Paris, Rome, New York and San Francisco throughout January and in some cases into February, whereas fact is that they stopped from 23rd January itself except some careers airlifting their citizens from Wuhan at request. Did other countries get enough time to take precautions and adopt measures? Yes, they did get over two months' time. Therefore, even if China tried to cover up the pandemic during its initial stage to 'save face' by hushing up 'rumor mongers', the seriousness and swift action it took thereafter, should have been an eye opener to other countries.

Second, in the history of epidemics no country has ever been blamed and asked to pay indemnities. For example, AIDS originated in the US, did the US compensate people who were infected by it across the globe? H1N1 or the swine flu that originated in Mexico and killed millions worldwide, did countries sue Mexico for compensation? The case is similar with Ebola and Mers and the list continues.

Third, look who is asking for indemnities? The same countries who forced China to pay an indemnity of US$ 21 million in the wake of the Opium War (1841); US$ 19 million to France and Britain after the Second Opium War (1860), US$ 333 million (the then exchange rate) to eight nations in the aftermath of the Boxer Rebellion. Besides, many coastal areas were ceded to Foreign powers. Hong Kong and Macao were returned to China only in 1997 and 1999 by the UK and Portugal respectively. Many areas in mainland China were turned into foreign enclaves by the US and European powers in the wake of the Opium Wars and remained so until the end of the Second World War.

If China suffered a century of humiliation, India suffered the humiliation of two centuries. India's GDP accounted for around 27 per cent of the world's economy prior to British colonisation, but was reduced to only 3 per cent when the British left India. In October 2019 while addressing the Atlantic Council in Washington DC, India's Minister of External Affairs, S. Jaishankar quoting a study stated that the wealth the British took from India was close to US$ 45 trillion in today's monetary value. And what about the loss of life in wars, the starvation the colonisers subjected Indian people to? The 1943 famine of Bengal caused an estimated death of 2-3 million people. The situation in other colonies was no different. No wonder that Europe's share of the world's GDP jumped from 20 per cent to 60 per cent!

Fourth, can the judicial institution of sovereign states exercise jurisdiction over other states? Obviously, China will pronounce the judgements as trash papers as it did over a South China Sea litigation with the Philippines. Moreover, can the unintentional transmission by individuals regarded as the action of a state? If so, what about the transmission of other epidemics that originated in different parts of the world?

Fifth, if we see the timing of these petitions, most of these have been filed in during the first and second week of April. Why not in January and February if these organisations believed China was the culprit? The petitioners are well aware that it would be extremely difficult to hold China responsible for the spread of the pandemic, therefore, the whole exercise is to stigmatise China nothing else. Furthermore, it is also to score political points and disguise their own incompetence in handling the pandemic by shifting blame on others.

Finally, as there are various conspiracy theories making rounds, including the one that COVID-19 in an outcome of the biological weapon program of China, I think we need to wait for the outcome of the 'serious investigations' being conducted by the Trump administration into China's response to the COVID-19 outbreak, until then, I believe countries across the globe need to come together and fight this pandemic united for the sake of humanity.

3

POST-CORONAVIRUS NEW WORLD DISORDER

On 11th February 2020, I wrote in the *Sunday Guardian* that given the intensity, lethality and speed of coronavirus's proliferation, it is no more a local problem of China, rather a global concern requiring global solutions. Two months down the line the virus has spread to 210 countries and territories around the world, with 2,000,243 confirmed cases and a death toll of 126,758 people (as of 15th April). The ground reality demonstrates that we are far from seeing global solidarity and global solutions in the fight against COVID-19. Moreover, in the absence of anyone filling the global leadership void in the post-COVID-19 world, especially when the credibility of global institutions is fast eroding, we are likely to witness the collapse of the liberal international order, a realignment of geopolitical and economic forces, perhaps bitter political struggles, the fall of regimes and even bigger racial and religious divides across the globe.

First of all, even though the struggle for hegemony between the US and China has already resulted in a bitter trade war between the two and the US pronouncing China as a free rider taking advantage of open democracies by way of its smart and sharp power, COVID-19 seems to have taken that strategic rivalry to new heights in terms of security and economics. Implying that the US has freed itself from the delusion of

China as a non-enemy and the misbelief that liberalisation and globalisation will affect a peaceful transition in China. It is in such a scenario that we will witness a hard decoupling of the US economy from China. It may not be a total decoupling but partial and selective decoupling in sectors such as telecom, electronics and ICT is imminent. Being a close US ally, Japan will follow suit, as could be seen from its announcement of allocating US$ 2.2 billion to help Japanese companies move their production out of China. As for the EU, though it has pronounced China as a "systemic rival" since 2019, whether a domino effect will occur, remains to be seen. At this point in time, it appears that Brussel is irked by China's "mask diplomacy" in Europe which is sending signals as if the EU was incompetent in handling and supporting its fellow members such as Italy and Spain in times of crisis. The decoupling will further impact adversely on the Chinese and global economy. The plunge in global economic growth could be worse than what has been suggested by the IMF recently.

Second, COVID-19 has proved that international order established in the wake of World War II is to serve the goals of the hegemon rather than serving humanity. Once the established hegemon realised that institutions it established with its allies have been encroached upon and rendered ineffective by the emerging hegemon, it has started to gradually withdraw from these. The US withdrawal from UNESCO, the Paris Agreement, the Trans Pacific Partnership, the Iran Nuclear Deal, and now threatening to quit from the WTO speaks volumes about the US retrenchment. China's alleged shadow over the WHO amidst the corona threat and China not favoring a debate on the virus in the UN has further undermined the role of these global bodies. The US in a fit of rage suspended funding of around US$ 500 million to the WHO on account of China's role in "severely mismanaging and covering up the spread of the coronavirus" on 15th April. Therefore, the credibility of the institutions of global governance will continue to erode as long as restructuring doesn't take place.

Third, the retrenchment, protectionism and nativism will further get strengthened in the western camp, and globalisation and liberalisation will witness a gradual retreat. This will result in exclusivism, racial discrimination, further divisions within diverse societies in the name of religious and other identities. No wonder racial attacks in the US, China and even in India have become the new normal. Religious and racial exclusivism will further sharpen contradictions between communities on the one hand and spur sub nationalistic tendencies in people rather than them integrating with the mainstream. While popular voices will call for supporting strong leaders, the same may result in authoritarianism, human rights violations, chaos and even the collapse of governments in many countries.

Fourth, the cold war between the US and China will intensify in various shapes and forms. Externally, China will continue to champion the cause of globalisation through its Belt and Road Initiative (BRI); the building of the Health Silk Road as pronounced by President Xi Jinping with Italian Prime Minister Giuseppe Conte on 16th March would be a new soft power tributary of the BRI. In response to US decoupling, China too will intensify relocation of its labor-intensive manufacturing supply chains to other countries, especially developing countries. In fact, the process of relocation by Chinese companies was triggered by the US-China trade war in order to avoid tariffs from the US. These have been relocated to Vietnam, Cambodia, Myanmar and Thailand in Southeast Asia and India and Bangladesh in South Asia.

With Chinese and western companies making headways to Southeast Asia, the region is likely to become the next 'factory' of the world after China. Meanwhile, the squaring of the "infrastructure deficit' by China in developing countries be it in South Asia, Central Asia, Middle East, Africa, East Europe and Latin America will continue albeit cautiously in sectors such as rail and roads, ports, telecom and power as it remains a win-win proposition for all stakeholders. The 'debt trap' narrative has not stopped these countries from inviting Chinese investment for capacity building in these sectors. But, will China remember Deng Xiaoping's words (Selected Works of Deng Xiaoping, 116-17): "never ever attempt to be the leader of the poor countries, all they want is your money"? Gauging the relocation of China's enterprises and composition of its trade, Asia is going to be the focus of China's economic activities, and Africa for executing various projects. Even here I think the countries would be happy to go along with

China's BRI in terms of economic assistance and capacity building, although they will continue to maintain social distance with China on matters pertaining to national security. Internally, China will be more inward looking, more authoritarian; witness sharper contradictions between the reformists and radicals and even revisit the class struggle depending on the turns in micro and macro environments post-COVID-19.

Finally, as for India, the post-COVID-19 period will throw unprecedented challenges. Internally, to realise the dream of becoming a US$ 5 trillion economy by 2024 will be a distant dream. Though the present economic structure may enable it to rebound quickly, the damage done to the industrial and agricultural sector will require years to recover. The divide between rich and poor will further widen and society may witness further polarization in the name of religion, caste and ethnicity. Externally, India-US security partnership will be further strengthened. The Indo-Pacific Strategy is likely to gain traction and trade and investment will witness an incremental rise. Nonetheless, like the Southeast Asian countries, India doesn't want to be caught in a zero-sum geopolitical contest between the two hegemons. Economically, India is likely to benefit from the decoupling of the western countries from China, as well as from China's economic rebalancing in the region. Though the China baiters may suggest India's 'decoupling' from China, there isn't much to 'decouple'. Though multilateralism will get a beating, nonetheless, India's engagement with China in the BRICS, the Shanghai Cooperation Organisation (SCO), the BRICS New Development Bank (NDB), Asian Infrastructure Investment Bank (AIIB), etc. will continue. Needless to say, India ought to correctly understand, promptly react and formulate feasible strategies to deal with the post-COVID-19 challenges.

4

CHINA'S "TWO SESSIONS" AND POST-COVID-19 BLUEPRINT

"Two Sessions" refers to the convening of the annual meetings of the National People's Congress (NPC) and the Chinese People's Political Consultative Conference (CPPCC). The former has close to 3000 deputies 'elected' by provincial people's congresses and according to China's constitution is the highest organ of state power, and the latter with over 2000 representatives is the NPC's advisory body consisting of eminent personalities from "political parties" and civil society. The real power, however, is wielded by the one, who holds the posts of President, General Secretary of the Communist Party (CPC) and Chairman of the Central Military Commission (CMC). Usually convened in March, this year's "Two Sessions" were delayed by the outbreak of COVID-19 and are being held from 21st and 22nd May simultaneously, an indication that it is business as usual in Beijing, or is it so?

At the outset, as international political and economic pressure builds on China in the wake of COVID-19, President Xi Jinping, at least since early February has been at the forefront of the "people's war" against the coronavirus. The "mishandling" of the corona crisis by the West, which China pronounces as "incompetence" has indeed turned away the wrath of Chinese people against their leaders' initial laxity in fighting the virus and a possible "cover up" as alleged by the West. Thus, reinforcing the narrative that only the development path, system and ideology chosen by China (also pronounced as four confidences including culture) has the capacity and capability to deal with a crisis of such magnitude, mobilise people and resources, which no other country can match. Without any doubt, the "two sessions" have reiterated their faith in Xi Jinping as a "core leader."

Second, two major goals identified for the first centenary in 2021 are – to double the 2010 GDP of China and make China a moderately prosperous society by totally eradicating poverty have been achieved. In fact, China has achieved both goals in advance. In 2010 China's GDP was 6.09 trillion US dollars, which in 2020 has been projected at 13.9 trillion US dollars. As regards poverty, China alleviated 800 million people in the last 70 years, lifting almost 70 per cent of the world's poor population, and meeting the objectives of SDGs almost a decade ahead. The real challenge in post-COVID-19, however, would be the realisation of the second centenary, especially when the US and the West have labelled China as a "free rider" using its "sharp power" to penetrate deep into the ecosystems of open democracies while denying them the access in many sectors.

Therefore, the real worry for China, would be, how to put its economy back on track as economy shrunk by 6.8 per cent in the first quarter of 2020. As projected by the IMF China like other Asian countries may see very little or zero growth in 2020. During the Asian Financial crisis in 2008, China's stimulus stood at 586 billion US dollars, since the magnitude of economic depression is much larger, stimulus could be 2-3 times bigger than the year 2008. China is likely to identify key sectors mostly from its "Made in China 2025" strategy or the so called "new infrastructure" focusing on technology innovation and information networks to support high-quality growth. China is estimated to spend 1.4 trillion US dollars in these sectors by the year 2025, aiming to achieve 40 per cent "self-sufficiency" by 2020, and 70 per cent "self-sufficiency" by 2025. This could be a herculean task, especially when the US has banned 33 of China's "new infrastructure" companies from buying crucial components from the US. Added to this, rising unemployment (pegged at around 6 per cent), 25 million workers sitting in their homes in rural areas, and another 75 million working from home on slashed salaries, plunging retail and investment, weak global demand etc. will be riders to recovery. Though China has revealed to create 9 million new jobs in 2020 in the face of the above facts, it will be a difficult target to accomplish.

Third, as China comes under attack from the global community and its rivalry grows with the US in the Asia Pacific, it's behavior would be more assertive, as has been reflected in its "wolf warrior diplomacy" at the diplomatic front, opening up new hotspots along the borders at the military front, and trying to rename areas which it perceives belong to it at the cultural front. Surprisingly, the Government Work Report of Premier Li Keqiang has recommended 6.6 per cent of the GDP (US$ 178.2 billion) for the People's Liberation Army, not a significant decrease from last year (7.5 per cent), especially when growth has dipped to negative. It is also believed that real spending is much higher than the officially declared budget. For example, in 2019, the SIPRI pegged China's nominal defense spending at US$ 261 billion, 1.5 times larger than the official figure of US$ 177.5 billion. Nevertheless, China will not go whole hog as far as the reclamation of territories like Taiwan, Senkaku, Spratly and other contested border areas are concerned. China knows it is not there as yet, and hence they are long-term goals for the second centenary. It will also not prefer a military confrontation with the US.

Fourth, in the face of the West's threat of decoupling with China, which at this stage remains exaggerated, China will do its best to keep its industrial and supply chains stable, prop up foreign capital utilisation in free trade ports like Hainan, and other regions such as the Greater Bay and Xiong'an areas. The Greater Bay Area has certain advantages as 20 of world's top 500 enterprises in sectors such as telecom, finance, automobiles, real estate and home appliances are based here, and are fed by around 15 innovation centers all over China. These areas along with other nodes in the coastal belt and hinterland will be instrumental in supporting the Belt and Road initiative of the Chinese government on the one hand and emerge as new innovation centers for supporting "new infrastructure" on the other. However, the perennial Hong Kong democracy movement, and a new security law (read sedition) proposed by the NPC on 22nd April for Hong

Kong may impact the region negatively. As China believes that the trouble makers behind the protests are foreign forces, especially the US and UK, it has deemed it fit to circumvent Hong Kong and bring in the new law. China seems to be readying for using force in the near future in Hong Kong.

Finally, as the US falters from assuming global leadership and continues to move away from multilateralism, weaken global institutions, and embrace protectionism and nativism, China will not shy away from stepping in and filling the vacuum. For example, when the US suspended aid to the WHO, China announced aid of 20 million US dollars followed by US$ 2 billion to the United Nations. Internally too, China has earmarked 141 billion US dollars to fight COVID-19. It has already advocated the notion of community of shared future which has found greater appeal in developing countries. When UN's sustainable development goals (SDGs) such as poverty alleviation, universal education, gender equality, child mortality, pandemics like HIV, environmental protection, global partnership for development are still around us and many countries are finding it difficult to get rid of them, a collective approach in dealing with these that is inclusive, and open ended, will bring mutual benefits and common development. China has benefitted immensely from the liberal order; therefore, it will continue to support international organisations and call for greater cooperation against the pandemic in various groupings like SCO, BRICS and G20 etc.

5

TRACING THE ORIGIN OF COVID-19

COVID-19 first appeared in Wuhan, China, and has subsequently spread to 220 countries and territories around the world. To date, the virus infected more than 173 million people and taken lives of 3.72 million people. Of these, almost 38 per cent fatalities took place in the US, Brazil and India, India alone accounted for almost 10 per cent of all global deaths. People's lives have been disrupted, economic activities have come to a grinding halt, and trillions of dollars have been lost as economies registered negative growth as high as 7.3 per cent in case of India, millions of jobs have been lost and millions have been pushed below the poverty line. Even after 18 months since its outbreak, the world is clueless about its origin as well as its end. As regards the origin of the virus, the zoonotic and lab accident theories are making rounds. The former, gained currency during the first wave of the virus, however, as the variants became deadlier in subsequent waves killing people of all age groups, the latter has gained traction and the US president Joe Biden has even directed his intelligence agencies to submit a report within 3 months. Why have events taken such a sharp turn? What are the plausible scenarios emerging out of the COVID-19 origin investigations?

First of all, if the lab-accident hypothesis is true, the credibility of the some of the leading virologists, science journals, and the World Health Organisation (WHO) will take a beating. This will also demonstrate that China's penetration of the U.S. goes beyond Wall Street and Washington, and perhaps Xi Jinping was right when he told Jo Biden in 2015 that "China will own America" by 2035, albeit in a light hearted mood. Nevertheless, U.S.'s heavy reliance on Chinese supply chains in some sectors including pharmaceuticals has been exposed amidst the pandemic. In the same vein, a quantum jump in China's farmland purchases, real estate investments, and business stakes of the owners of mainstream U.S. media at minimum vindicate the China buying America view. Now examine this: when Dr. Shi Zhengli, the "bat women" of China published a paper in *Nature* on 3 February 2020 advocating the zoonotic origin theory of the Wuhan Coronavirus spread, she was supported by 27 public health scientists in a statement published by *Lancet* on 19 February 2020. The scientists said they were in "solidarity with all scientists and health professionals in China who continue to save lives and protect global health during the challenge of the COVID-19 outbreak." The WHO also took this line and ruled out that the virus originated from lab-accident in its *Report* issued in February 2021 after their investigations in Wuhan. This line of thinking was projected in the mainstream media globally, especially in the U.S. and any attempt to circulate news related to the lab accident hypothesis was completely blocked, including from social medias like Facebook, so much so the accounts of the "spreaders" of such a "conspiracy theory" were also closed temporarily.

Two, an article by Nicholas Wade, a science writer associated with the *Nature, Lancet* and *New York Times* on 5 May 2021 in the *Bulletin of the Atomic Scientists* weighs the zoonotic as well as lab-leak hypotheses and inclines towards the latter. The argument is supported vehemently by the British Professor Angus Dalgleish and Norwegian scientist Dr. Birger Sørensen, in a paper accessed by the *Daily Mail* of the U.K. The duo argue that they have had "prima facie evidence of retro-engineering in China for a year." The scientists also concluded that that the "SARS-Coronavirus-2 has no credible natural ancestor." Indian researchers in a paper titled "Uncanny similarity of unique inserts in the 2019-nCoV spike protein to HIV-1 gp120 and Gag" had argued that they have "found that the 2019-

nCoV spike glycoprotein contains 4 insertions," but the paper had to be withdrawn. Dr. Luc Montagnier, a 2008 Nobel Prize winner for Medicine has supported this argument by pointing to "molecular tinkering" with the spike proteins and that the virus is "manipulated and accidentally released from a laboratory in Wuhan."

This has created a storm in China and the rest of the world. China published a series of editorials blaming the U.S. of "politicisation" of the virus. As for the U.S virologists, who hereunto were adhering to the zoonotic hypotheses, now argued that there could be a possibility of lab-leak, therefore further investigations were required. Even the Biden administration that issued an executive order banning the use of terms such as "China virus" and "Wuhan virus" when referring to COVID-19 in January 2021, has now ordered an investigation into the origin of the virus. The U.S. Secretary of State, Antony Blinken vowed to hold China accountable to origin of the virus in an interview given to the Axion HBO on 7 June 2021.

If this is the case, why did Dr. Anthony Fauci, the director of the National Institute of Allergy and Infectious Diseases, and Dr. Peter Daszak, of the EcoHealth Alliance, U.S.A and many other scientists give in to the zoonotic theory so quickly? Why is the U.S mainstream media doing a volte-face now? If the Fox News anchor, Tucker Carlson's story is to be believed, the US has gathered credible information from a "highest-level Chinese defector" to the U.S., who is believed to be cooperating with the National Defense Intelligence Agency (DIA). If this is a credible piece of information, the Biden Administration has been forced to take a tougher stand, who hitherto appeared to be giving a respectful burial to the virus origin. This was in contrast to the Trump administration's investigations and calling the virus a "China virus." It was perceived that President Biden didn't want to rock the troubled boat of the U.S.-China relationship beyond castigating China's assertiveness in the Taiwan Strait and human right issues in Xinjiang, Tibet and Hong Kong. Remember his son, Hunter Biden still holds 10 per cent stakes in a Chinese equity firm named Bohai Harvest RST Equity Investment Fund Management Co. Notwithstanding Biden's intentions, things don't look good given the geopolitical rivalry between the established hegemon and the challenger.

Three, the investigations will also implicate the U.S., for it points fingers towards the U.S. virologists and state organs that funded dangerous "gain of function" research in China's Wuhan Institute of Virology (WIV), which is banned in the U.S. U.S. top virologists like Dr. Ralph Baric have been collaborating with Dr. Shi Zhengli for many years. In late May, in a Senate hearing, Dr. Fauci told lawmakers that the U.S. granted $600,000 in funding to the WIV for coronavirus research through Peter Daszak's non-profit EcoHealth Alliance. The Daily Mail also reveals that between 2013 and 2019, the Pentagon gave $39 million to EcoHealth Alliance. Dr. Fauci's emails from last year reveal that he didn't entertain the idea that the novel coronavirus could've leaked from a lab, contrary to the views of a fellow scientist Kristian Andersen, a virologist at the Scripps Research Institute in California who did point out that "some of the features (potentially) look engineered." Furthermore, emails also establish Dr. Fauci's cordial relations with Chinese government officials such as George Gao Fu, director of the Chinese Centre of Disease Control and Prevention. Given this nexus between the U.S. Virologists, government entities and organisations with their counterparts in Wuhan, and also as to why the US was encouraging and conducting hazardous "gain of function" research when the same is banned in the U.S., it could be deduced why U.S virologists tried to put a lid on the lab-accident theory.

Four, so even if both the zoonotic and lab-leak hypotheses have not been proved right to date, nevertheless, public opinion at this point in time is right in demanding free and fair investigations. However, even if the origin of the virus is established, at maximum voices asking for trillions of dollars in compensation, as Donald Trump has been asking recently, will become louder. But who has paid compensation for the origin of pandemics? In the history of epidemics, no country has ever been blamed and asked to pay indemnities. AIDS originated in the U.S., did the U.S. compensate people who were infected or killed by it across the globe? H1N1 or the swine flu that originated in Mexico and killed millions worldwide, did countries sue Mexico for compensation? Similar is the case with Ebola and Mers and the list continues. Even if the political slug is dragged to the International Court of Justice, who abides by the ruling nowadays? This may be followed by sanctions, but the same have been imposed on Russia for other reasons obviously. These may have hurt Russia economically to some extent, but did they diminish Russia's role or influence? What the likely scenario is therefore, is that it may hasten China's economic decoupling from the West, which in certain hi-tech sectors is already happening. It will also intensify the cold war between the U.S. and China and turn the Indo-Pacific more volatile and fraught with dangers of armed conflict.

Finally, the lab-accidents do happen, however, whether they are part of other conspiracy theories, including the one that COVID-19 is an outcome of the "biological weapon program of China" which so far has not gained credence, needs to be investigated. Nepenthes, the U.S. and its allies cornering China on the virus origin and human rights issue, has certainly mellowed down the "wolf-warrior" approach of China, and Present Xi Jinping has called on the Communist Party leaders to project a "trustworthy, loveable and admirable" image of China in a speech on 31 May 2021. The unfolding of events in the U.S. recently establishes the fact that conflicts of interest are certainly at the centre of all narratives. It is owing to these conflicts of interests that a certain narrative is created and sold. So much so that social media and some reputed science journals have blocked information or forced scholars to withdraw their findings that are antithetical to the mainstream narrative.

VIII
CHINA'S GOVERNANCE

1

Understanding China

China takes pride in its 5000-year-old history and civilisation, and its contribution to mankind. One of the most prominent features of the Chinese civilisation has been its unusually strong textual tradition. One is amazed to see the compilation of *Four Books* (Analects of Confucius, Great Learning, Means and Mencius) and *Five Classics* (Book of History, Book of Odes, Book of Rites, Book of Change, Spring and Autumn Annals) much before the invention of paper in China around 105 AD. This forms the core of China's cultural capital that nurtured Chinese intelligentsia, dynasty after dynasty until the monarchy was overthrown in 1911.

The roots of Confucian tradition are so strong that rulers like Qin Shihuang (221 BC–210 BC) and Mao Zedong (1893-1976) failed to uproot it from society. Not only did they fail, Confucianism bounced back as a state philosophy during the Han dynasty (206 BC-220 AD), and has been instrumental in projecting China's soft power in the post-Mao era. The *Three Character Classic* (San zijing) that had been banned, has made a comeback, and can now be found in every household as Xi Jinping calls to foster and practice 'socialist core values' which are heavily borrowed from the several millennia old value system, which according to Xi has deep roots in the Chinese people's mentality, influencing their way of thinking and behaviour. Obviously, there are many other philosophies, but

Confucianism and Legalism have found much currency in Chinese society throughout history, thanks to their utilitarian nature. It is for this textual and legalist tradition that China has made use of historical and legal claims as far as its territorial interests on land and sea are concerned even though the first *Map of Imperial China* only came into being in 1708 through the help of foreign missionaries!

If ancient history has been glorified by China, a century of its modern history (1840-1949) has been portrayed as one of humiliation and lost opportunities. This was the time when China was humiliated, its sovereignty infringed upon, and its people bullied by foreigners—a clear reference to China's defeat in the Opium Wars (1840, 1856), the Sino-French War (1875), the Sino-Japanese War (1895), and the drubbing China got from Japan between 1931 and 1945. Largely this is the period when China talks about signing humiliating and unequal treaties with foreign powers and losing three precious opportunities to rise as a power. For example, it argues that between 1842 and 1895, Japan and Russia could modernise but not China; between 1912 and 1945 China established a republic but could not modernise, even though late entrants like Turkey did turn over their economies in this period. Another lost opportunity which is now being discussed is between 1957 and 1978 when the labour-intensive industries moved from developed countries to developing countries. China lost, but Korea, Singapore and Taiwan developed rapidly. The Chinese however, do believe in their own saying that 'the crop that is sown late ripens early,' for it took the UK and US almost 150 years to realise modernisation; Germany, France and other European countries did it in 70 years; Japan did it in 40 years, and China is confident that they will do it even faster.

Therefore, ever since China has "stood up," its overall foreign policy has become the reversion of the national humiliation inflicted on it by the foreign powers. Transforming the image of China from a weak, bullied and humiliated one to a strong and self-confident China was projected as China's domestic as well as foreign policy goals. According to Wu Yuanli, "This goal consisted of three parts: military, to be second to none; territorially, to settle all border disputes with neighbours and to regain "territorial integrity" (including Tibet and Taiwan and now the South China Sea); and emotionally, to win back self-esteem, which is often identified with foreign respect." With this reversion, the victim's mentality was brought to full play while dealing with neighbours and great powers. This is demonstrated by China fighting the US in the Korean War (1950-54), the border conflicts with India (1962) and the USSR (1969), and its invasion of Vietnam (1979) although there were many other factors which were at play and responsible for this Chinese behaviour. Conversely, China's very turbulent history and isolation drove home the point that confrontation was not the way. If China wished to realise a great national rejuvenation, she must seek common development by reserving its differences with neighbours.

Hence started the period of reforms and opening up. China indeed became the largest country to benefit from globalisation in the shortest possible time alleviating 700 million people from poverty. As China's state capitalism paid dividends, long-term planning was initiated. In 1987, a three-step strategy (62 year modernisation plan) was drawn for making China a moderately developed country by 2049 when China would celebrate 100 years of the establishment of the People's Republic of China. Another centenary was added to this by Xi Jinping in 2012—that is, in 2021, when the Communist Party of China celebrates the 100th anniversary of its foundation, China will have doubled its 2010 GDP and made China a 'moderately well off' society. This in other words has been pronounced as China's dream of the great rejuvenation of the Chinese nation. According to Xi Jinping, "Our struggles in the 170 plus years since the Opium War have created bright prospects for achieving the rejuvenation of the Chinese nation. We are now closer to this goal, and we are more confident and capable of achieving it than at any other time in history." China has certainly ushered in a new era of assertiveness.

The shift was visible as China successfully conducted the 2008 Olympic Games, and more so since Xi Jinping took over the reins in China in 2012. Though China pledged that its rise would be peaceful, that it would advocate greater economic integration of China with the global ecosystem, it has also said that it will not be a moot spectator to global affairs and aspire for a democratic, peaceful and multi-polar world order. With more military and economic muscle, China has imposed ADIZ over the Senkakus/Diaoyu islands in the East China Sea, reclaimed isles and reefs in the South China Sea, and rolled out global goods and services in the form of the Belt and Road Initiative. It has emerged as one of the strongest challengers to American hegemony, which has forced the US to indulge in unprecedented disruptions as far as the global order is concerned. Given the nature of the Sino-US economic cold war, the economic slowdown in China and a poor global recovery, it is still too early to write off the existing global order and the emergence of a new economic model is still far away.

2

THE PHILOSOPHICAL FOUNDATIONS OF XI JINPING'S 'NEW ERA'

With the adoption of "Xi Jinping's Thought on Socialism with Chinese Characteristics for a New Era" by the 19th Party Congress of the Communist Party of China in 2017, China officially entered a new phase. Adhering to the notion of Chinese thought of continuity, president Xi sees the development of socialism as a continuous phenomenon that has been advanced by all his predecessors irrespective of differences in guiding principles, thinking and policies during the revolution, socialist construction and reforms etc. phases. During the first stage of the 'New Era' between 2020 and 2035, Xi envisages basically realising socialist modernisation, and during the second from 2035 to 2050 developing China into a great modern socialist country.

What would be the philosophical foundations of Xi Jinping's 'New Era'? Many scholars inside and outside China have been debating this question. Neo leftists like Wang Shaoguang, professor at the Chinese University of Hong Kong have endorsed the idea of a party-state, where the state is responsive to the needs of the people; neo Confucians like Chen Ming of Capital Normal University bring in Confucian morality and even Confucianism as a religion to the party-state; neo liberals like Xu Jilin, professor of history at East China Normal University are propounding new Chinese universalism with Confucian civility at its core; Jiang Shigong, professor of Law at Peking University puts Socialism with Chinese characteristics as a political theory, which borrows heavily from the core values of Chinese civilisation as the pillar of philosophical foundations of the 'New Era.' Foreign scholars such as Sam Crane of Contemporary Chinese Politics and Ancient Chinese Philosophy at Williams College, US in a recent article have argued that the philosophical foundations of Xi Jinping's 'New Era' would be legalist rather than Confucian albeit he agrees that Xi has borrowed anecdotes from the Confucian classics selectively.

Professor Crane's main argument is that Xi is the center of China both administratively and spiritually, at the helm of a monocratic power structure. He argues that such concentration of power is not inherent in Confucian thought but rather stems from the political thinking of legalists like Shang Yang and Hanfezi who laid emphasis on the law to safeguard the decrees of the sovereign, employment of tactics to weed out the treacherous and promote able people in bureaucracy, and the absolute power of the monarch. I believe that it is not so simple to define the philosophical foundations of China in the 'New Era', for these are intertwined with the historical journey of China and the path, thought and system it has chosen during different phases of history. In the 'New Era' too, Xi Jinping has categorically emphasised that the path will be economic development (read 'wealth and power') guided by the theory developed by his generation of the Chinese leadership, and guaranteed by a political and economic system that is rule based. It is the thought and the system that has generated much heat inside and outside China.

As regards the thought, Xi Jinping has emphasised the communist principles which is understandable in a party-state configuration; to this end, he has always reminded the party and the people not to forget the 'original intentions' or the basis on which the party was founded. This is also employed to avert an ideological contest between reformers and the radicals. The celebration of the 200th birth anniversary of Karl Marx in early May this year could also be seen in this context albeit China has long abandoned the Marxist theories of 'class struggle' and 'proletarian revolution'. Moreover, since the Sinification of socialism or communist ideology has been the goal of the Chinese leadership, it has tried to infuse the core values of Chinese civilisation in it for its legitimacy and turning it into an acceptable spiritual belief not only inside China but globally too. It is for this reason that while cultivating socialist core values (prosperity, democracy, civility, harmony, freedom, equality, justice, the rule of law, patriotism, dedication, integrity and friendliness) Xi Jinping seeks shelter in traditional Chinese philosophical foundations that emphasise continuity, dynamism, relativity, relationships, and totality.

In this context, Chen Lai, the writer of the *Core Values of Chinese Civilisation*, which has been translated into Hindi from Chinese by one of my students and I recently, sums up the Chinese philosophical foundation as: morality is more important than law, the community more important than the individual, the spiritual more important than the material, responsibility more important than rights, the wellbeing of the people more important than democracy, order more important than freedom, this life more important than the afterlife, harmony more valuable than conflict, civilisation more valuable than impoverishment, and family more valuable than social class. These are not only based on Confucian humaneness or *ren* but also on legalist, Taoist, and Buddhist values. No wonder Xi Jinping has placed the 'people at the core' and has been advocating the building of communities of shared future in the region and beyond in terms of connectivity, economics and security.

As regards the system or the nature of the structure of state, China toyed with the idea of blurring the boundaries of the party and government during the Mao era, and then introduced divisions between the party and government during the reform era under Deng Xiaoping. In the new era, Xi Jinping is trying to modernise the state governance by making the party take absolute control. Here again, though the party asserts a leadership role over everything in China including the army, government and people, which gives Xi Jinping free hand to consolidate his power synonymous to the legalist approach of governance, however, by reforming the state apparatus and setting up institutions like the National Supervisory Commission to reign in corrupt practices in governance, Xi Jinping is trying to imbue Confucian virtues alongside legalist measures to the rule of law, thus making governance acceptable to the people. This is an extremely difficult task; it remains to be seen if the Chinese people will accept Xi as a 'sage king' having morality and righteousness to govern. If yes, the path, thought and the system in the 'New Era' will succeed and so will the Chinese dream of national rejuvenation.

3

China's Constitutional Amendments for 'Longlasting Security of the Party - State'

On 11th March 2018, the National People's Congress (NPC), the Chinese legislature amended the 33-page constitution of the People's Republic of China (PRC) literally making Xi Jinping president for life and incorporating most of his vision for the governance of China. The PRC Constitution was enacted in 1954. The current amendments have been carried out in the Constitution adopted in 1982; previously the Constitution was amended in 1988, 1993, 1999 and 2004. The amendments essentially reflect tremendous changes China has undergone since revolution, construction and reform. Most of the amendments have been carried out in the last 40 years of reform, for example between 1988 and 1999 these included the inclusion of a 'socialist market economy' in place of a 'planned economy', reform of land use rights, legalisation of the private economy, Deng Xiaoping's theory of building socialism with Chinese characteristics etc. The 2004 amendment included the private property protection provision as well as Jiang Zemin's theory of 'Three Represents' without putting his name, the same goes for Hu Jintao, when 'Scientific Outlook' gets added this time. Let's examine what amendments have been carried out in 2018.

The 1982 constitution has a table of contents, preamble, and 4 chapters. Chapter 1 is on general principles; chapter 2 on the fundamental rights and duties of citizens; chapter 3 on the structure of the state, which is the most elaborate with 7 sections, and finally chapter 4 is related to the national flag, the national anthem, the national emblem and the capital. The 2018 amendments add a section under chapter 3 in the contents thus making the number of sections 8. The new section The Supervisory Commission has been inserted as section 7 above the People's Courts and the People's Procuratorates, obviously making it more powerful. The sixth paragraph in the preamble: "Both the victory of China's new-democratic revolution ...culture and democracy" has been amended. Some of the new additions in specific lines are:

The basic task of the nation is to concentrate its efforts on socialist modernisation along the road of Chinese-style socialism. Under the leadership of the Communist Party of China and the guidance of Marxism-Leninism, Mao Zedong Thought, Deng Xiaoping Theory, the important Theory of "Three Represents," scientific outlook 科学发展观, and Xi Jinping's Thought on Socialism with Chinese Characteristics for the New Era 习近平新时代中国特色社会主义思 the Chinese people of all nationalities will continue to adhere to the people's democratic dictatorship, follow the socialist road, persist in reform and opening-up, steadily improve socialist institutions, develop a socialist market economy, advance socialist democracy, improve the socialist rule of law instead of the legal system, implement the new development concept 贯彻新发展理念 and work hard and self-reliantly to modernise industry, agriculture, national defence and science and technology step by step, promote the coordinated development of the material, political, spiritual civilisations, social civilisation 社会文明 ecological civilisation 生态文明 and turn China into a great modern socialist country that is prosperous, strong, democratic, culturally advanced, harmonious, and beautiful and realise the great cause of national rejuvenation 民主文明和谐美丽的社会主义现代化强国,实现中华民族伟大复兴. Another major change in the second last paragraph, a new line reflecting Xi's ideas has been inserted: China adheres to an independent foreign policy as well as to the five principles of mutual respect for sovereignty and territorial integrity, mutual non-aggression, non-interference in each other's internal affairs, equality and mutual benefit, and peaceful coexistence, peaceful development path, mutual benefits and win-win strategy of opening up 坚持和平发展道路,坚持互利共赢开放战略 in developing diplomatic relations and economic and cultural exchanges with other countries, and promoting and building communities of shared future 推动构建人类命运共同体. Apart from these major changes in the preamble, there are other minor changes, for example the reform period has been added to the stages of revolution and construction, indicating that there would be a demarcation between the 40 years of reforms and the 'new era' under Xi Jinping.

In Chapter 1, a new line has been inserted in Article 1 as 'Leadership of the Communist Party of China is the most essential feature of socialism with Chinese characteristics' 中国共产党领导是中国特色社会主义最本质的特征. In Article 24 the advocacy of socialist core values 倡导社会主义核心价值观 has been added to other civic virtues of love for the motherland, for the people, for labour, for science and for socialism etc. Article 27 adds on assuming office any government functionary must publicly administer a constitutional oath in accordance with the law 国家工作人员就职时应当依照法律规定公开进行宪法宣誓. Chapter 2 has no amendments. Chapter 3 under Article 62 at number 7, the NPC is also exercising the functions and power of electing the director of the National Supervisory Commission 选举国家监察委员会主任 has been added. The same has been added in Articles 63 and 67 and elaborated under Section 7 of the same chapter. The establishment of the Supervisory Commission is a new state organ that will give it sweeping powers to supervise malpractices related to corruption and other misconduct not only within the Party but across the entire government machinery. Fighting the 'tigers and flies' during the last five years has been extremely successful. Recent figures released by China's state media, say that in the last five years, 1.4 million party officials have been investigated for corruption. It's not that China is setting up such a commission all of a sudden, pilot work was going on in some areas including Beijing. Once the organ is established across provinces, municipalities and counties, various overlapping functions of other supervisory agencies would be done away with, thus bringing these functions under the ambit of one authority which would be more effective and efficient at the same time. Article 100 under Section 5 has an addition relating to formulating laws by provincial governments and reporting the same to higher levels.

The most talked about and debated, however, is Article 79 under section 2 on the President of the People's Republic of China of Chapter 3. The third paragraph thus has been changed to "The term of office of the President and Vice-President of the People's Republic of China is the same as that of the National People's Congress. They shall serve no more than two consecutive terms stands deleted 连续任职不得超过两届. In the words of Xi Jinping, to amend part of the Constitution is a major decision made by the CPC Central Committee from the overall strategic height of upholding and developing socialism with Chinese characteristics in the new era. It is the blueprint which he has made for realising the two centenaries of China that the amendments in all the sections have been carried out. Nevertheless, the post of president and vice president in China are titular ones, they do not control the party, army and neither have any say in constituting the State Council. Given the structure of the Party and state in China, it is the general secretary of the CPC who wields real power, and moreover, the Party constitution does not restrict or limit the general secretary or the chairman of the military commission to hold office for more than ten years. However, the amendments and doing away with the tenure does guarantee that the path, theory and the system as advocated by the present leadership is maintained for a certain period of time, so as the bi centenary goals of making China in to a moderately prosperous society, realising the socialist modernisation, and making China a developed society are met with.

4

Xi Jinping's Governance of China

I have been watching China since the late 1980s, and of late have been associated with the translation of Xi Jinping's *The Governance of China* (Chinese edition) into Hindi, I believe those who deem his speeches as stereotypical are grossly mistaken. I have found them reflecting the historical and present realities of China, reflecting a strong sense of continuity and connectivity, be it Chinese society, the Communist Party, or China's relations with its neighbours and major powers. It remains a must read not only for the domestic but especially for the foreign audience who would like to understand where China is heading.

First and foremost, I believe 'people oriented thought' remains at the core of Xi Jinping's governance, essentially the reinforcement of China's ancient philosophical thought. The Chinese dream, the goal of 'two centenaries', his tirade against the 'tigers and flies', reinforcing the 'mass line' as a fundamental of the Party, providing the best public services and goods in the form of state of the art infrastructure including high-speed rails, the length of which was more than doubled during his first term, as well as promoting close people-to-people relations as far as China's relations with foreign countries are concerned should be viewed in this context.

Second, he makes it clear that the development path of China would remain socialism with Chinese characteristics and must not be abandoned. This again he attributes to historical explorations and choices made by the Chinese people. Adhering to the notion of Chinese thought of continuity, president Xi sees the development of socialism as a continuous phenomenon that has been advanced by all his predecessors irrespective of differences in guiding principles, thinking and policies during the revolution, development and reforms etc. phases. Therefore, it will remain the path, theory, and system for a long time to come. The path which is economic development remains the main priority guided by the theory developed by his generation of the Chinese leadership, and is guaranteed by a political and economic system that is rule based. The system has been successful in guaranteeing unity, diversity, social cohesion and peaceful development, therefore, rather than abandoning the system, it would be further improved, and perfected albeit requiring discipline from party and government officials. The search for a rule based system and society continues.

Third, as China continues to advance economically and endeavors towards realising the two centenaries, Xi Jinping sees the stimuli in China's traditional value system and cultural soft power. So much so, while cultivating socialist core values, Xi Jinping seeks shelter in traditional Chinese culture. He also dumps the 'clash of civilisations' theory for 'learning from civilisations.' According to him, it is civilisational interaction that has enriched cultures and civilisations and enhanced understanding between peoples and nations. Therefore, it is of little surprise that Xi has been invoking the Spirit of Chinese culture as well as the 'Silk Road Spirit' which he says favours peace and cooperation, openness and inclusiveness, mutual learning and mutual benefits. This is the spirt that is at the core of his neighbourhood policy too.

Fourth, Xi Jinping envisions common development, common prosperity and common security in the region, beyond and between nations. This, he has been referring to as building communities of shared future for mankind in his speeches. The notion will lead to integrating regional development, integrating markets and thus bringing nations and people closer to each other. Various connectivity initiatives across Asia, Europe and Africa by way of the Belt and Road Initiative (BRI) advocated by him, and China's free trade agreements with various countries have demonstrated this fact, albeit many have seen the BRI as China's grand strategy to capture markets and pose a security threat to their interests in the regions. It is in this context that the rise of China has been seen as a threat not only by some of China's neighbours but also by the established hegemon, the US. In order to build a relationship that is devoid of historical clashes and confrontation, Xi has advocated the building of a new model of Major country relationship by dialogues, promoting trust, expanding cooperation and controlling disputes. Meanwhile, Xi has advocated building a strong national defence and military forces. In order to enhance the combat capacity of the PLA, he created a new command system intended to integrate and rebalance land, air and naval forces, which is understandable given the sprawling interests of China across the continents.

Finally, Xi Jinping remains a man of actions. We will see that what he has said in his speeches, he has carried into actions. China's global rebalancing in the form of the Belt and Road initiative in the face of western retrenchment and protectionism is demonstrative of this fact. The building of the US$ 51 billion Silk Road Fund, the foundation of Asia Infrastructure Investment Bank, New Development Bank etc. reinforces the fact that China remains committed to shouldering greater global responsibilities by substantiating existing institutions of global governance. His anti-corruption drive aimed to cleanse the system from corrupt officials at all levels, and his commitment to the deepening of reforms on the one hand and restructuring Chinese economy aimed at maintaining the equilibrium between industry, services and agriculture through innovation is another example. Xi's domestic as well as global assertiveness has undoubtedly raised hopes as well as concerns across continents. I believe by going through his *Governance of China* people certainly will have a better understanding of the most powerful leader in recent times as well as the direction China will take in the years to come.

5

CHINA'S RISE AND 40 YEARS OF REFORMS

As China marks 40 years of reforms and opening up, many analysts are taking stock of the path China has treaded and the strides it has made in socio-economic and technological areas. I myself being a student of China studies since 1986 and a witness to the earthshaking changes since 1991 when I visited China for the first time have been mystified by the developments in China, and have no definite answers as my understanding remains inconclusive and incomprehensive, albeit I am not in the category of those who characterised the reforms in China as westernisation, and predicted the disintegration of China, or China moving towards western democracy. The following figures answer some questions partially.

After 40 years of reforms and opening up, China's per capita GDP reached over 9000 US dollars in 2018 from the meagre 384 US dollars in 1978. As revealed by President Xi Jinping in his speech marking the 40th anniversary of reforms and opening up on 18th December 2018, the share of China's GDP in global GDP has risen from 1.8 per cent at the beginning of reform and opening up to 15.2 per cent, and its contribution to world economic growth has exceeded 30 per cent over the years. The total import and export volume of China's goods has increased from 20.6 billion US dollars to more than 4 trillion US dollars. In the last 40 years, 740 million people have been alleviated from the poverty, and urbanisation has reached

55.26 per cent. Today China boasts 22,000 kilometres of Hi-Speed railways (largest in the world), 123,000 kilometres of expressways non-existent prior to the reforms. Prior to the reforms China didn't have a single private enterprise, at present there are over 20 million!

The figures reveal that the growth story in China has been phenomenal, unprecedented in the history of humankind. How did it happen? First and foremost, institutional changes are behind unleashing the productive forces in China. For example, the initial thrust of the reforms was in rural areas, where a 'contract household responsibility system' was implemented that linked remuneration to output. Between 1982 and 2008 a series of administrative reforms were introduced to create a leaner government structure, and bureaucracy was downsized almost 50 per cent from a whopping 10 million people. During the 3rd Plenary Session of the 12th Central Committee in 1984, reforms were taken to urban areas, and various systems of ownership such as collectively owned enterprises, individual, private and foreign owned enterprises were introduced and encouraged. The Southeast Coastal Priority Development Strategy was unfolded that saw the establishment of special economic zones, the experimental zone, the free trade zone, and the free ports that enabled some people to get rich first.

Second, as China created new institutions and institutionalised reforms, it drew long-term strategic goals for country's development. For example, during the 13th National Congress of the CPC held in 1987, a three-stage modernisation formula (*sanbuzou*) for the next 62 years was unrolled. The goals included, doubling the 1980 GDP to end shortages of food and clothing (*jiejue wenbao wenti*); quadrupling the 1980 GDP by the end of the 20th century and achieving the level of a moderately prosperous society (*dadao xiaokang xueping*); raising the per capita GDP to that of moderately developed countries (*dadao zhongdeng fada guojia de shuiping*). To everyone's surprise, China achieved the first stage by the end of the 1980s and the second stage in 1995 ahead of schedule. This vision continues and could also be seen in the 'Two Step' formula for China's development between 2020 and 2050 advocated by Xi Jinping during the 19th Party Congress. By 2035 China will basically realise the socialist modernisation, and by the middle of the 21st century, "China will develop into a great modern socialist country that is prosperous, strong, democratic, culturally advanced, harmonious and beautiful" to quote from Xi Jinping's 19th Party Congress Report.

Third, strides in infrastructure and manufacturing lead to technological breakthrough and innovations. The industrial shift in the wake of reforms aided by higher labour costs and energy prices resulted in a manufacturing boom in China making it the 'factory of the world'. Manufacturing and infrastructural development was primarily driven by a whopping 300 million migrant workers, who were responsible for creating wonders across China such as Pudong in Shanghai. However, as the labour cost gradually went up, China took advantage of the new information technology and made huge strides in telecom, energy, finance etc. sectors. Today, China has made huge strides in artificial intelligence and quantum computing, automated machine tools and robotics, aerospace and aeronautical equipment, maritime equipment and high-tech shipping, modern rail transport equipment, new-energy vehicles, power equipment, agricultural equipment, biopharma and advanced medical products. Enterprises such as Ali Baba, Tencent, and Huawei etc. are at the forefront of this new industrial revolution.

Fourth, though the liberals may not agree with the institutionalisation of 'political meritocracy' in China in the wake of reforms, however, it has proved a success albeit there remain gaps between the ideal and the practice. In order to cater to the needs of reforms and opening up, the Communist Party of China right from the lower rungs to the higher echelons of power demonstrated merit to achieve goals. This resulted in regional economic decentralisation and determined the political mobility of leaders through performance. Many politicians ranging from Jiang Zemin, Hu Jintao including Xi Jinping indeed were provincial leaders in Shangahi, Guizhou/Tibet, and Fujian/Zhejiang respectively.

Finally, since the blueprint for the future could be realised in a peaceful surrounding only, therefore, China in the last 40 years pursued the policy of good neighbourliness, obviously, Deng's dictum, 'bide your time and hide your capabilities was at play'. Deng's notion of maintaining a 'favourable environment' was changed to the policy of "good neighbourliness' during Jiang Zemin, and to 'harmonious peripheral diplomacy' during Hu Jintao's time. Xi Jinping further intends to deepen relations with China's neighbours in accordance with the 'principle of amity, sincerity, mutual benefit, and inclusiveness and the policy of forging friendship and partnership.'

6

THE 19ᵀᴴ PARTY CONGRESS:
CLEARING FACTIONAL FOG AND XI JINPING'S 'DOCTRINE'

Although it may not be entirely correct to reduce Chinese politics to a binary of factional power struggle, if we glance over the powerful Politburo Standing Committee of the Communist Party of China (CPC) we find Xi and Wang Qishan against heavy odds from the 'Shanghai clique' once headed by Jiang Zemin. In the same vein, Xi battles it out in the Politburo with the 'League faction' once headed by Hu Jintao. It becomes clear that factions are formulated by affiliation, patronage and experience. It is interesting to note that the existence of factions has been acknowledged by the CPC News Agency, *Xinhua* in some of its commentaries in January 2015. On 3 January 2015, the Agency flagged out three such factions, namely "mishubang" (secretaries gang), "shiyoubang" (petroleum gang) and "shanxibang" (Shanxi gang). It pointed out that while the man behind the first two gangs was once a powerful petroleum and security czar, Zhou Yongkang; Ling Jihua, former director of the Central Committee General Office was behind the "Shanxi gang." Another commentary on the CPC website on January 5ᵗʰ once again referred to these gangs and factions and stated that "Beneath the old tigers, there are big tigers, and behind the big tigers there are foxes and rats. Where gangs form, there are also gang lords;

where there are cliques, there are also 'mountain tops,' and these kinds of 'mountain tops' are very harmful to our party."

Undoubtedly, Xi Jinping with the help of Wang Qishan a close Xi ally and Secretary of the powerful Central Commission for Discipline Inspection (CCDI), fought the 'tigers and flies' during the first five years of his regime, thus consolidating his position fairly well. Recent figures released by China's state media, reveals that in the last five years, 1.4 million party officials have been investigated for corruption. Some of the fallen 'tigers' are Zhou Yongkang, Bo Xilai, Guo Boxiong, Xu Caihou, Ling Jihua, Fang Fenghui, and Sun Zhengcai. Notable are the fall of Guo Boxiong, Xu Caihou, and now the removal of General Fang Fenghui, former head of the CMC's Joint Staff Department, and General Zhang Yang, former head of the commission's Political Work Department. Xi has replaced General Fang with General Li Zuocheng, and appointed Admiral Miao Hua, as head of the Political Work Department thus further consolidating his position and hold over the People's Liberation Army (PLA). We will further see huge churnings in the composition of the Central Military Commission, headed by Xi Jinping.

Although Xi Jinping has not associated himself with any faction, analysts are of the view that Xi has gradually created a 'Fujian faction.' The appointments of Wang Xiaohong, vice mayor of Beijing and since 2016 vice-minister of the Ministry of Public Security; Deng Weiping, secretary of the Party Disciplinary Commission of the Public Security Ministry, and Chen Min'er, party secretary of Chongqing are some of the people who have worked for Xi Jinping in various capacities. While Wang and Deng have never been nominated to the Central Committee, Chen is likely to be inducted in the Politburo this time. It is believed that Xi may groom Chen as his ultimate successor, albeit it is too early to say as Xi has 5 more years to go.

China under Xi Jinping has done extremely well if the statistics are to be believed. Most outstanding is China's burgeoning economic strength which was catapulted to US$ 11.2 trillion from around US$ 8.5 trillion when he took over in 2012. Per capita income of China rose from around US$ 6000 to over US$ 8000 in recent times, a further 55.5 million people were alleviated from poverty. This is impressive, for the global economic recovery remains sluggish and countries across the globe reels under economic recession. More importantly, this is occuring at a time when China herself is undergoing economic readjustments and striking a balance between manufacturing, services and agriculture. Hi-speed rail tracks were expanded from 9,300 kilometers in 2012 to over 22,000 kilometers at present. In the same vein, China ranked first in the world in having constructed state of the art expressways totaling 123,000 kilometers. China's internet consumers also jumped to 730 million from a mere 420 million in 2012, implying that at present around 53 per cent of the Chinese population is wired. Needless to say, China has maintained its leading position as the world's largest exporter, producer of food grains, steel, coal, electricity etc. Very cleverly, Xi Jinping unfolded a development agenda that forced reformers as well as conservatives to lend their support to him. For example, his pet project the Chinese Dream that advocates the rejuvenation of the Chinese nation (making China rich and powerful) has been a hit in China although it has raised nationalistic tendencies too. *In the same vein, Xi took the notion of 'Silk Road Economic Belt and the 21st Century Maritime Silk Road' an idea of the reformists that is being increasingly seen as a game changer as far as geo-economics and geopolitics across continents is concerned.*

Second, in order to diminish the influence of Zhou Yongkang's in China's security apparatus, in an unprecedented move Xi created the National Security Commission, which controls the police, intelligence and judicial apparatuses and became its Chairman. In order to keep the reformists under his command, he created the Central Leading Group for Comprehensibly Deepening Reforms and became its head. In order to take ultimate control of the People's Liberation Army, he reorganised the previous seven military regions into five theatre commands, and assumed the title of commander in chief of the PLA. *Xi, therefore, has displayed enormous wisdom, patience and ultimate art of statecraft, and has emerged as the strongest leaders of the CPC since Mao Zedong.*

As far as Xi's legacy is concerned, it has been agreed by the Party that his ideas on China's governance would be written in the Party Constitution. In the line of Jiang Zemin's 'Three Represents', and Hu Jintao's 'Scientific development', Xi has propounded 'Four Comprehensives' that call to comprehensively to build a moderately prosperous society, deepen reforms, govern the nationa according to rule of law, and strictly govern the Party. Many have speculated that if the constitution is amended it would include Xi's ideas as 'ism' or 'thought' alike. I personally believe, it would neither be 'ism' nor 'thought' for in the case of the former it will supersede both Mao's Thought and Deng's Theory while the later latter will put him at par with Mao. If at all, the CPC would like him to leave his mark on history, it would be Xi Jinping's Doctrine, a level up from Deng Xiaoping's theory and a notch down from Mao's thought.

7

MADE IN CHINA 2025:
CAUSE FOR A COLD WAR BETWEEN CHINA AND THE US?

Why did a simple domestic economic strategy rolled out by Premier Li Keqiang in May 2015 to upgrade Chinese industry face such backlash from the West culminating in the US-China trade war? If we go through the full text of the "Made in China 2025" released by the State Council on 8th May 2015 and the "Made in China 2025" Green Paper on Technological Innovations in Key Areas, it becomes clear that the initiative is geared towards letting Chinese manufacturing move up the value chain in production and innovation during Xi Jinping's "New Era" from the labor intensive and low end manufacturing of the reform era (1978-2012).

One of the most ambitious goals it has identified is to achieve 40 per cent "self-sufficiency" by 2020, and 70 per cent "self-sufficiency" by 2025 in core components and critical materials in a wide range of industries, including aerospace and telecommunications equipment and achieve international recognition for Chinese brands. Ten core areas the strategy has identified are: (1) New advanced information technology, including artificial intelligence and quantum computing, (2) Automated machine tools and robotics, (3) Aerospace and aeronautical equipment, (4) Maritime equipment and high-tech shipping, (5) Modern rail transport equipment,

(6) Self-driving and new-energy vehicles, (7) Power equipment, (8) Agricultural equipment, (9) New materials, and (10) Biopharma and advanced medical products. Of these China has already made huge inroads in artificial intelligence (AI), robotics, high-speed rail and aerospace. Chinese ambitions have been pronounced as "bad for America" by US officials, and the Trump administration has justified the need for a US military space force by 2020.

In China, people argue that even though it has become the world's largest manufacturer, it cannot be considered "manufacturing power" *(zhizao qiangguo)*, for it lags behind developed countries especially in areas such as innovation, efficiency and efficacy, quality, IT level and overall industrial structure. The "Made in China 2025" addresses these concerns by following a "Three Step Strategy" *(sanbuzou)*, a decade attributed to each phase from 2015 to 2045. The strategy is roughly in sync with president Xi's economic development plan in two phases for China, i.e. by 2035 China will basically realise socialist modernisation, and by the middle of the 21st century, "China will develop into a great modern socialist country that is prosperous, strong, democratic, culturally advanced, harmonious and beautiful" to quote from Xi Jinping's 19th Party Congress Report. Though China has tried to convince the developed nations that the "Made in China 2025" strategy is open, inclusive, transparent, conforms to the WTO norms, and above all is devised to turn China from the "world factory" to a "manufacturing power" so as to avoid the "middle income trap", it appears that the West, especially the US is not buying the Chinese argument. China believes that the hawks in the US are hell bent on preventing the rise of China. Therefore, even if there are no talks of direct military conflict, the war over trade, technology, IPR, cyberspace etc. is becoming increasingly intense and leading to an unpronounced cold war.

As regards the progress made by "Made in China 2025" in the last three years, various innovation centers with massive capital have been established across China. According to Lai Ning of the Strategic Planning & Management Office, Shanghai Branch, Hitachi (China) Research & Development Corporation, by 2020 national innovation centers would be established in 15 locations; besides 19 provincial-level innovation centers have also been approved. For example, the National Power Battery

Innovation Center, China's first national manufacturing innovation center was established in Beijing on June 30, 2016, with the National Additive Manufacturing and New Material Innovation Center in Xi'an in 2017. Some other innovation centers established since 2017 include the National Manufacturing Innovation Center, High-end Equipment Manufacturing Innovation Project, and New Materials Industry Innovation Project etc. Various cities across China have submitted applications to be pilot cities for the "Made in China 2025" strategy, it is estimated that about 30 cities would be designated as pilot cities for the strategy. Ningbo was the first to be designated followed by Guangdong, Chengdu, the cluster of five cities in south Jiangsu province, and six in the west coast of the Zhujiang river, Wuhan in central China, Shenyang and Changchun in the northeast, and Qingdao in Shandong are some others in the lineup. What is interesting is that these would be integrated with the pivot cities designated for the Belt and Road Initiative.

In order to bridge the technological gap, China has promoted foreign acquisitions and transfers of technology agreements. However, these have been dubbed as coercive and predatory by the US and its allies. China's tech giants such as Baidu, Alibaba, Tencent, Huawei and ZTE are facing backlash and resistance in the US and Europe. "Findings of the investigation into China's acts, policies, and practices related to technology transfer, intellectual property, and innovation under section 301 of the trade act of 1974", a report prepared by the Office of the United States Trade Representative executive office of the President or the so called "Section 301" report released in March 2018 has accused China of stealing trade secrets and forcing the acquisition and transfer of technologies and intellectual property to Chinese companies. The Trump administration is convinced that by way of "Made in China 2025" China desires to penetrate deep into the open economies while denying similar access to foreign companies in the Chinese market. It desires to assume leadership in the above-mentioned core sectors and replace the established giants, the US and other players like Germany, Japan and South Korea.

Therefore, the US-China trade war is not about the US$ 375 billion trade deficit with China alone but a future hegemonic contest between the two rivals, in which hi-tech leadership is just one field. Early in June when president Trump announced that the US will increase the scope of tariffs on Chinese goods from US$ 50 billion to US$ 250 and ultimately to US$ 500, "Made in China 2025" was in the back of his mind. It is also perhaps for this reason that the Chinese government has lowered its pitch on "Made in China 2025" but the strategy is being unfolded uninterrupted. Essentially it remains a blueprint for transforming China's labor intensive manufacturing to high end products, which has threatened the technological leadership of the West and hence triggered an attempt to stop China's rise by initiating a trade war.

8

Destruction and Construction in China:
A 'Millennium Plan' for Building Xiongan—
A New Area and a New Capital City

During the Second World War, when the US planned the bombardment of Japan, it sought the help of a Chinese architect from Tsinghua University, as to which areas should be protected and spared from destruction. The architect was none other than Liang Sicheng 'the father of modern architecture, the son of one of the tallest intellectuals of the 20th century China, Liang Qichao, who not only set aside Kyoto, Nara and Osaka but also marked precisely the location of the ancient architectural wonders in these cities and requested the US to spare these. Liang Sicheng succeeded in protecting these cities but could not protect Beijing from destruction in the wake of communist victory in 1949.

After liberation, Liang Sicheng was appointed as the Deputy Director of Beijing Metropolitan Planning Commission and proposed that the ancient city be kept intact in totality and that the administrative Centre may be constructed on the western suburbs of Beijing. He proposed that Beijing must be a political and cultural centre as opposed to a industrial centre. However, his proposals were rebuffed by the then Beijing mayor, Peng Zhen, for Peng described them as the 'symbols of feudalism' which must be toppled. He told Liang that it was Chairman Mao's desire to see chimneys all around from the Tiananmen rostrum. Thus started the colossal destruction of old Beijing: in 1953 Left Anmen was flattened, in 1954 the Qingshou twin pagodas were pulled down, in 1956 Zhonghuamen was destroyed, in 1957 Yongdingmen, Guangqumen, Chaoyangmen etc. towers were leveled. The fury of destruction continued into the mid and late 1960s that witnessed the destruction of Dongzhimen, Xuanwumen, Chongwenmen, Andingmen, Fuchengmen, Xizhimen etc places which were reduced to mere names of many metro stations along line 2 in Beijing. Imagine the grandeur of Beijing had these structures been spared by the leaders of New China who wanted to convert Beijing into another Kremlin for mass gatherings!

If Deng Xiaoping envisioned the development of Shenzhen and Putong, and if Hu Jintao and Wen Jiabao designed the development of the Beijing-Tianjin plan, Xi Jinping's plan for XNA is as grandiose as his 'China Dream' and 'great rejuvenation ton of the Chinese nation.'

If these were the ambitions of the first generation communist leaders in China, the ambitions of the fifth generation leadership are equally grandiose but diametrically different. Xi Jinping, perhaps has seen the logic in Liang Sicheng's vision. On April 1, 2017, the Central Committee of the Communist Party of China and the State Council decided to establish Xiongan New Area (XNA) in Hebei province. It wasn't an April fool, but a serious and even more ambitious developmental plan that will exceed the scale of the Shenzhen Special Economic Zone (SSEZ) and the Shanghai Pudong New Area (SPNA), according to the State Council. The Xinhua News Agency of China has termed it as a 'Millennium plan and a mega event of national significance.' It is being reported that Xi Jinping chose the area after visiting Anxin in February this year.

If Deng Xiaoping envisioned the development of Shenzhen and Putong, and if Hu Jintao and Wen Jiabao designed the development of Beijing-Tianjin plan, Xi Jinping's plan for XNA is as grandiose as his 'China Dream' and 'great rejuvenation of the Chinese nation.' SSEZ was built on 196 square kilometers of land, SPNA in 1210 square kilometers, and XNA would be built in 2000 square kilometer. It will span the counties of

Xiongxian, Rongcheng and Anxin, which are at the center of the triangular area formed by Beijing, Tianjin and Hebei's provincial capital Shijiazhuang. According to initial reports, some 87 industries from Beijing, most of them educational institutions, hospitals, schools and administrative divisions would be relocated to the XNA.

Essentially, XNA would serve as the sub capital of China. The decision marks China's efforts to solve problems facing mega cities, like education, health, traffic, pollution, and heavy smog. Some analysts also see political and economic security reasons in the move. Some also view that since South-North water diversion that affects over 400 million people would also incur a huge financial burden, and since the diversion is against the laws of nature it may have huge implications in future. XNA on the contrary would be a green and ecological project that will see the economic integration of Beijing-Tianjin and Hebei. There is another viewpoint that since successful reforms have bred various interest groups in Beijing, in order to break their monopoly; it would be desirable to build a new capital. Still others argue that since the model of establishing municipalities directly under central control has not worked out well, the establishment of a sub capital will provide a new direction to reforms.

With the announcement of the XNA, it has been reported that real estate magnates are already scrambling for prime properties in the area, catapulting the existing per square meters rates manifold. The officials from Xiong and Anxin counties have imposed a ban on any property sale in the area. Social media too is abuzz with the establishment of the XNA. Many parochial views have also been aired. For example drawing parallels between Shanghai Pudong and Shenzhen, one netizen says it is because the people in the south are apt for economic construction not the people from the north. He fears that the massive funds allocated by the central government along with property speculation will result in the building of another mega ghost city. Five more years to rule China, Xi Jinping has initiated mega projects, will he enter the annals of history and CPC constitution the way Mao and Deng made their legacies? Or will he require three decades to transform China as both Mao and Deng got?

9

CHINA'S FOREIGN POLICY IN THE LAST 70 YEARS

At the time of its inception, China's overall foreign policy was the reversion of national humiliation that western countries including Japan had inflicted on it since the mid 19th century. Transforming the image of China from a weak, bullied and humiliated one to a strong and self-confident China, was projected as China's domestic as well as foreign policy goal. Militarily, China's goal was to be second to none; territorially, China wished to settle its border with neighbouring countries and regain all territories including Tibet and Taiwan it claimed; and economically, turn China into a rich and prosperous country. Today, China appears to have realised most of its foreign policy goals cut out at its inception.

Immediately after its inception in 1949, since China was completely ostracized by the western world, it at once found refuge in the communist bloc formed by the Soviet Union and its satellites, thus becoming an important constituent of the communist camp, having diplomatic relations with only 18 countries. While elucidating China's foreign policy, Zhou Enlai remarked on 8 November 1949 that "Our foreign policy should be twofold, i.e. alliance [*lianhe*] and struggle [*douzheng*]. Alliance with our brotherly states, however, in tactic we must reserve criticism; struggle against imperialism, but our tactic should be to join hands with them on certain issues."

China's "leaning to the one side" forced China to venture on a strategy that would at minimum neutralise the Asian and African countries on the one hand, and render the western economic embargo against it ineffective on the other. This would allow China to engage in economic construction that was in shambles after the Sino-Japanese (1931-45) and the civil wars (1946-49). It is clearly reflected from China's handling of the Korean, Indo-China crisis, and its positioning at the Asian-African Conference in Bandung. However, the extreme leftist errors that resulted in manmade disasters like three years of prolonged famine, which killed millions of people in the wake of the "Great Leap Forward" plunged China into crisis internally and conflicts with its neighbours externally. China's "democratic reforms" in Tibet that resulted in the Tibetan Uprising and flight of the Dalai Lama in 1959 deteriorated its relations with India and culminated in China's India war in 1962. As the Soviet Union initiated de-Stalinization after Stalin's death, the Chinese denounced Soviet Union as revisionist and competed with it for ideological leadership of the world communism. This resulted in China's bloody conflict with the Soviet Union in 1969 and the Sino-US rapprochement, restoration of its membership to the United Nations, and its invasion of Vietnam in 1979. There was a time when China ridiculed and undermined the role of the United Nation, but now it is one of the staunchest supporters of the UN and the second largest contributor to its peacekeeping operations.

With the de-Maoization since 1978, China embarked on the path of opening and reform policy. Relying on the "bide your time and hide your capabilities" strategy, China under Deng Xiaoping made great strides. With the Sino-US rapprochement, a number of countries establishing diplomatic relations with China increased from 18 to 179 to date. In order to see the smooth return of Hong Kong and Macau in 1997 and 1999, China promised and implemented the "One Country, Two Systems" policy. As regards Taiwan, China continues to struggle with "foreign interference" however, was successful in convincing the Kuomintang (KMT) Party in Taiwan to accept the 1992 "One China" principle, which is being resisted tooth and nail by President Cai Yingwen's Democratic Progressive Party, flaring up tensions across the straits. Moreover, the lingering turmoil in

Hong Kong has posed serious challenges to China's peaceful unification with Taiwan.

As the focus was to nurture its relationship with major powers, China during the 1990s under Jiang Zemin advocated "a new security concept" centered around "mutual trust, mutual benefits, equality, cooperation and coordination" and partnerships with countries that were non-aligned, non-conflictual, and not directed towards any other country. The last three were further elaborated and incorporated into a "New type of major power relationship" in an article on China's peaceful rise in the *Study Times* brought out by the CPC's Party School. It was during the second round of China's strategic and economic dialogue in 2005 that China's state counsellor, Dai Bingguo officially spelled out that the "New type of major power relationship" between China and the US should be built on the basis of "mutual respect, harmonious coexistence, and win-win cooperation." In early 2012, the then vice president of China, Xi Jinping during his visit to the US expounded that both China and the US must endeavor to build a new 21st century type of major power relationship. The above contents of the "New type of major power relationship" were incorporated by Hu Jintao in his speech during the fourth round of the China-US security and economic dialogue in May 2012 and a few months later by the 18th Party Congress of the CPC.

This concept of relationship proposed by China has never been accepted by the US. As argued by eminent Chinese scholar Yan Xuetong, the US will never consider China fit for an equal footing in the Asia Pacific as well as globally. If it does, its strategic relationship with some of its allies, say Japan and South Korea will necessarily be "downgraded." And moreover, since the new type of major power relationship calls for "mutual respect" the honor and hubris of US hegemony will not deem China fit for that respect. From China's perspective, the rationale behind this new type of relationship is to avoid the kind of conflict the bipolar world witnessed during the Cold War, and try to learn from the relationship the US and the UK established after World War II. However, this is not possible, as the focal point of China's new type relationship is "peaceful strategic competition" rather than the "comprehensive strategic cooperation" that resulted between the US and the UK. As US-China relations ran into rough weather due to strategic rivalry demonstrated by the trade war, China's strategic relationship with Russia is on an upward and solid trajectory, and there is a rebalancing towards India and Japan.

With the ascendance of Xi Jinping on the political stage in China, China abandoned the Deng era "bide your time and hide your capabilities" demonstrated by its assertiveness over the Senkaku Islands in the East China Sea, the reclamation and militarisation of some of the islands and archipelagos in the South China Sea, and more recently by displaying an array of new types of weaponry including the DF-17, DF-26, DF-41 ICBM, Gongji 11 attack UAV, Julang-2 SLBM etc. that will challenge US dominance in the Indo-Pacific on the one hand, and effect the forceful unification of Taiwan on the other if necessary. While enhancing China's defense capabilities, President Xi Jinping has advocated grandiose concepts like "Building communities of shared future" and the "Belt and Road Initiative" (BRI), essentially a surgical strike on de-globalisation, protectionism and the rebalancing to Asia strategy of the US. In the past six years, China has signed cooperation agreements with more than 160 countries and international organisations during the two BRI forums for international cooperation in 2017 and 2019. As China's trade with the BRI countries exceeded US$ 6 trillion, the China club, as many have referred to it, is undoubtedly becoming more and more attractive to countries across the globe including Italy and Switzerland, new entrants to the BRI from Europe.

Indeed, by way of peaceful strategic competition, China has trounced the US as a major trading nation across the continents albeit it still needs to strive hard to become a global market. It has also infuriated the US by challenging the Bretton Woods institutions of global governance and establishing its own, such as the Asia Infrastructure Investment Bank, New Development Bank of the BRICS, the prospective Shanghai Cooperation Organisation Development Bank; besides, China drew many US allies lining up for the membership of these institutions. Nonetheless, China has argued that it is supplementing existing institutions and sharing greater responsibility in global governance. China's share of voting rights in the World Bank and the International Monetary Fund has remarkably risen to third place. It successfully hosted a number of summits such as the G20, APEC, Shanghai Cooperation Organisation, and BRICS, the BRI Forums, and Dialogue of the Asian Civilisation thus expanding its friend circle. It remains the staunchest supporter of the existing international order, as it has immensely benefitted China in becoming the second largest economy in the world and alleviating some 800 million people from poverty in the last 70 years.

Finally, if the first three decades of the People's Republic were full of internal strife and external conflicts, the last four decades witnessed China pursuing the policy of "good neighbourliness" during Jiang Zemin's time, "harmonious peripheral diplomacy" during Hu Jintao's time, and the "principle of amity, sincerity, mutual benefit, inclusiveness and the policy of forging friendship and partnership" during the New Era of Xi Jinping. Undoubtedly, China's historic leap from "standing up, getting rich to becoming strong in one way also explains its diplomacy in the last 70 years. However, "becoming strong" has also brought China into direct conflict with the established hegemon and the contest which will be protracted has been unfolding in various shapes and forms, the trade war between them is just one manifestation.

10

China's War on Poverty

In the period of deep globalisation, even though humankind made huge strides in poverty alleviation, according to a recent World Bank Report entitled *Poverty and Shared Prosperity 2020: Reversals of Fortune*, the world is not on track to meet the global goal of reducing extreme poverty to 3 per cent by 2030 and warns that extreme poverty is expected to rise this year for the first time in over 20 years owing to the COVID-19 pandemic and global economic slump. With the worsening economic situation around the globe, the report estimates that an additional 88 million people will live in extreme poverty in 2020. It says that the total number of people living in extreme poverty globally will be between 703 and 729 million, and some other estimates put them at the one billion mark.

Confucius (551 BC–479 BC) once said that "In a country well governed, poverty is something to be ashamed of. In a country badly governed, wealth is something to be ashamed of." In other words, good governance is directly proportional to the increase in standard of living of the population, needless to say this results from the moral responsibility of the government towards the wellbeing of its citizens. From this perspective, China's poverty alleviation achievements have been impressive; especially in the last 40 years of reforms, China reduced the rate from 90 per cent in 1981 to 0.5 per cent in 2020. This is tantamount to alleviating around

850 million people from extreme poverty as per the World Banks spending benchmark. The poverty line set US$ 1.90 could be subject to interpretations, however, the larger picture of one time China's agrarian challenge is very different today. How did it happen and what lessons can we draw from the Chinese experience?

At the outset, it is owing to the concerted efforts of the Chinese political leadership and people alike that these results have been achieved. The "Three Rurals" (Agriculture, countryside and peasants) dominating the agenda of rural reforms for decades is at the heart of poverty reduction in China. First of all, if the Household Responsibility System of the late 1970s revolutionised agriculture production and made China self-sufficient in food grain production, the land contracting system facilitated the mechanisation of farming and enabled peasants to engage in off-farm income opportunities in the 2000s. The mushrooming of cooperatives and e-commerce platforms that connected peasants' products to markets and brought in new technologies and training programmes, catapulted peasants' income to new levels. The rural healthcare system initiated in the mid 2000s could be another guarantor of peasants' income. Obviously, the peasant resistance in the late 1990s and early 2000s was also instrumental in reforming the agrarian sector in China. For example, in 1996-97 alone, 380,000 peasants participated in public protests across China resulting in 7,400 fatalities. In 2005, a year before when China abolished agricultural taxes and levies altogether, peasants' protests across China numbered 87,000.

Second, achievements cannot be separated from China's development path and system with Chinese characteristics in which the Communist Party plays a pivotal role. These are closely connected to the formulation and implementation of policies such as "The Five-sphere Integrated Plan" proposed in November 2012 at the 18th National Congress of the CPC aiming at the development of socialism with Chinese characteristics encompassing economic, political, cultural, social and ecological development; "Targeted poverty alleviation Strategy" pronounced in 2013; "Four-pronged Comprehensive Strategy" proposed in December 2014, which is aimed at comprehensively building a moderately prosperous society in all respects, expanding in-depth reform, promoting law-based governance, and enforcing strict Party self-governance; and identification of anti-poverty as one of three "tough battles" for 2017 to 2020 pronounced by president Xi Jinping. No wonder ever since he took over in 2012, about 100 million Chinese people have been uplifted from poverty.

Third, particularly noteworthy is the "Targeted Poverty Alleviation" programme, which has been instrumental in changing the social landscape of rural China. Under this programme, China has set clear poverty reduction goals. Thanks to the great leap China has taken in building big data and e-governance a database of 128,000 poverty-stricken villages, 29.48 million poor households and 89.62 million impoverished people was constructed. This was made possible by sending a massive 775,000 officials to be stationed in villages for a period of 1 to 3 years, and Party secretaries at the provincial, municipal, county, township and village levels were held accountable for poverty alleviation. Between August 2015 and June 2016 an additional 2 million people were mobilised for the task. This is perhaps the second "back to the countryside" movement since the Cultural Revolution with totally different goals. It was in the wake of such a movement and database building exercise that the "five-batch" policy through industrial development, relocation, compensation, education, and social security could be identified and implemented. For the purpose of relocation alone, the Chinese government earmarked 250 billion yuan (US$ 38 billion) outlay for provinces and an additional 170.6 billion yuan (US$ 24.3 billion) was offered to poverty stricken people in form of microcredit.

Fourth, as hinted above, it would not have been possible without hefty spending from the central government. For example, the Chinese government allocated 91 billion RMB (US$ 13 billion) to poverty alleviation funds for the year 2019 alone. The Chinese Development Bank pledged 400 billion RMB (US$ 57 billion) to fund poverty alleviation projects. At the same time, strict supervision over poverty alleviation funds has been the norm, no wonder more than 60,000 cases of corruption and misappropriation of funds have been discovered and thousands are being tried in the court of law.

Fifth, China's poverty alleviation has made huge contributions towards global poverty eradication goals. China lifting 850 million people out of poverty translates into alleviating more than 70 per cent of the world's poor out of poverty. It has offered hope, especially to developing and least developed countries with dense populations that they too can dream of throwing off the yoke of poverty in a time bound framework. China could be instrumental in building capacities in developing and least developed countries by sharing its experience. Having gotten rid of poverty at home, China since 2015, has assisted other developing countries through 180 poverty reduction projects, 118 agricultural cooperation projects, 178 aid-for-trade projects, and 103 projects concerning ecological conservation and climate change. In September 2020, during the 75th session of the United Nations General Assembly, Xi Jinping pledged to provide 50 million US dollars to the China-FAO South-South Cooperation Trust Fund that is supporting 80 projects in more than 30 developing countries. Moreover, the Belt and Road Initiative, the Asian Infrastructure Investment Bank, BRICS New Development Bank etc. institutions are also instrumental in generating employment and providing funds for various sustainable development projects across the globe.

Finally, it is owing to the free flow of goods, commodities, technologies and people under the ambit of globalisation and multilateralism that has made poverty reduction possible in China and India. This was supported by professor Kishore Mehbubani during the the plenary session of the recently concluded "International Forum on Sharing Poverty Reduction Experience", organised by the Chinese Academy of Social Sciences in collaboration with China Media Group, China Development Bank, and China International Poverty Reduction Centre on 15 December by pointing out statistics to prove his point. According to him, in 1992 China and India's international trade stood at US$ 166 and US$ 45 billion respectively, which rose to US$ 4.6 trillion and US$ 949 billion respectively in 2018. The poverty rate in 1992 for China and India stood at 56.7 per cent and 46 per cent respectively, which in 2018 has been reduced to 0.5 per cent and less than 7 per cent respectively. Therefore, the kind of protectionist, retrenchment, populist and unilateral tendencies we have been witnessing of late will do more harm to the cause of poverty reduction than good. I hope that the year 2021 will augur well for world poverty reduction programs as well as international trade and multilateralism.

11

THE TWO SESSIONS FURTHER CONSOLIDATE XI JINPING'S POWER

From 4 to 11 March 2021, more than 5,000 of China's political, business, and social elite congregated in Beijing for the two annual plenary sessions of the National People's Congress (NPC) and the Chinese People's Political Consultative Conference (CPPCC). Popularly known as "Two Sessions" (两会), they are of interest to the strategic community, policymakers, economists and investors, for these reveal China's priorities for economic development for the next five years and beyond, defence spending, veiled insights into China's factional feud, and more importantly overall policy direction of the country.

Picking figures from various reports presented during the sessions, analysts have mostly focused on China's 2.3 per cent economic growth in 2020, projected growth of over 6 per cent for 2021 against IMF's projections of 8.1 per cent, generating 11 million new jobs, and spending 6.8 per cent of the GDP (209 billion USD) on defence, which anyhow is way less if expenditure on military research and development, Chinese People's Armed Police Force and allocation pertaining to defence to other ministries is concerned. One thing which many China watchers has missed is one of the agendas (number 5) of the NPC titled "Deliberate on proposals submitted by the Standing Committee of the NPC for deliberation of the Organic Law of the NPC (Revised Draft)".

The Organic Law (组织法) of the NPC was adopted at the Fifth Session of the Fifth National People's Congress and promulgated for implementation by the proclamation of the National People's Congress on 10 December 1982. The Organic Law has four chapters and runs into 46 articles. A total of 37 new amendments proposed by Wang Chen, Vice Chairman of the Standing Committee of the National People's Congress on 6 March undoubtedly bear the imprimatur of the core leader, Xi Jinping. The 25th and 26th amendments may be of particular interest as these reveal the undercurrents of factional feud, the leadership succession, Xi Jinping's vulnerabilities, and further consolidation of his grip over the party state.

A new chapter entitled "General Provisions" (总则) has been added that stipulates that the NPC and its Standing Committee must adhere to the leadership of the Communist Party of China (CPC), Marxism-Leninism, Mao Zedong Thought, Deng Xiaoping Theory, the "Three Represents", scientific outlook, and Xi Jinping's thought on socialism with Chinese characteristics for a new era as the torchbearer (Article 3 of the revised draft); the provisions also talk about building China into a "socialist country ruled by law" (Article 5 of the draft amendment), as well as reiteration of "democratic centralism" (Article 6 of the revised draft) that was almost forgotten during the reform era.

The most important components are Articles 25 and 26 of the draft amendment pertaining to the appointment and removal of individuals from the State Council as well as the Central Military Commission (CMC) by the Standing Committee of the NPC. The amendments stipulate: First, the Standing Committee may decide on the appointment and removal of other members of the State Council on the recommendations of the Premier of the State Council when the NPC is not in session. The same provision has been extended to the appointment and removal of individuals from the CMC (Article 25 of the draft amendment). In another clause, the removal of the portfolios could be at the recommendations of both the Chairman's committee as well as the Premier, the same has been extended to the removal of portfolios in the CMC (Article 26 of the draft amendment).

Though the amendments have been carried out in order to "promote the modernization of the national governance system and governance capabilities", however, it is visible that Xi Jinping wants to assert greater control in the highest organ of the state power, which in fact also demonstrates his uneasiness with "other members" of the State Council, ostensibly the Vice Premiers. Having Li Zhanshu as the Chairman of the Standing Committee of the NPC, the removal of names would be possible even when the NPC is not in session (闭会期间). We have seen how Premier Li Keqiang contradicted President Xi Jinping on poverty alleviation, when he said during a press briefing that "China has over 600 million people whose monthly income is barely 1,000 yuan (USD 140) and their lives have further been affected by the coronavirus pandemic". On 11 March 2021, during a press briefing, Li Keqiang dropped yet another bombshell by declaring that there are over 200 million Chinese people doing "flexijobs" (灵活就业), implying that these many people are doing more than one or two jobs at a time in order to secure their livelihood. Premier Li Keqiang advocated that these people should be brought under the social security net and offered state subsidies. The above revelations of Li Keqiang demonstrate that he contradicts his boss' line on poverty eradication in China. Therefore, Xi Jinping would be extremely cautious to the names recommended by Li Keqiang in the State Council. Though the possibility of Li Keqiang recommending someone not liked by Xi Jinping is remote, but even if it happens Xi could strike them down through new amendments.

Furthermore, the undercurrents of factional feud are visible in Xi Jinping clipping the wings of the Shanghai clique by way of striking hard on their investments in entities like Jack Ma's Ant Group. It may be a matter of time when Vice Premiers like Han Zheng and Sun Chunlan are shown the door owing to their allegiance to the Shanghai clique. It is believed that Xi Jinping is extremely unhappy with the role the two played during Hong Kong's democracy movement and the US-China trade war. Hu Chunhua, being from the League faction (团派), could be next in the line of fire. Liu He perhaps is the safest as he is Xi Jinping's man and his economic advisor too. It is understood that it's not only the Shangai clique that is at loggerheads with Xi Jinping, but some of the princelings (太子党) too have turned their back on him. Therefore, in the face of such undercurrents inside and outside the Party, Xi Jinping is further consolidating his power.

*

Index

Act East Policy, 5, 55, 166, 201
Active Pharmaceutical Ingredients (APIs), 78
Af-Pak, 168
Africa, 50, 195, 224
AIDS, 220
Air Defence Identification Zone (ADIZ), 141, 239
Aksai Chin, 10
Alibaba, 261
Amdo, 39
Anglo-Nepalese War, 45
Arial Route, 50
Arthasastra, 153
    kauseyam cinapattasca cinabhumijah, 57, 91
ASEAN, 5, 55, 129, 142, 165, 201
ASEAN+3+3, 140
Asia Infrastructure Investment Bank (AIIB), 3, 34, 60, 170, 174, 187, 202, 204, 250
Asian Infrastructure Investment Bank (AIIB), 226
Asian NATO, 142
Asian Premium, 191
Asian Relations Conference, 66
Atamnirbhar (self-reliance) *Bharat* programme, 77
Atlantic Daily, 171
Aurobindo Ashram, 111
Australia, 129, 138
Austria-Hungary, 219
Axial Age, 111

Ayodhya, Ram Temple, 97
Azad Kashmir, 42

BAA2, 76
BAA3, 76
Baidu, 261
Balance China's rise, 165
Bangladesh, 54
Bangladesh-China-India-Myanmar (BCIM), 196-97
    Economic Corridor, 51, 200, 211
Bangu's
    Han Annals, 58
Bara Hoti, 9
Barakatullah, 93
Basic Exchange and Cooperation Agreement (BECA), 121, 128
Bedbugs (*chouchong*), 22
Beijing, 33
    Consensus, 15
Belgium, 219
Belt and Road Forum for International Cooperation, 203
Belt and Road Initiative (BRI), 46, 54, 47, 73, 129, 141, 165, 174, 187, 189, 195, 197, 203, 204, 205, 206, 207, 208, 224, 249, 269, 270
Belt and Road Study Network (BRSN), 211
Bhagavad-Gita, 102, 111-12
Bharat Mala, 5, 55
Bhutan, 33
Biden, Joe, US President, 230

Bilaspur-Manali-Leh, 10
BIMSTEC, 5, 55
Blinken, Antony, US Secretary of State, 232
Blue Dot Initiative, 136
Blue Dot Network, 141
Bodhidhrma, 59
Border Provocations, 24
Bose, Rash Behari, 93
Boycotting Chinese goods, 24
Brazil, 186
BREXIT, 185
BRIC first Regional Center of the New Development Bank, 183
BRICS, 3, 60, 85, 126, 174, 179, 184-85, 187, 190, 225, 270
    Achievements, 183
    Contingency Reserve Arrangement, 183
    Emerging Markets, 183
    Friends Circle, 186
    New Development Bank (NDB), 3, 34, 170, 185, 204, 226
    Rating Agency, 183
    University League, 183, 187
BRICS+, 186
Buddhism, 100, 117
Buddhist iconography, 95
Bulletin of the Atomic Scientists, 231

Cai Tieying
    Epiphany and Immortality: A Biography of Cheng'en, 115
Cambodia, 77, 224
Carter, Ashton, US Defence Secretary, 124
Cdr. Gurpreet S Khurana, 163
Central Asia, 180, 195, 224
Central Asian Republics (CARs), 180
Central Commission for Discipline Inspection (CCDI), 256
Central Global Television Network (CGTN), 18, 142
Century of humiliation, 70
Chaoyangmen, 264
Cheers to Chill, 136

Chen Hao, 111
Chen Lai
    Core Values of Chinese Civilisation, 243
Chen Yi, 111
Chen Yinke, 110
Cheng Xizhong, 41
Chennai Connect, 12
Chiang Kai-shek Government, 66
Chiang Kai-shek's Secret Agents, 71
China, 6, 9-10, 23, 28, 34, 38-39, 47, 50-51, 54-56, 59-60, 63, 65, 67, 70-73, 84-85, 90, 103-04, 110-12, 125, 135-36, 147, 152, 158, 163-64, 173-74, 180, 182, 187, 189-90, 195, 201, 211, 216-17, 222, 224, 227-28, 260-61
    Card, 45
    Dream, 15
    Focus, 132
    Rise, 129
China Central Television (CCTV), 146
China Daily, 43, 146
China Global Television Network (CGTN), 17
China Myanmar Economic Corridor (CMEC), 54
China's
    Burgeoning Economic and Military Muscle, 141
    FDI, 69, 73
    GDP, 251
    Health Commission, 215
    MG Motors, 78
    Poverty Alleviation, 273
    Poverty Line, 272
China's National Development and Reform Commission (NDRC), 41
China's Institute of Contemporary International Relations (CICIR), 139-40
China-ASEAN Free Trade Area (CAFTA), 196
China-FAO South-South Cooperation Trust Fund, 274
China-Laos Railway, 204
China-Myanmar, 49

China-Myanmar Economic Corridor (CMEC), 49-51, 209
China-Myanmar Oil and Gas Pipeline, 50, 54
China-Pakistan Axis, 61
China-Pakistan Economic Corridor (CPEC), 49, 51, 54, 73, 132, 182, 200, 202, 204
China-Thai Railway, 204
Chinese Civilisation, 88-89
Chinese Communist Party (CCP), 23
Chinese Investment in India, 77
Chinese People's Political Consultative Conference (CPPCC), 226, 275
Chinese Silk Handicrafts, 91
Christopher Walker, 146, 155
Chumar/Demchok, 4
Civilisational Dialogue, 94
Clash of Civilisations, 84, 87, 189, 249
Classic of Odes, 103
Cold War, 86, 154, 173, 190
Collected Works of Xu Fancheng, 111
Combating Global Warming, 186
Communications Compatibility and Security Agreement (COMCASA), 133
Communications Interoperability and Security Memorandum of Agreement (CISMOA), 121, 128
Communist Party of China (CPC), 172, 239
  18th Party Congress, 172, 272
  19th Party Congress, 241, 252-53, 255
Comprehensive Global Partnership, 134
Confidence Building Measures (CBMs), 12-14, 21, 72-73
Confucian Classics, 86
Confucius, 271
Conspiracy Theory, 231
Contingency Reserve Fund, 185
Counter Terrorism, 186
COVID-19, 6, 10-11, 27, 75-76, 78, 134, 218, 221-22, 229-30, 232, 234, 271
Crayon Xiaoqiu, 22

Dai Bingguo, 13

Daily Mail, 231, 233
Dairy products, 63
Dalai Lama, 37-40, 53
  visited Tawang, 153
Darbuk-Shayok-Daulat Beg Oldie (DS-DBO), 9
David Shambaugh, 171
DBO-Depsang, 4
Defence Industrial Base, 126
Defence Technology and Trade Initiative (DTTI), 121, 128
de-Maoization, 267
demilitarized zone (DMZ), 24
Deng Xiaoping, 13, 52, 72, 224, 244, 264
  Spiritual civilisation, 146
Dharchula-Lipulekh, 4
Dialogue of civilisations, 90
Digital India, 60, 69, 77-78, 94, 189
Djibouti, 129
Doka La, 32
Doklam, 10, 17, 27-28, 31, 61, 73, 136
  Infringement, 141
Doval, Ajit, National Security Advisor, 127
Dr. Anthony Fauci, 232
Dr. Kotnis, 94
Dr. Peter Daszak, 232
Dr. Ralph Baric, 233
Dr. Shi Zhengli, 231
Dr. Zhong Nanshan, 219
Dragon-Elephant Contest, 29
Dream of the Red Mansion, 95
Durban-Shyok-DBO, 4

East Asia Summit, 60
East China Sea, 141
East Europe, 224
Economic Times, 78
Egypt, 90
Eighth Route Army, 94
EU, 223
Eurasian Economic Union (EEU), 201
Europe, 50, 145, 195

Fang Bing, 41
Favourable environment, 253

Feng Chuanlu, 27-29
Fenghuang Net, 24
Finger 3, 17, 21
Finger 4, 8, 23
Finger 8, 21, 23
First United Front in China, 93
First War of Indian Independence, 93
Five Classics, 237
Five Connectivity, 209
Flaring up anti-China sentiments, 24
Foreign Direct Investment (FDI), 50, 76
Four Books of Confucianism, 95
Four Books, 237
Four Comprehensives, 258
France, 52, 219
Free and Open Indo-Pacific (FOIP), 141, 164
Free Trade Area (FTA), 169
Fujian, 105, 256

G2, 68, 173
G20, 60, 126, 160-61, 187, 269
Galwan, 4, 6-10, 12, 17, 66, 73-75
Gandhi, Rajiv,
    visited China, 72
gedou (gladiator), 14
Geng Shuang, 36
Gengzinian, 219
Genuine autonomy, 40
Germany, 219
Gilgit-Baltistan, 73
Global Britain, Global Broker, 6
Global rebalancing, 60
Global Times, 16, 18-19, 33, 64, 165
Globalisation vs. De-globalisation, 185
Golden Age of Rama, 100
Graham T. Allison, 171
Granules India, 78
Great Leap Forward, 267
Great Wall Motors, 78
Greater Bay Area, 228
Greater Mekong Sub-regional Economic Cooperation Plan, 195
Greco-Roman cultural system, 87-88
Guangqumen, 264
Guanyin (Avalokitesvara), 106

Gu-Chu-Sum Movement (GCSM), 40
Gwadar, 54, 129

H1N1, 220, 233
Haley, Nikki, 132
Han Dynasty, 106, 237
Haqqani Network, 136
Harmonious Peripheral Diplomacy, 270
Henry Jackson Society, 218
High Quality Development, 209-10
Himalayan blunder, 67
Hinduism, 100
Hindustan Seva Dal, 217
Hong Kong, 145, 220
Hot Spring, 4
Hot Springs, 17
Hu Chirui, 107
Hu Chunhua, 277
Hu Jintao, 253
    Harmonious World, 146
    Scientific Outlook, 244
Hu Shi, 115
Hu Shisheng, 29
Hu Zhiyong of Shanghai Academy of Social Sciences, 29
Hua Chunying, 154
Huang Baosheng, 103, 112
Huang Hancheng, 28
Huawei, 77, 261
Hubei, 217
Hungary-Serbia Railway, 204
Hybrid theory, 115-16

India, 6, 9-10, 13, 23, 28, 34, 48, 50-52, 55, 63-64, 67, 73, 76, 90, 125-26, 129, 135, 138, 152, 169, 187, 189, 200, 206, 224, 239
India's Air Defense, 42
India's Air Strikes Balakot, 41
India's Economic Growth, 69
India's Economic Measures against China, 29
India's Indo-Pacific strategy, 64
India's Telecom Sector, 69
India-Afghanistan
    Strategic Partnership Council, 130

India-China Bilateral Trade, 59
India-China Boundary Question, 14
India-China High Level Mechanism, 83
India-China Regional Trading Arrangement (RTA), 73
India-China, 66, 93, 126, 166, 191
  Trade, 94
India-China-Bhutan, 32
India-Myanmar-Thailand Trilateral Highway, 201
Indian Ocean Region (IOR), 122, 164
Indian Ocean Rim Association (IORA), 141
Indian Ocean Strategy, 166
India-US 2+2 Dialogue, 131
India-US Defence Relationship, 121, 128
India-US Relations, 130
India-US Security Partnership, 225
India-US Strategic and Commercial Dialogue, 131
India-US Strategic Partnership, 134
Indispensible Partner, 169
Indo-Japanese Asia-Africa Growth Corridor, 129
Indo-Pacific Economic Corridor, 129
Indo-Pacific, 10, 129, 163, 165
  Strategy, 5, 132, 136, 166
Industrial Parks, 123
International Criminal Court (ICC), 219
International Department of the Central Committee of the Communist Party of China (IDCPC), 196
International Tibet Support Network (ITSN), 40
Italy, 219

Jack Ma's Ant Group, 24, 277
Jaishankar, S., India's Minister of External Affairs, 30, 216, 220
Jakarta-Bandung High-speed Railway, 204
Japan, 34, 52, 76, 122, 129, 135, 138, 145, 169, 219, 223
Jataka Stories, 98
Java, 99
Jessica Ludwig, 146, 155

Ji Xianlin, 99-100, 102, 112-13, 116
Jiang Jingkui, 103, 112
Jiang Zemin, 172, 253
  Three Represents, 244-45, 257, 276
Jin Dinghan, 103, 112
Jin Kemu, 103, 112-14, 116
Jinri Toutiao, 24
Joint Study Group (JSG), 73
Joint Task Force (JTF), 73
Journey to the West, 116-17

Kabir Granthavali, 102
Kadeer, Rebiya, 38
Kaladan Multimodal Transit Transport Project, 201
Kalidasa's
  Abhijnanashakuntala, 102
  Meghaduta, 102, 111
Kargil Conflict, 72
Karl Marx, 242
Kathasagar, 102
Kazakhstan, 180, 182
Kenneth Juster, 5
Key Starting Materials (KSMs), 78
Kham, 39
Kim Jong Un, North Korean leader, 148, 152
Kirghizstan, 182
Kongka La, 13
Korean War, 239
Kunming-Kyaukpyu Railway Line, 50, 54
Kunming-Tengchong-Myitkyina-India, 196
Kuomintang (KMT) Party, 267
Kyaukpyu Deep Sea Water Port, 50, 54
Kyaukpyu SEZ, 50, 54
Kyaukpyu-Nay Pyi Taw Highway Project, 50, 54
Kyrgyz Republic, 205
Kyrgyzstan, 180

Ladakh, 29
Lala Lajpat Rai, 93
Lan Jianxue, 29
Lancet, 231

langyabang (wolf teeth iron maces), 14
Laos, 205
Lapthal, 9
Latin America, 224
Laurus, 78
Learning from Civilisations, 84, 94
Legal Instruments, 37
Letpadaung Copper Mine Project, 50, 54
Lhasa-Kathmandu Rail Link, 46
Li Bingxian, 27
Li Keqiang, Government Work Report, 228
Li Muyang, 22
Li Tieh-Tseng in his book The Historical Status of, 37
Liang Qichao, 106, 264
Liang Sicheng, 263, 264
Line of Actual Control (LAC), 4, 9-10, 14-17, 20, 24, 27-28, 66, 68, 73-74
Liu A'ming, 140
Liu Anwu's, 103, 112
   Comparative Studies of Indian and Chinese Literature, 116
Liu Zhaohua, 106, 108
Logistics Exchange Memorandum of Agreement (LEMOA), 121-22, 124-25, 133
Logistics Parks, 123
Logistics Support Agreement (LSA), 121, 124-25, 133
Long Xingchun, 131
Longju, 13
Look North Policy, 201
Lt Gen Y.K. Joshi, 21
Lu Xun, 114-15
   A Brief History of Chinese Fiction, 114
Lu Yang of Tsinghua University, 29

Ma Xiaolin, 165
Macao, 220
Made in China 2025, 161, 189, 205, 259-60
Mahaballipuram, 10
Mahabharata, 99, 102
Major Defense Partner, 127-28
Make in India, 60, 94, 189, 201

Malaysia, 206
Mandalay Yida Economic and Trade Cooperation Zone, 50, 54
Mandalay-Tigyaing-Muse Express Way, 50, 54
Mansergh, Nicolas, 53
Manufacturing power, 260
Manusmriti, 102
Mao Keji, 64
Mao Zedong, 89, 110, 237
Maritime India Summit, 2016, 123
Maritime Silk Road (MSR), 123
Mask Diplomacy, 223
Matteo Ricci, 103
Mattis, James, US Secretary of Defense, visited India, 127, 132
Maxwell, Neville, 8
McMahon Line, 8
Mekong-India Corridor, 201
Melamchi Water Supply Project, 46, 54
Meng Wanzhou, 160
Meng Zhaoyi
   Mahabharata and *Ramayana*, 97
Mexico, 168
Mi Video Call, 75
Middle East, 50, 168, 224
Ming Dynasty, 103, 114
Mini Asian NATO, 140
Mini NATO, 4, 23
Misamari-Tenga-Tawang, 10
Missile Technology Control Regime (MTCR), 125
Modern Xuanzang, 113
Modi, Narendra, India's Prime Minister, 9, 47, 56-57, 59, 62, 83, 91, 123, 127, 217
   Government, 46, 121, 123, 128
   Visited US, 164
Mongolia, 205
Moody's Investor Services, 76
Moon Jae-in, South Korean President, 148
Mulian (Maudgalyayana), 106
Mumbai Terror Attack, 72
Myanmar Investment and Corporate Administration, 50

Myanmar, 50, 54, 77, 99, 197, 224
　　Government, 51

Nail House (*dingzihu*), 63
Naku La, 4, 8, 10
NAM, 53
National Advanced Surface to Air Missile System-II (NASAMSII), 133
National Defense Intelligence Agency, 232
National Democratic Party of Tibet (NDPT), 40
National K-12 Foreign Language Enrollment Survey Report,, 84
National People's Congress (NPC), 226, 244, 246-47, 277
　　General Provisions, 276
　　Organic Law, 276
National Supervisory Commission, 246
NATO, 121, 124-25, 133
Nature, 231
Neighbouring Country, 42
Nepal Investment Summit, 46
Nepal, 28, 45, 47, 54-55, 209
Netherlands, 219
New Development Bank, 174, 206, 250
New Education Policy 2020, 101
New Silk Road, 129
New York Times, 231
Nibbling Chinese territory, 21, 27
Nilang-Jadang, 8
Ning Jizhen, 204
North Korea, 149, 151
North Korean Nuclear Issue, 141
North Korea-US Joint Statement, 149
North Lakhimpur-Bame-Silapathar, 10
Northeast India, 55
North-South Transport Corridor (NSTC), 180
Norway, 219
Nuclear Suppliers Group (NSG), 67, 73-74, 125, 136

Obsession (*zhinian*), 27
Oby Ezekwesili, 219
Oli, Nepali Prime Minister, 46
One China policy, 67
One Touch AppLabs, 75
Opium War, 220, 238
Oppo, 77

Pacific Command (PACOM), 164
Pacific country, 165
Pakistan Occupied Kashmir (POK), 67, 73, 122, 124, 209, 200
Pakistan, 28, 54, 68, 182, 205
Pallava Dynasty, 58
Panchtantra, 102
Pangong Dao, 17
Pangong Tso, 4, 20, 26, 28
Papua New Guinea, 161
Paris Climate Change Accord, 130
Paris Climate Change Agreement, 185
Parrikar, Manohar, the then India's Defence Minister, visited US, 124
Pasighat-Teju-Parsuram Kund-Rupai, 10
Peaceful Development, 172
Peaceful Rise, 172
Peak Pegasus, 157
Pence, Mike, US Vice President, 161
People's Bank of China, 76
People's Courts, 245
People's Daily, 22, 33, 75, 146
People's Liberation Army (PLA), 7-8, 14, 21-22, 26, 181, 228, 257
People's Procuratorates, 245
People's Republic of China (PRC), 9, 37, 244
People's War, 134, 226
People-to-People Dialogue, 86
People-to-People Exchange, 187
PLA Daily, 22
PLA Institute of International Relations, 104
PLA Paper, 22
Pompeo Mike, US Secretary of State, 132
Port based Smart Cities, 123
Portugal, 219
post-COVID-19, 4, 225, 227
Prasad, S.N., 7
Prof. Ji Xianlin, 98
Prof. Liu Anwu, 116

Prof. Crane, 242
Prof. Feng DaHsuan, 180
Prof. P.A. Stobdan, 8
Prof. Yu Longyu, 106, 116
  History of Oriental Literature, 97
Prof. Yu Longyu, 108
Prof. Zhang Guihong, 133
Provoking the Incident, 9
Puncog, 39

Qin Shihuang, 237
Qing dynasty, 103
Qing Emperor Qianlong, 37
Qu Yuan
  Heaven Questioned, 92
  Questions to Heaven, 57
Quad, 5, 61, 69, 74, 136, 138, 140, 142, 164, 166
Quadrilateral Security Dialogue (Quad) Summit, 138
Quadrilateral Traffic in Transit Agreement (QTTA), 182
Quality Infrastructure, 210

Ramaphosa, Cyril, South African President, 135
Ramayana, 98, 100, 102, 115-17
  in China, 97
Ramcharitmans, 102
Rashtriya Swayamsevak Sangh (RSS), 63
Records of the Western Regions during Great Tang, 95
Red Star News, 27
Referendum, 40
Regional Comprehensive Economic Partnership (RCEP), 5, 55, 62-65
Reliance Jio, 77
Remove China App, 75
Ren Zhengfei, 160
Retaliatory Strikes, 42
Reuters, 36
Rituals and Historical Conventions, 37
Roy, M.N., 93
Russia, 125, 180, 186, 187, 202, 219
Russian president Vladimir Putin, 201

SAARC, 5
SAGAR, 166
Sagarmala, 5, 189, 201
Samudra Manthan, 58
Sanbuqu (*Trilogy*), 39
Sangchamalla, 9
Saran, Shyam, 8
SARS-Coronavirus-2, 231
Scientific Development, 257
Second Belt and Road Forum for International Cooperation, 208
Security and Growth for All in the Region, 166
Self-sufficiency, 227, 259
Senkaku, 228
Shanghai Cooperation Organisation (SCO), 3, 34, 60, 85, 126, 174, 179, 181, 190, 201, 226, 270
Shanghai Cooperation Organisation Development Bank, 174
Shanghai Five, 180
Shanghai Joint Publishing Company, 111
Shanghai Pudong New Area (SPNA), 264
Shangri-La Dialogue, 132
Shankracharya, 102
Sharp Power, 146
Shen Dan, 22-23
Sheng Tai, 32
Shenzhen Special Economic Zone (SSEZ), 264
Shinzo Abe, the then Japanese Prime Minister, 139
Shipki La, 9
Sikkim-Tibet boundary. Article 1, 32
Silk Road Economic Belt, 180
Silk Road Fund, 187, 203, 250
Silk Road Spirit, 88, 94, 199, 204, 207
Singh, Rajnath, Minister of Defence (MoD), 20
Sino-French War, 238
Sino-Japanese War, 238
Six Dynasties, 110
Six Philosophical Schools of India, 102
Social Media, 148
Soft Power, 146

Solara Active Pharma, 78
South Asia, 196, 224
South China Sea (SCS), 4, 23, 122, 129, 141, 153, 167
South Korea, 135, 145, 169
South-China Sea, 164
Southeast Asia, 166, 196
Southern Silk Route, 92
South-South Cooperation, 185-86
Spain, 219
Special Economic Zone (SEZ), 49, 123
Special Representative (SR) Mechanism, 13
Spiti, 9
Spratly, 228
Sri Lanka, 54, 205
String of Pearls, 54
Students for a Free Tibet (SFT), 40
Study Times, 172, 268
Sun Tse [Zi],
    The Art of War, 101
Sun Weidong, 216
Sun Wukong, 114-15
Sun Xiao, 7
Sun Yat-Sen, 93
Sunday Guardian, 222
Surendermohan Bose, 93
Sursagar, 102
Sustainable Development Goals (SDGs), 229
Sutra Translation, 105-06
Swadeshi Jagran Manch (SJM), 64, 75
Swadeshi Self-Reliance Campaign, 75
Swaraj, Sushma, the then India's Foreign Minister, 83
Sweden, 219
Systemic Rival, 223

Tagaung Taung Nickel Industry Development Project, 50, 54
Taiping Uprising, 93
Taiwan, 15, 67, 70, 145, 228
Taiwan Straits, 4
Tajikistan, 180, 205
Taliban, 182
Tang Dynasty, 58, 88, 92, 106

Tang Seng, 114
Taoguang Yanghui, 175
Targeted Poverty Alleviation, 273
TASS Report, 22
Tencent News, 43, 261
Territorial Integrity, 70
Text based Negotiations, 62
Thailand, 77, 99, 224
The Romance of Three Kingdoms, 95
The Scholars, 95
The Washington Post, 219
Three Character Classic (San zijing), 237
Three Communiqués, 169
Three Rurals, 272
Three Step Strategy, 23, 260
Thucydides
    The History of the Peloponnesian War, 171
Tibet, 7, 9, 14-15, 31, 37, 39-40, 45, 70, 72, 74
Tibet Autonomous Region (TAR), 39
Tibetan Independence, 38, 40
Tibetan Women's Association (TWA), 40
Tibetan Writers Organisation (TWO), 40
Tibetan Youth Congress (TYC), 40
TikTok, 75
Tillerson, Rex, the then US Secretary of State, 173
Tourism and Pilgrimage, 86, 94
Trade Promotion Council of India (TCPI), 78
Trans-Asia Railway (TAR), 195
Trans-Pacific Partnership (TPP), 64, 168
Transport Corridors, 123
Tributary State, 45
Trump Administration, 158, 168
    Afghanistan Policy, 129
    Rule based Global Trading System, 154
    Unilateralism, 154
    Zero-sum Mentality, 154
Trump, Donald, the then US President, 160, 167, 171, 174
Trump's India visit, 135
Trump-Xi Meeting, 152

Trustworthy, Loveable and Admirable, 234
TTP, 136

U Tsang, 39
UC Browser, 75
UN General Assembly, 188
UN Security Council, 44
UN, 71, 223
UNESCO, 223
United Kingdom (UK), 44, 219
    Terrestrial Military, 174
UNSC, 67, 74
Upanishads, 102, 111-12
US, 34, 44, 52, 69, 76, 121-23, 125-26, 129, 133, 135, 138, 145, 147, 157, 162, 165, 168-69, 173, 175, 209-10, 220, 223-24, 228
    Military, 71
    Pivot to Asia, 124
    Strategic Framework for the Indo-Pacific, 5
    Indo-Pacific Strategy, 140
    Think Tank, CSIS, 139
US Indo-Pacific Command (USIPC), 164
US-China Economy, 155
US-China Trade War, 157, 161, 224, 261
US-India Defense Technology and Trade Initiative, 128
US-India Economic and Trade Relations, 136
US-Japan-India-Australia, 136
USS Carl Vinson, 152
USSR, 239
Uygur, 38

Vajpayee, A.B., the then India's Foreign Minister, 13
Vedas, 111
Vietnam, 34, 77, 122, 224, 239
Vimalkirti, 106
Visva-Bharati, 111
Vivo, 77

Wade, Nicholas, 231
Wall Street Journal, 161

Wang Bangwei, 112
Wang Dehua, 9, 27, 29
Wang Guowei
    Study in History, 88
Wang Hongwei, 27, 71
Wang Mingyuan, 148
Wang Shuying, 103, 112
Wang Wenbin, 20
Wang Yi, 30, 83, 142
War of Resistance, 93
    Against Japanese Aggression, 53
Washington Consensus, 15
Wei, 114
Well-known Zed (Zhiming Zed), 22
Wen Shuo, 31
West, 70, 103, 219, 226-28, 234
Western Development Campaign, 195
Western Sector, 8-9, 13, 25, 30
Wilhelm von Humboldt, 105
Wolfish Nature (langzi yexin), 27
Wolf-warrior, 4, 234
World Bank, 187
    Report, 271
World Health Organisation (WHO), 216, 219, 229, 231
World Literature, 89
World Trade Organisation (WTO), 64, 156-57, 159, 223
World War II, 93, 173, 223, 220, 263
Wu Qian, 20
Wu Yuanli, 238
Wuhan, 215-16, 219
    Museum, 57
    Spirit, 12, 83
    Summit, 59
Wuhan Institute of Virology (WIV), 233

Xi Jinping, 12, 49, 54, 83, 87-89, 91, 94, 132, 141, 148, 151, 159-60, 171-72, 175, 180, 188, 199-201, 203, 205, 208, 210-11, 215, 217, 224, 226, 227, 231, 239, 241-43, 247, 249-50, 253, 256, 269, 274, 277
    Cultural Soft Power, 146
    Core Socialist Values, 146
    New Era, 241-43, 259

Xiamen, 184
Xiaomi, 77
Xinhua News Agency, 22, 43, 135, 255
Xinjiang, 7, 9, 14-15, 74, 100
Xiongan New Area (XNA), 264-65
Xu Dishan, 110
Xu Fancheng, 103, 110-13, 116
Xuan Zang, 106, 112
Xue Keqiao, 103

Yama Ribbon, 185
Yan Xuetong, 173
Yang Gongsu, 27, 70
Yaoxing, 105
Yijing, 112
Yongdingmen, 264
Yu Longyu, 103, 112
Yunnan, 195

Zan Ning, 106
Zhang Feng, 165
Zhang Taiyan, 93
Zhang Yu'an and Xiao Xiaorui's
  The Story of Rama and Southeast Asian Literature, 117
Zhang Zai, 111
Zhao Gancheng, 29
Zhonghuamen, 264
Zhou Bo, 142
Zhou Dunyi
  Book of Zhou Zitong, 111
Zhou Enlai, 25, 38, 71, 200, 266
  visited India, 13
Zhou Yongkang, 257
Zhu Weiqun, 38
Zhu Xi, 111
ZTE, 261

*